T0284867

**Watching While Black
Rebooted!**

Watching While Black Rebooted!

The Television and Digitality of Black Audiences

EDITED BY BERETTA E. SMITH-SHOMADE

Foreword by Herman S. Gray

Rutgers University Press

New Brunswick, Camden, and Newark, New Jersey

London and Oxford

Rutgers University Press is a department of Rutgers, The State University of New Jersey, one of the leading public research universities in the nation. By publishing worldwide, it furthers the University's mission of dedication to excellence in teaching, scholarship, research, and clinical care.

978-1-9788-3003-5 (cloth)
978-1-9788-3002-8 (paper)
978-1-9788-3004-2 (epub)

Cataloging-in-publication data is available from the Library of Congress.
Library of Congress Control Number: 2023944844

A British Cataloging-in-Publication record for this book is available from the British Library.

This collection copyright © 2024 by Rutgers, The State University of New Jersey
Individual chapters copyright © 2024 in the names of their authors
All rights reserved
No part of this book may be reproduced or utilized in any form or by any means, electronic or mechanical, or by any information storage and retrieval system, without written permission from the publisher. Please contact Rutgers University Press, 106 Somerset Street, New Brunswick, NJ 08901. The only exception to this prohibition is "fair use" as defined by U.S. copyright law.

References to internet websites (URLs) were accurate at the time of writing. Neither the author nor Rutgers University Press is responsible for URLs that may have expired or changed since the manuscript was prepared.

♾ The paper used in this publication meets the requirements of the American National Standard for Information Sciences—Permanence of Paper for Printed Library Materials, ANSI Z39.48-1992.

rutgersuniversitypress.org

For Gen-Z and my two favorites, Salmoncain and Zolacatherine

Contents

Foreword

HERMAN S. GRAY

> For bell hooks and Greg Tate,
> two of the most powerful truth-seekers
> and storytellers we have produced

Blackness and Television

What possibilities does Blackness engender in television in the third decade of the twenty-first century?[1] How does Blackness engage with the possibilities created by streaming technologies, social media platforms, and the production practices and logics associated with the digital capabilities of television? As Marlon Riggs details in his classic documentary *Color Adjustment* and Terence Nance so poignantly illustrates in his groundbreaking series *Random Acts of Flyness*, television plays a pivotal role in conditioning, shaping, and sustaining representations of Blackness and Black people. From the early decades of its formation when the medium depicted Blackness through blatant stereotypes into the golden years of television, which were dominated by invisibility and indifference, television representations of Black people and Black experiences have been put in service of what the late scholar Cedric Robinson called "forgeries and theft" designed to contain, exploit, and provide an alibi for white supremacy as normative. Although the introduction of cable and satellite distribution technologies in the 1980s momentarily opened the way to new and more diverse themes, stories, and representations, this moment was at best transitional, anticipating the current ecologies of streaming and the proliferation of platforms devoted to binge watching, global distribution, and atomized viewing.

Along with social shifts in the organization of production and technological innovations in the distribution of content came changes in the field of vision, meaning, and looking relations around Blackness, *especially* for Black viewers and audiences. That is, with the increases in Black-themed content and Black creative personnel came gradual changes in the field of vision, the point of view, the challenges, and the burdens of representation for Black people. In other words, with the proliferation and intensification of Black stories and characters on-screen, a certain level of visibility was realized. Yet disputes over how Blackness is represented and how it is deployed remain contested.

In 2023, with so much creative content, endless possibilities for new platform synergies, and millions in corporate money invested in controlling the digital ecologies of social media and streaming platforms, the potential for Black creative content seems limitless. As we learned in previous boom (and bust) cycles of Black-themed content on television and in film, the social context, political conditions, and economic investment in Black content create powerful incentives and constraints for content geared toward Black audiences. It is hard not to be skeptical of boom and bust cycles from the mid-twentieth century to the early decades of the twenty-first century or not to regard them as just structural features of American (and global) television and its relationship to Black representations.

Enriched by attention to institutional formations, the history of the medium, the discursivity of Blackness, and industrial organization and production practices, criticism and the scholarly regard for television are energized and complicated by new questions, foci, and challenges. For example, there is considerable promise in the new directions charted by scholars like Ralina Joseph, Racquel Gates, and Michael Gillespie, who are writing about the importance of Black content creators and scholars exceeding the instrumentalism of mimetic commitments or observing the fidelity of positive image construc-tions of Blackness; AJ Christian, Alfred Martin, Kristen Warner, and Khadijah Costley White are alert to production practices and institutional formations (of legacy networks and digital ecologies) and the role of race in the history and formation of the medium as well as the history of media and television studies concerning race, difference, and power.

Neither ought we take for granted the social and cultural common sense through which Blackness is constructed and represented in television. Take for granted, that is (and here I am drawing on Édouard Glissant's poignant idea of opacity), in the sense of Blackness as a discursive and historical formation (including pleasures, knowledge, meanings, and disputes) and Black people as social, political, and cultural subjects who are known through empirical mea-sures, economic value, or cultural signifiers. In fact, Black viewing positions are complex, intersecting, dynamic, and irreducible to preconfigured categories or some popular racial common sense. In addition, it is more useful to explore the complex history and expression of Black joy, pleasure, trauma, and world-making through and across Black differences. Asking critical questions with these assumptions in mind or from the vantage point of Black opacity broadens our reach and deepens our understandings of Black audiences and their intertextual and dialogical viewing practices.

Television and Blackness

In the case of television (at least as we now know it), there are points of access, places of connection, and practices of reading Black world-making with and through television that we have only begun to apprehend and experience. With streaming, social media, and related lines of access, forms of engagement, Black viewing practices, and sense-making are generative, expansive, and connected in ways heretofore seldom seen. Asking what is Black, what it means, and how it signifies in the television universe of streaming, social media, and platforms opens both television and Blackness to new questions, practices, meanings, and disputes.

At one level, these questions invite us to respond in terms of funding models and profit margins, audience share, and measurement metrics. At another, they ask who Black subjects are; what do Black subjectivities and subject positions imply about who reads, who sees, who hears, and what meanings they produce? For instance, the subject position of the ideal viewer anchoring Black-cast and -themed historical dramas like *Underground*, *The Underground Railroad*, and *Watchmen* makes visible—perhaps for the first time—a conception of Black trauma operating both on the screen and off. With the insights of Black critics, journalists, and scholars, these programs help tutor and heighten our sensibilities and approaches to watching, listening to, and participating in different modalities and screen depictions of Blackness. The meaning of Blackness posited in these and other Black-themed and Black-cast programs illustrate the multiple, interlocking, and dynamic conceptions of Blackness and the histories of trauma and pain that are traced and registered televisually.

With programs like *Lovecraft Country*, *Small Axe*, *13th*, *Random Acts of Flyness*, and *Exterminate All the Brutes*, writers, showrunners, and producers critique white supremacy, racism, and forms of sexual, class, and gender oppression and their instantiation in media. Their attention to memory, trauma, identification, and belonging also generate (and promise) forms of connection, recuperation, repair, and community that come through centering Blackness as a discursive subject and object. Instead of producing nostalgic yearnings for a utopian and romantic unity to which limited conceptions of screen Blackness can appeal, these responses do not obscure the fundamental role of difference and the critical disputes and struggles over and within Blackness that heterogeneity mobilizes. Expressions of various registers of Black diasporic connection, identification, and belonging take place through explorations of differences that Black folks engage through Black looking relations, including disidentification, reading against the grain, and recoding. So for example, with media coverage of the murders of Sandra Bland, George Floyd, and so many others, Black television

viewers often respond with complex emotions to repeated televisual rehears-
als and displays of violence perpetrated against Black folks and inflicted at the
hands of police. At the same time, dramatizations of police violence in scripted
television shows like *Atlanta* and *When They See Us* work through forms of
identification and healing, care and intimacy.

With the advent of digital technologies and ecologies, Black viewers have
generated new lines and maps of connection, meaning, and engagement that
television scholar Beretta Smith-Shomade calls "watching while Black." This
sprawling and often illegible (to some) formation of Black viewership, looking
relations, and dialogic practice generates conversation and pleasures across emotional, psychological, cultural, and political horizons. Many of these engagements and the meanings they conjure are historical in theme and perspective
(addressing, for example, issues of enslavement and Jim Crow trauma), while
in other cases, it is Black memory and imagination that are being mapped and
remapped, explored and stretched through genres like science fiction, animation, and horror.

Whatever the case, these forms of connection look, feel, and sound Black
but not so much by reducing Blackness to its role in critiquing regimes of white
supremacy, exploitation, and terror. Rather, these connections spring from the
willingness of Black directors, showrunners, producers, and writers and the organizations they work with to center Blackness, Black stories, and Black subjectivities and to insist that they matter in the quotidian experiences of Black viewers.
Centering Blackness offers Black viewers Black mattering maps that exceed the
discipling gaze of whiteness and the corporate conceit of television that reduces
Blackness to a financial investment in search of a profitable return.[2]

These mattering maps signify differently now than they did when Black viewers were so starved for images and representations of ourselves that we invested
in media legibility and visibility as ends in themselves. In this historical moment
of very real assault stemming from the deliberate instability and chaos of white
nationalism, the rise of authoritarian regimes, threats to liberal democratic
governance, the climate crisis, and a global health pandemic, just what kind of
Black social and cultural mattering maps do we have and need? What kind
of meaning maps help us to see and hear, understand and participate in the
media and television's production of Blackness? Who and what matters in a television ecosystem where value is extracted from clicks and visits, where Blackness
moves across legacy media, archives, streaming platforms, social media sites,
and any place where visits and clicks are the keys to building and monetizing
(self) brands? The conditions that shape the relationships and spaces among,
between, and within these ever-changing and complex environments beckon
for ways of apprehending and making sense of Blackness and television.

Watching While Black Rebooted! appears during the realignment among these
platforms, content, subject positions, and Black viewers, which suggests that at
the very least, our understanding of this realignment may need to be rethought

to account for the shifting dynamics and positions with Blackness and television and what they both mean now. How do we take account of the shifts in not just viewing practices and circumstances (including Black Twitter, visualization of talk radio, and networks of affiliation) but the very meaning of Blackness and how it is mobilized and where it is deployed culturally, politically, and socially?

As I have noted already, new conditions require new questions and different approaches (whose emergence and necessity we can track historically). In the mid and late decades of the twentieth century, with the expansion of rights and access to opportunity as the driving moral and political claim, movements for social and racial justice insisted on the visibility and representations of Black people in the civic vision of a shared social, cultural, and political "public." Now with the proliferation of images of Blackness and the platforms to circulate them, there is a significant increase in the sheer amount and varieties of Black content and the number of content producers, including showrunners, producers, writers, and talent. And yet, both television and social media are regularly mobilized and used by deeply sinister politicians and racist forces to place Blackness in service of fueling white anger and grievance about the perceived loss of white privilege and status.

These conditions require a different set of analytic and political moves—that is, away from thinking strategically about Black participation in primarily terms of parity and from emphasizing representation, visibility, and the legibility of Blackness as productive routes to social equality. Perhaps the ethical and political demands of the moment require us to widen our analytic focus to include *other* indicators, registers, and conceptual frames such as those affective conditions of feeling, care, and concern and the forms of expression and attraction they generate both on and off the screen.

Every few years journalists, activists, scholars, and critics raise questions about television and the status of Black images on television. Hence the questions of who is represented and how, who is visible and recognized, and who is not remain largely at the center of our media, cultural, and political discourse about the politics of representation. And television continues as a primary means of representation and point of access. Along with social media, television is especially crucial for seeing and "feeling" the disproportionate impact of race on issues like mass incarceration, policing and the criminal justice system, economic inequality, and fairness in our social, economic, and political life.

True to our enduring commitments to social, racial, gender, and economic justice, media scholars (especially women and scholars of color) are concerned with and continue to produce, assess, and consult yearly statistical and qualitative inventories of Black, Asian, Latinx, and LGBTQ+ images according to casting, characters, and production personnel. These annual inventories provide invaluable data for scholars, activists, and industry decision-makers on progress (or lack of progress) and participation on-screen and off by race, gender, and sexual identification. As measures of progress, recognition, and regard, we might include expressions of cultural recognition and prestige ritualized in annual celebrations of craft, critical, and popular television awards.[3]

Moreover, on the academic front, scholarly meetings, professional conventions, and informal networks of scholars and researchers convene to identify, collect, judge, analyze, and index the state of affairs in television. Regional and national organizations like the Society for Cinema and Media Studies, American Studies Association, National Communication Association, and Consoling Passions among many other regional scholarly organizations convene meetings around social activities, networks, panels, conference papers, newsletters, and blogs in order to comment on, present, assess, and discuss research on the state of television, including the field of television studies. Not to be forgotten either is the rapid growth of popular comment and public opinion passing for television criticism and making everyone a TV critic jockeying for attention in a crowded information field of clicks, posts, blogs, and tweets. Although it is hard to avoid, especially on social media platforms, this genre of vernacular criticism exists in a robust field of professional television critics and journalists who write and broadcast for National Public Radio, the *New Yorker*, the *New York Times*, the *Los Angeles Times*, and other major national outlets maintaining regular television beats and coverage.

So in the third decade of the twenty-first century, we appear to be in yet another boom cycle of critical recognition and regard for Black television content, fueled by a new generation of talented Black creative personnel and bolstered by the realization among some executives in the television industry of the social and economic value of the Black audience. A number of programs—both narrative and nonnarrative—with Black-themed content, Black casts, and Black showrunners continue to enjoy some measure of popular recognition, even critical regard. The critical and perhaps even cynical question must be posed nonetheless: In the cacophony of reports, studies, data, papers, books, prizes, and deals, is this yet another boom-bust cycle of extracting Black value and buying time until the industry restructures or finds a more lucrative audience?

Critical Black Television Studies

I'd like to turn finally to the issue of the intellectual and professional tendency (perhaps even formation) of what I am calling critical Black television studies (CBTS) and the possibilities (including television and Blackness) that condition and prompt considering such a tendency now. The promise of such a formation or something like it rests with the potential to identify, network, and map the work of critical scholars, researchers, archivists, publishers, journals, and critics (especially senior scholars) whose work authorizes, evaluates, and builds a discursive practice and cultural politics around understanding the nexus of Blackness, power, race, television, and difference.

More ambitiously, such an intellectual formation helps prepare the (organizational and institutional) conditions necessary to reproduce itself as a network around a set of objects, questions, and approaches that can serve as building blocks for graduate student training, research, and scholarship. Such an emergent formation (or at the very least formalizing the existing network) has the potential benefit of recognizing the crucial work of its practitioners to graduate schools, archives, industry personnel, publishers, fellowships awards, prizes, and tenure and promotion committees. The itineraries and conditions that prefigure, shape, and commend such a configuration—its objects, subjects, perspectives, methods, and insights—draw from existing fields and disciplines in the social sciences, the humanities, the arts, and transdisciplinary studies, including Black, media, cultural, feminist, queer, and technology.

However, the main distinction is that such a formation does so with a *difference*. That is, the field of inquiry, objects, subjects, and participants are distinct from any one discipline, field, or subfield, especially when animated and framed through the epistemologies, methods, theories, and debates with Blackness and television at its center. Rather than being additive, this emergent intellectual arrangement is constituted by subjects and objects that are not reducible to merely adding Blackness, Black people, or race to the existing disciplinary order of things. Neither is "the thing" under study reducible to any of the constitutive elements that appear under the sign of such a tendency.

Moving from conceptual to practical matters brings with it the challenges of methods, objects, theorization, policy, and politics. In other words, one might ask, What is to be gained by designating CBTS as an emergent intellectual assemblage now? For both CBTS and adjacent fields, one obvious analytic and conceptual benefit is the elimination of single-object and axis formulations and explanations. That is, single-axis accounts and objects like race or Black characters, themes, and narratives elide complex and mutually constitutive relationships and dynamic differences like gender identities, social class, and ethnicity within and among Black people. Rather, the objective is thinking relationally and intersectionally through both specificity and multiplicities of objects, subjects, differences, and locations as well as formal elements, industrial logics, and reception. Thinking of Blackness and television together through differences also enables researchers and scholars to trace the histories of Blackness as objects of study without reducing our takes to mere aesthetic choices or financial instrumentality. Similarly, the history and meaning of what we call television now in relation to Blackness necessarily center Black people and our related histories of critical reception, institutional and organizational challenges, political disputes about coverage and representations of race, and regulatory public policies aimed at broadcasters.

In this respect, U.S. television and the readings we make of it with regard to Blackness are connected to histories and meaning maps across Black diasporic worlds—including Europe, the Caribbean, and Latin America—and heretofore operate within a nexus of finance, production centers, and reception capacities that are not merely local, national, or regional. Because of finance and distribution capacities made possible by digital technologies, they are often all three at once. Indeed, one cannot see Blackness produced in the United States in isolation from production centers and reception in other parts of the globe, especially Asia, India, Africa, and Latin America. The potential of such a formation then bears directly on how Black-themed content, audiences, and creative personnel regard and are regarded at home and elsewhere given the proliferation of platforms, international financing partnerships, and dynamic communities of reception, evaluation, and anointment. A multiaxial approach to subject-object relations within the dynamics of difference and power more specifically means attending to mutually constitutive, historically specific operations of race, gender, and class (displacement, migrations, and extraction) as a social, cultural, and economic system of power; it means viewing television as an industrial and cultural system *and* as a technology of race and race-making.

Within this rubric, one can then locate various axes of difference, power, hierarchies, practices, and relations that increase the analytic precision and specificity of relations among, within, and across (Black) differences. Difference in this formulation acquires more specificity as an analytic concept that is helpful in detailing particular subjects and practices (both organizational and signifying) and their relationship to television and Blackness. To take but one example, for all its productive potential, even the single-axis concept of Blackness, as Alfred Martin shows, is limited in what it allows us to say and see about the nuance of distinctions among gender, gender identification, sexuality, sexual identification, and various forms of attachment and belonging; but it is also limited in helping us see how these understandings, practices, and identities are structured within and by systems of power and hetero/ homonormativity that are normalized and routinized in television. Race as an analytic is not just reductive, but it also cannot pick up on such nuances. And where it does, it is wholly incapable of doing so with descriptive and analytic precision.

Thinking through the rubric of an intellectual disposition, archive, and discursive practice has the potential to increase some of the descriptive accuracy, conceptual force, and analytic importance of a relational approach to Blackness, television, and difference. To be sure, there is also some gain in multiple and detailed accounts of how systems of social hierarchy work within and through groups without flattening the specificity of relations within and among ethnic, racial, gender, and sexual politics. In short, it is important to avoid reducing Blackness and debates about representation and visibility to race and vice versa. As well, it is important to identify and name the practices that organize and present whiteness, white supremacy, and the institutional-industrial, social, and cultural forms that normalize and sustain cultural and social systems of racial inequality. This critical approach avoids a tendency toward a hierarchy of oppressions and relying on race as a one-concept-fits-all approach to critical understandings of Blackness and television.

Specifying the location, circumstance, power dynamics, and histories of Black, Latinx, Asian American, Native, and particular axes of difference among and within each group affords an analysis that emphasizes the specific histories and conditions of encounter with television and the politics of representation that operate in such encounters. Working through the history and specificity of social, cultural, and economic relations of engagement with media has the added advantage of identifying the production of normative whiteness in its material and cultural forms. In the end, this approach avoids the reductionist or zero-sum models of racial analysis by positing a series of relational understandings of racial systems, group location, and power relations; similarly, this approach posits an account of television as a technology of race and a signifying system through which struggle and transformation can occur.

While the suggestion of such a formation might be perceived as a form of intellectual enclosure and needless compartmentalization, I offer it as a rather more capacious way to organize, circulate, and advance insights about how the relationship between television and social difference, especially Blackness, is coproduced within fields of power. Thinking historically and relationally about television and Blackness avoids the temptation to engage in creating "cheering fictions," as Stuart Hall once put it, about the promise of visibility and the politics of representation in cultural systems like television and cinema; rather, approaching these issues relationally and historically encourages critical questions, research projects, and collaborations that reframe the relationship between television and race as interlocking systems focused on particular and specific histories, practices, and struggles over the politics of representation, visibility, demographic parity, and meaning.

Watching While Black Rebooted! then appears at an opportune and challenging time in the history and future of the emergent scholarly arrangement that I am calling, for lack of a better formulation, CBTS. The book builds on over three decades of robust creative, important, and lasting scholarship that has heretofore remained at the level of informal networks, conference panels, occasional book series, and special journal issues. Foundational to the book's appearance is a generation of scholars (primarily women) who have curated and produced research, mentored several generations of scholars and students, and achieved some measure of public recognition. With the accumulation of the impressive body of scholarship, the proliferation of Black-themed television content, and the politics of representation gaining a foothold in the popular consciousness enabled by media activists, Black Lives Matter, and the campaigns against white supremacy in American media and culture, we face the challenge and opportunity of (re)imagining the field and the promise it offers. Indeed, this promise is one of the major possibilities conditioning a way forward; CBTS is a pitch as well to connect research and scholarship like that showcased in *Watching While*

Black Rebooted! to a broader set of histories, resources, questions, and networks. These opportunities are valuable now in a moment of excitement and possibility that is rich with content, interest, and seeming support for Black creative work and scholarship. But such a project is also crucial in those fallow times as well when there are limited opportunities to conduct research, to present and circulate work, and to teach and train a new generation of scholars.

Notes

1 The possibilities conditioning Blackness are of course themselves shaped by social and cultural events: global mass mobilizations for social justice and against racial violence in the wake of the George Floyd murder; the radicalization of white nationalism fueled by white resentment and grievance; and acceleration and intensification of disruptions, displacements, migrations, and precarity facing many thousands of people and wildlife related to climate change. Then there is the militarization, fortification, and use of technologies by nation-states, police, and forces of authority for the management and containment of domestic populations.

2 But let's not forget too that attracting Black viewers is profitable for studios and media companies.

3 These televised awards are handed out by, among others, Black Entertainment Television, NAACP, Peabody, Emmy, Golden Globe, the Screen Actors Guild, and the Writers Guild that all present annual prizes for the best work in television.

**Watching While Black
Rebooted!**

Introduction

● ●

I Still See Black People . . .
Everywhere

> Blackness is its own class.
> —Marsha Warfield[1]

Dear Generation Next,

Here we stand in the 2020s. What a time and place to start anything. The beginning finds us enduring widescale calamity with continued disregard and antipathy for Black life; the pandemic of COVID-19 and the deaths and destitution it causes, the economic tragedy of joblessness and shuttered businesses; and the lingering news cycle featuring an angry and petulant head of state. These states of affairs get illustrated in a multiplicity of ways, but none is more pervasive than on our television screens and through our social media. And while media scholar Herman Gray rightly ponders and critiques whether academicians have gotten it right by only addressing and complicating the visual, we know help and/or justice would not have come for the residents of the Gulf South or George Floyd or Ahmaud Arbery had we not had the ability to see it televisually or digitally and raise our voices in protest of what we saw.

In this time, we witness Black Lives Matter marshal a multiracial, multiethnic, and multicultural coalition of people who shout and demand change. We get a differently, digitally articulated education and cultural cybersphere leading to new and often viable forms of connection—a connection that also highlights the many problems within U.S. educational systems. We work in an exposed gig economy. And we enjoy voluminous televisual and digital content via the new-new streaming services and flowering of technology like YouTube and Tik-Tok. Despite this changed mediascape and culture, it remains important and necessary to think about and explore the content, industrial strategies, and logics that Black audiences, consumers, and users contend with for visual pleasure, companionship, refuge, information, retribution, branding, remembrance, justice, and entertainment.

And in the twenty-third year of this century, we return to television and digital spaces (those spaces relying on televisual content) to think anew about what engages and captures Black audiences (and users) and, more, why it matters. Ten-plus years past *Watching While Black: Centering the Television of Black Audiences*, the televisual landscape has changed exponentially. Since 2012, we've witnessed (and paid for) the rise of Netflix from a DVD mail company to the big-boy streaming platform and originator of content, the flowering of Hulu, Amazon Prime, HBO Max (now Max), Disney+, and the short-lived Quibi. Creators and showrunners Shonda Rhimes, Tyler Perry, Kenya Barris, and Ava DuVernay continue to dominate and shape the larger televisual landscape, especially for Black audiences. Yet old and newcomers such as Felicia D. Henderson, Mara Brock Akil, Issa Rae, Misha Green, Katori Hall, and even Jada Pinkett Smith on Facebook Live also flex their muscles and flower (or reseed) in ground laid ripe and hungry for Black content (well honestly, any content).

The added movers and shakers and platforms and makers fail to even account for the overwhelming deluge of content, everywhere. For 2023, six hundred scripted series are on tap for the broadcast, cable, and streaming platforms. This comes behind numbers of four hundred and five hundred annual contributions. These numbers suggest that either audiences do nothing else but watch television content or many shows go unseen by large numbers of people. Critically acclaimed and scholarly noticed series such as *Lovecraft Country* (HBO, 2020), appear and disappear as quickly as quirky but longer-lived ones like *Woke* (Hulu, 2020–2022) and *The Carmichael Show* (NBC, 2015–2017) with two and three seasons, respectively. Deals such as the 2012 one between Oprah Winfrey and Tyler Perry to create for and air his works on OWN make Black televisual content readily available, and several scholars have rightly examined this particular partnership for its content and industrial strategy over the years. Yet that is not all that has impacted and shaped the television targeting Black audience.

Social media plays a critical role in shaping, critiquing, and adding to what becomes screened and listened to as we share TikTok vignettes of our daily lives on that platform and the algorithmic equivalents on others. While fascinating and fabulous on one hand, these technological shifts afford us the ability to live and understand the world in alternate universes. Our shared viewing experience has completely shattered into countless different ways of seeing. In addition—as I forecasted in my first monograph, *Shaded Lives: African-American Women and Television*—much of the television content we consume is the same: programs simply recycled across various networks and streaming platforms. Thus, critical questions are very different and yet still similar, as the more things change, the more they remain the same.

The ways in which audiences and scholars grapple with the largesse of Blackness in all its splendidness are intriguing. As comedienne Marsha Warfield observes, Blackness really is its own class. With so much content and so many platforms, the productive and sometimes fantastical ways they are put into conversation, collusion, and collision not only fascinate but also cultivate potential career paths for you, Generation Next. Especially enthralling is the right-now tension between nonacademic watchers (and commentators) and media scholars. In places like Walmart, Old Navy, on MARTA, and the park, Black folks talk about media expertly. Combing carefully through Generation X– and millennial-driven Facebook groups of nonacademics and leaning into what Gen Z students and my children talk about and share on their platforms of choice, especially my Black TV freshperson students, provide insights about how and why people take up televisual tools in this moment. I believe listening to, watching, and discerning the voices and visions of how people understand and share, especially outside of academia, are paramount in making mediated scholarship continually viable, relevant, and useful.

In fact, I suggest apps and platforms alongside traditional television programs provide grounding and sense-making for many—not in a nostalgic sort of way necessarily but in one where narratives and technology resonate together. While most content creators, TikTokers, and Instagrammers feature makeup, fashion, hair, food, lifestyle, or fitness, some use the technology to move generations into a different level of consciousness. For example, Black creator Lynae Vanee (Bogues) talks "Parking Lot Pimpin" on Instagram, where she weekly critiques and explains systems of multiple oppressions—whether it be the Georgia runoff election, the HBCU bill, Supreme Court decisions, intersectional invisibility, or believing Black women.[2] Or, Angela Barnes and Paul Fox's 2020 getyourbootytothepoll.com campaign uses YouTube to get Black men in particular to vote. This campaign targets a rarely addressed demographic with spaces and places some might appreciate like the strip club.[3] In other words, creatives can now put information where people can get it, and they do it in ways already recognizable to and appreciated by audiences and users.

Generation Next, I keep thinking about what meanings we are discerning in this moment and why they matter—most directly, to our lived lives, our activism, and our making this world different, better. Not one for a whole lot of intellectualisms for the sake of it, I consider ways to push through minutiae to give voice to you who are coming up—to encourage, help shape, and provide tools, insights, and gumption to go further than just talk. The preeminent Herman Gray, whose works and generosity many of us stand on the back of, poses a way for media scholars to mesh our talents and concerns through his CBTS (Critical Black Television Studies). But it is challenging. The COVID-19 pandemic and the visualized murder of George Floyd laid bare that some of the ways we conduct business are not only antiquated but also unnecessary (and don't work). This hypermediated time also demonstrates how far apart we are ideologically, even as we share the need for community. So it is crucial to wonder aloud what these situations and shifts mean for Black people directly, Black popular culture in general, Black television and digital media specifically, and you, Generation Next.

Many argue that urban (Black) culture is the number one exported commodity of the United States. Apparently, knowing the heart of that culture can allow for the harnessing of a certain energy, talent, and star-power to yield revenue for those who produce it while affirming those who consume it. For example, the televised, streamed, and memed 2022 Super Bowl Halftime Show provided a blackity-Black salute to old-school hip-hop. It reaffirmed that California really knew how to party but, more, the centrality of Black music makers and Black popular culture to larger U.S. culture. However, a divided audience response along racial lines not only reflects different ways of seeing but also surfaces the court battle that the NFL faced then as a league where nearly 70 percent of its central employees (the players) are Black and 98 percent of its coaches are not. In larger Black popular culture, conundrums like these provide concrete rationales for why artists such as Beyoncé and Erykah Badu keep close reign on their brands or why NILs (name, image, and likeness rights) are now retained by collegiate athletes—any exposure potentially impacts their cash flow and ability to profit from their talents.

Thinking about the late 2021 selections Hulu picked and emailed "just for you [me]," I'm struck by the number and variety of selections offered. Series from the 1990s such as *My Wife and Kids* and *All of Us* are positioned next to the twenty-first-century *Claws*, *mixed-ish*, *Black Love*, and *Wu-Tang: An American Saga*. As a Black Generation X (boomer-adjacent) woman and audience member, I now have many choices about where I see and watch Black, while Black. But now I wonder, will there be anyone for me to talk to about all this televisual content? Deloitte Consulting produced a 2021 study that listed the five media places cornering the attention of Generation Z. As reported in the *Los Angeles Times*, "Twenty six percent of Gen Zers in the survey cited playing video games as their favorite entertainment activity, compared to 14% for listening to music, 12% for browsing the internet and 11% for engaging on social media. Only 10% said they would rather watch a movie or TV show at home."[4] Ten percent. In the last two years of teaching about television to over one hundred students (and mostly online), only three actually owned a television set, and all of them watched TV via a streaming platform. This sobering scenario must be considered and taken up within the scholarship and with how the work gets done by television and digital media scholars, as the likelihood of audience reversal is slim.

But despite these stats, broadcast and cable television still live. As Parrot Analytics asserts in their 2022 Value of Broadcast TV report, "Broadcast consistently appeals to broad audiences—at a fraction of the cost—at a time when streamers are battling for every subscriber in a hyper competitive market."[5] While people may not be at home watching television as much, they are still audiences watching televisual content, intently. Streamers host syndicated programming from broadcast and cable networks, while others like Netflix produce thousands of hours of original television content targeting global audiences. And more important to this project, 2019 data suggests that streamers' "diverse" debuts have been more in-demand than those that aren't, leading by more than 42 percent.[6] These figures suggest that the prediction of television's death is grossly exaggerated. Moreover, as scholar Kristen Warner reminded me, to sustain monetization, streamers are returning to advertising models and the television flow of the past. Thus, Generation Next, your gaming, music, internet, social media, and television may start to resemble the television of your grandparents—just digital, mobile, and prettier. And bountiful Black lives may see greater televisual light because of it all.

What Next Scholarship Looks Like

Watching While Black Rebooted! brings together a diverse set of critical media voices to examine what watching and living while Black and gendered, while Black and sexual, while Black and gaming, and while Black and confronting life can mean right now. The contributors, respected senior and up-and-coming-junior scholars, traverse larger television landscapes to interrogate issues of industry, transmediation, and content for Black audiences and those who command their attention. The chapters explore superheroism in series such as *Watchmen*, historic traumas as shown in the 1977 miniseries *Roots* and reimagined for the enslaved in the 2016 series *Underground*, machinima of the murder of Trayvon Martin, and queer possibilities in *Being Mary Jane*. The book provides an introspection of Blackness, visuality, and feeling in this moment, both broadly and specifically construed, that allows for generative ways of thinking about meaning and mattering in television media. Overall, *Watching While Black Rebooted!* tackles what the future looks like now.

The anthology is divided into four sections that overlap, bump up against one another, and speak to one another as part of a larger Black televisual conversation. The first section, **HISTORICIZING BLACK**, delves into the intersection of representation, recording, and recompense. Meaning, the writers in this section pose and answer critical questions about the intersections of real-lived Black experiences, their television representations, and industrial strategies that lean toward the status quo from the viewpoint of historical distance. The four chapters traverse time, genre, and larger cultural engagements to grapple with America's historic lies and broken promises about and to Black people. They think through the way television attempts to balance contest and complacency.

Eric Pierson addresses "Audiences and the Televisual Slavery-Narrative" by considering the ways in which television periodically turns to slavery as the focus of its scripted narrative programming. Through these programs, U.S. audiences get to wrestle with "original sin," and the stories become instrumental in initiating and shaping public discourse around slavery. Looking at the miniseries *Roots* as he did within the first version of this anthology, Pierson puts it in conversation with Misha Green and Joe Pokaski's series *Underground* (WGN America, 2016–2017) and Barry Jenkins's eleven-episode *The Underground Railroad* (Amazon Prime Video, 2021). He believes thinking through these series in tandem can be very instructive regarding the willingness of U.S. culture to engage in difficult dialogues around the impact of slavery on African-Americans as well as its willingness to tackle the present-day remnants of Black enslavement.

Moving forward in time but connected to contemporary enslavement, Christine Acham writes about "History, Trauma, and Healing in Ava DuVernay's *13th* and *When They See Us*." She believes that the eight minutes and forty-six seconds of George Floyd's murder awakened mainstream America to what has been the reality of Black life in this country since slavery. In her chapter, Acham analyzes the Netflix television texts *13th* (2016), *When They See Us* (2019), and the surrounding paratext of Oprah Winfrey's interview with the Exonerated Five in *When They See Us Now* (2019). In looking at these programs, she questions the relationship between Black stories, television, and history and whether viewers can really contend with Black history when so much of it is entwined with right-now violence, criminalization, trauma, and death.

Michael Boyce Gillespie leads a critical conversation with scholars in his "Thinking about *Watchmen* with Jonathan W. Gray, Rebecca A. Wanzo, and Kristen Warner." During this robust exchange, they think through medium, genre, fandom, and African-American history in the highly regarded HBO series *Watchmen* (2019). The scholars characterize the series as a disobedient adaptation, one that modifies, extends, and redirects the world-making of its source material—the famed twelve-issue comic-book series of the same name. Gillespie et al. explore the ways in which *Watchmen* remediates American historical legacies of racism and war that often serve as historical and ideological triggers. In so doing, they argue for *Watchmen*'s significance as some of the most consequential television of the century to date.

Finally, in a very different vein but with the same eye toward the importance of historical knowledge and understanding, Felicia D. Henderson writes about her own work as a television writer and showrunner. In her dual position as television scholar and practitioner, she employs a self-reflexive production studies approach to illuminate the five-season run of her one-hour drama *Soul Food* (Showtime, 2000–2004). The chapter, "From Sitcom Girl to Drama Queen," forces audiences and scholars to think about *Soul Food*'s role in foregrounding the current television landscape of Black-themed dramas across network, cable, and streaming platforms. Henderson addresses the absence of scholarly examination around the successful series and Black dramatic content in general while placing it in conversation with the current crop of now deemed successful, Black-themed televisual dramas.

In the second section, **ATTENDING BLACK**, scholars interrogate the ways in which televisual content not only migrates to other platforms and media (and vice versa) but does so with the well-being of Black people in mind. They consider what these platform and technology shifts mean for intent, Black audience address, and care. Using a variety of approaches, the scholars in "Attending Black" demonstrate how Black televisual media often moves beyond just entertainment, impacting the ways communities deal with trauma, professionalism, and ways of being seen both directly and covertly, tangibly and ephemerally. Beginning with TreaAndrea Russworm's "Gaming as Trayvon: #BlackLivesMatter Machinima and the Queer Metagames of Black Death," this section examines Black audiences and users beyond traditional television screens.

In her chapter, Russworm examines some of the ways in which Black gamers, both as new media content creators and as spectators, remediate Black televisual and digital culture. She focuses on a game that centers the horror of Trayvon Martin's murder from the perspective of players serving as witnesses. Closely examining original machinima ("machine cinema" that repurposes video game footage) and YouTube channels, she explores how their creators' actions encourage players, users, and audiences to complicate popular assumptions about the cultural life of video games. Their actions also help update approaches to the study of Blackness and media spectatorship.

The live-action televisual world returns with Nghana Lewis's "'Trying to Find Relief': Seeing Black Women through the Lens of Mental Health and Wellness in *Being Mary Jane* and *Insecure*." In this chapter, Lewis examines the space that creators Mara Brock Akil and Issa Rae construct for leading Black women to develop their identities, especially through the lens of mental health and wellness. Brock Akil and Rae create characters whose encounters with crisis and conflict in their professional and personal lives reveal behaviors and decision-making that are both self-affirming and self-destructive. Lewis argues that Brock Akil and Rae provide complex portraits of Black women's tremendous capacity to seek balance and find relief through self-definition. She highlights how these definitions map onto real-lived and necessary work being done in many spaces around Black women's health and well-being—areas that are contemporarily assessed as lacking for Black women within U.S. health-care systems.

Finally, the idea of Attending Black comes through updated industrial forums as Adrien Sebro introduces the concept of visual radio. Often overlooked in academic media discussions, Sebro outlines how radio continues to evolve with syndicated programming in his chapter "On Air Black: *The Breakfast Club*, Visual Radio, and Spreadable Media." According to Nielsen Media, Black audiences still listen to radio at higher rates than all audiences, with 91 percent of all Black Americans listening. Through radio, these audiences can engage in discussions of Black life and culture through sound and now by sight as programs expand their reach through YouTube and other platforms. With a particular focus on Black radio, its history, and shifts to the visual, Sebro writes specifically on how the syndicated show *The Breakfast Club* (2010–) attends to a contemporary, millennial, and tech-savvy Black audience and gains national attention in the process. Attending Black through media is a continued critical (or at least voiced) aspect of Black media business enterprises. It also serves as an integral and sophisticated component of monetizing Black audiences.

Thus, the section **MONETIZING BLACK** focuses on the ways Black audiences get commodified through and within Black content. With ever-changing and developing technologies, the economic, production, and representational models of televisual content stay in flux. However, this expanded televisual landscape allows Blackness to recur more frequently and readily. When it comes to how content gets monetized and how Black audiences are reached, different models and updated strategies are being deployed to capture the still-coveted eighteen-to-forty-nine market. And within this demographic, Black women audience members retain their most-targeted status. Television research leans heavily into data analytics of audience composition and address. Contemporary research provides several relevant findings: (1) authentic stories resonate with audiences, (2) audiences are socially conscious, and (3) contentment engagement continues to rise.[7] These findings suggest that corporations, studios, and production companies must deploy their resources toward and be much more conscientious about content that jives with audiences' vision of a more progressive (and actual) United States. The chapters in this section delve into how the new media landscape actualizes Black audience monetization in different ways.

In the first chapter of this section, Alfred Martin writes about "Black Women, Audiences, and the Queer Possibilities of the Black-Cast Melodrama." He suggests that since the 1970s, Black gayness gets addressed only episodically within Black-cast sitcoms and as undifferentiated in its characterization. However, as networks and advertisers began to deal with audience "nichification," rather than turn to the larger Blackness paradigm as they so often do, some networks turned to Black *women* audiences to introduce queer narratives. Using the series *Being Mary Jane* (BET, 2013–2019) and *The Haves and the Have Nots* (OWN, 2013–2021) as examples, Martin explores how the industrial imaginings and address of Black women audiences enliven Black gayness in Black television drama.

This sort of attention to industrial spectatorship leads to Briana Barner's "In a '90s Kind of World, I'm Glad I Got My Shows! Digital Streaming and Black Nostalgia." With the July 2020 Netflix announcement introducing their Strong Black Lead marketing plan, Black audiences received what seemed to be a response to their pleas for older, Black-cast series to appear on the streamer. This chapter explores how Black audiences' demand for inclusion in the television nostalgia boom helped bring a slate of shows to the platform, particularly in the aftermath of the civil unrest following the murders of Breonna Taylor and George Floyd. The inclusion of these series helps strengthen Netflix's subbranding of Strong Black Lead, courts Black audiences, and increases Netflix's quest for diverse representations. In this shifting climate, monetization in terms of brand and diversity may even now encourage a sort of reversal, or at least the potential for it, as shown in the final chapter of the Monetizing Black section.

Shelleen Greene's "*Tyler Perry's Too Close to Home*: Black Audiences in the Post-Network Era" thinks through Perry's target audience in this series as part of a changed media economic landscape. Running for two seasons, *Too Close to Home* (2016–2017) was the first scripted program for TLC. As opposed to race, this series foregrounds intersections of class, gender, and sexuality as a way to differently monetize and extend the Perry brand. Unlike all his other series that cater to and center Black lives, the protagonists of *Too Close to Home* are largely white. In her chapter, Greene discusses the ways in which Perry attempts to extend his brand to white audiences and explores how his industrial approach within and outside of this narrative both addresses and repels his core audience—a Black core audience that certainly expects him to champion them. The affective resonance Perry's work typically engenders with Black audiences brings the *Reboot* to its final section, Feeling Black.

While this fourth and final section of the book could have easily been titled Intersectional Black or even Blackity Black, **FEELING BLACK** most affectively captures Blackness through industrial, cultural, and theoretical lenses. Affective discourses have permeated television studies for nearly forty years, forcefully over the last twenty. This theoretical frame of feeling and in-betweenness draws not only on phenomenological work but also on the ways in which Black scholars have consistently valued, highlighted, and made knowable interiority, culture, and emotional resonance in the conception of Black audiences. This feeling comes through a deep and unrepented understanding and privileging of Black cultural points of view. Whether appearing in something like *A Black Lady Sketch Show* (HBO, 2019–), where they feature a "Hertep Homecoming," or the Black and brown *Pose* (FX, 2018–2021) narratives, centering queer life of color, making the lives of Black folks visible beyond BET and TVOne and more than surface-level are part of the new televisual reality. In tandem, the chapters in Feeling Black tackle how contemporary television and digital media provide a deeper look into Black interiority and culture—the ways creators make audiences feel Black.

The section starts with Brandy Monk-Payton, who offers "'I'm Trying to Make People Feel Black': Affective Authenticity in *Atlanta*." In this chapter, she considers the series *Atlanta*'s affective authenticity by thinking through the program's promotion of an unapologetic, Southern Black, poor and working-class audiovisual vernacular—a vernacular that has increasingly gone viral in current digital media culture. Monk-Payton maintains that audiences must do more than watch with *Atlanta* (FX, 2016–2022); they must connect with the stories and the people of the text to move within and through the millennial and Black structures Donald Glover attempts to establish. This need for audiences to connect culturally, to really feel and relate to what's happening, finds its way into the next chapter as well.

In Beretta E. Smith-Shomade's "I'm Digging You: Television's Turn to Dirty South Blackness," I explore media's scripted capturing of a new Black Dirty South and its embodiment of the people there. Specifically, I think through the re-migrated Black Dirty South as shown in the narratives of OWN's *Queen Sugar* (2016–2022) and Starz's *P-Valley* (2020–). I consider not only who's watching but also why these audiences watch rural, Black and poor, Black and striving, and Black and surviving people and their stories. Looking pointedly through the frames of queerness and informal work economies, I highlight some of the ways this new Black Dirty South gets understood and felt through a limitedly seen cultural lens.

To bring the *Reboot* home, Jacqueline Johnson emotes "I Feel Conflicted as F*ck: Netflix's *Dear White People* and Re-presenting Black Viewing Communities." This chapter extends important research on Black audiences by analyzing how audiences themselves are rendered on-screen. Asserting that *Dear White People*'s depiction of Black spectatorship uniquely portrays the anxieties of Black viewers while also effectively working to dismantle binary understandings of media images, Johnson uses the Netflix series (2017–2021) as a case study to engage broader conversations about relationships between race, spectatorship, and media representation. She also theorizes and elevates Black spectatorship through contemporary Black television audiences' imaginings. Johnson provides a fitting conclusion to thinking about Black audiences' navigation of television and digital media and an apt direction for where audiences and scholars might go next.

Scholarship in the Time of Trauma

Watching While Black Rebooted! The Television and Digitality of Black Audiences provides present-day critical insights from media scholars who examine works targeted toward Black audiences. The large landscape from which we can now draw prevents covering all or even most of the significant works airing and streaming in this moment. Quinta Brunson's *Abbott Elementary*, an ABC sitcom that premiered in 2021, has become a critical and award-winning success by centering the lives of primarily Black working teachers, Black students, and their families. 50 Cent's *Power* block of shows continues to bring significant ratings for Starz. *Empire* (FOX, 2015–2020), *The Quad* (BET, 2017–2018), Spike Lee's *She's Gotta Have It* (Netflix, 2017–2019), and *Bel-Air* (Peacock, 2022–) all invoke "quality" dramatic Black television ascriptions across platforms. These offerings fail to even include nonscripted television aimed at Black audiences. These series seem to have perfected franchising with offerings such as *Love & Hip Hop*, *Love & Marriage*, and *Growing Up Hip Hop*; these as well as the emerging ways we might think about television through video games and social media storytelling are not robustly addressed.

Beyond these gaps, several other scholars were planned for inclusion in this reboot—mostly, but not exclusively, Black women whose voices are missed here. But scholarship in a time of trauma is hard-pressed and, for some, a lost endeavor. No one can fully account for the scares, the illnesses, the deaths, the agony, the murders, and the depression that color every aspect of our lives *still* in this moment. These also don't factor in the daily and continued microaggressions coming from colleagues, co-workers, students, and neighbors where we reside. Although I won't name you here, know that you are seen and valued. The world is lessened by not getting your voice and brilliance on this one—but next time.

Always,

Beretta E. Smith-Shomade

Notes

1 Quote from Marsha Warfield in *History of the Sitcom*, written by Robert Eaton, aired August 8, 2021, on CNN.
2 Bogues was nominated for a 2021 and 2022 NAACP Image Award for Outstanding Social Media Personality, losing to Laron Hines and Kevin Fredericks (Kevonstage), respectively.
3 See the commentary around getyourbootytothepoll.com (no longer extant) from Juana Summers, "Stripper Polls: The Racy Voting PSA That's Actually All about the Issues," NPR, October 5, 2020, https://www.npr.org/2020/10/05/918711192/stripper-polls-the-racy-voting-psa-thats-actually-all-about-the-issues.
4 Ryan Faughnder, "What Entertainment Does Gen Z Prefer? The Answer Isn't Good for Hollywood," *Los Angeles Times*, April 18, 2021, accessed February 15, 2022, https://www.latimes.com/entertainment-arts/business/story/2021-04-18/what-entertainment-does-gen-z-prefer-the-answer-isnt-good-for-hollywood.
5 Parrot Analytics, "The Value of Broadcast TV," October 26, 2022.
6 Parrot Analytics and Creative Artists Agency (CAA), "Measuring What Matters: The Impact of Talent Diversity on Audience Demand for Television," Marché International des Programmes de Communication (MIPCOM), October 11, 2020, https://insights.parrotanalytics.com/hubfs/Resources/whitepapers/Parrot%20Analytics%20-%20CAA%20-%20TV%20Diversity%20-%20MIPCOM%20Online+.pdf.
7 Parrot Analytics and CAA.

Part I

Historicizing Black

• •

1

Audiences and the
Televisual Slavery-Narrative

●●●●●●●●●●●●●●●●●●●●●●●

ERIC PIERSON

Periodically, the producers of television content turn their attention to slavery in America for narrative inspiration. These narratives become a nexus for dialogues that can touch upon several areas, such as history, politics, and social justice. Slavery-narratives may be anchored in a historical past, but they present an opportunity to explore the ways in which the remnants of the institution continue to have an impact on the cultural and political landscape. Beginning with the broadcast of *Roots*, through two seasons of *Underground* and the release of *The Underground Railroad* on Amazon Prime, slavery-narratives have always been about much more than slavery.

Beginning with the publication of Harriet Beecher Stowe's *Uncle Tom's Cabin* in 1852, slavery-narratives have been important to public discourse.[1] Stowe's novel was critical in establishing a set convention that would shape the structure of slavery-narratives. From *The Klansman*, published in 1905, through Margaret Mitchell's *Gone with the Wind*, first published in 1936, a series of solidified storytelling codes and conventions follow the slavery-narrative from novels to filmic and televisual presentations. The ways audiences respond to these narratives are shaped by the method of delivery and the cultural climate at the time of viewing.

Roots, first broadcast in 1977; *Underground*, which was a project connected to Superstation WGN, first aired in 2016; and *The Underground Railroad*, which began streaming on Amazon in May of 2021, all make use of the slavery-narrative conventions but in different ways. This interaction between narrative convention and audiences reflects the ways in which the discourse about the impact of slavery has evolved over time. These slavery-narratives are worthy of more extensive examination because of their ability to not just entertain but also shape and change public discourse around the lives of African Americans from the past, influence conversations in the present, and challenge the direction of the future.

Conventions

In this chapter, I focus on four conventions that have defined televisual slavery-narratives. This list is meant not to be exhaustive but to home in on those conventions that are most influential in televisual storytelling. These conventions include plantation as setting, the dramatic conflict between the enslaved in the fields and those in the house, the presentation of debates about slavery, and the act of bearing witness. On one level, the planation is the physical space in which the slavery-narrative primarily takes place. The plantation contains important narrative spaces like the big house, the slaves' quarters, and the fields where the enslaved labor. Beyond just the physical, the plantation functions as a symbolic representation of the master's influence and power, not just the power he wheeled over the enslaved but also the power he held within the community. The opulence of the big house is used to separate the master from the brutality of slavery.

The big house displays the slave hierarchy—a hierarchy where the enslaved are divided into factions of house slaves and field slaves. Those who work within the big house are better treated and are seen as of greater value than those who work in the fields. This conflict created among the slaves is often used to structure narrative tension as they are pitted against each other. This cultivates questions of to whom slaves owe their loyalty: to the master of the house or to others enslaved like themselves.

Debates on the merits of slavery are an integral convention and component of the slavery-narrative. Usually within these parleys, slave owners argue with other slave owners or slaves debate with other slaves. The wrangling on the merits of slavery seldom provides a discussion of the myriad forces that contribute to its maintenance like politicians, lawyers, bankers, and doctors. These conversations are less about the institutions surrounding slavery and tend to present the slavery conflict between good masters and bad masters. The enslaved themselves often argue the merits in terms of good versus bad treatment at the hands of the master.

The act of bearing witness carries an important role in the televisual presentation of the slavery-narrative. Violence visited upon Black bodies is a very familiar element of the slavery-narrative and is often described or presented in graphic detail. Alongside this violence, audiences get the reactions of those who witness these moments. They capture much of the pain of slavery. The use of the reaction shot can move the audience into a deeper connection to the narrative's presentation. Those watching become surrogates for the audience; their point of view becomes our point of view, and their helplessness to intervene is shared by the audience. The movement of the slavery-narrative to television put stress on these conventions as content creators and viewers understood that slavery-narratives were about more than a moment of history.

Roots

In January of 1977, ABC televised the miniseries *Roots* based on the novel *Roots: The Saga of an American Family* that had been published in August 1976 by Alex Haley. The narrative unfolded over eight nights, with the final night of the broadcast delivering a ratings share of 71 percent. The program received almost universal critical acclaim, receiving thirty-five Emmy nominations. Since its initial broadcast, it remains one of the most important miniseries in television history. *Roots* was not only a critical success, but it has also had a lasting cultural impact. The process of bringing *Roots* to television was complex. The production needed to be faithful to the novel, conform to production expectations of network television, and navigate the conventions of the slavery-narrative in the televisual setting. The success of *Roots* can be attributed to a deft balancing of these ofttimes competing expectations.

Roots began its march toward television when producer David L. Wolper purchased the rights to the unfinished novel. The publisher, Doubleday, sold the rights hoping to recoup some of the investment it had made in the novel. Haley had missed several of the publisher's deadlines, and there was concern that Haley may never finish the project. Wolper, who had produced several successful media projects, indicated that his goal was to make a series that was an immigrant family narrative. He saw the novel as not about slavery but instead about the strength of a family. Wolper's decision would have an impact on how the production would handle the convention of the slavery debate: *Roots* would not include a complex examination of the institutional structures of slavery. It would instead frame the debate as good participants in the institution versus bad ones. In the premiere episode, we are introduced to Captain Davies, played by Edward Asner, and Mr. Slater, played by Ralph Waite. Both are part of the slave trade but have very different views of slavery. Captain Davies is a religious man who wants to treat slaves as humans with souls, while Mr. Slater sees them simply as cargo. Throughout the production, the institution of slavery is reduced to the actions of good versus bad people.

While *Roots* centers a great deal of the narrative on the plantation and big house, the story begins in Africa. The beginning of the story on the continent of Africa is one of the elements of the narrative that would have a profound cultural impact. The slavery-narratives prior all begin with the institution of slavery in place and center themselves on the plantation. In the case of *Roots*, they present Africans as people and free. The series begins in Africa and introduces the audience to a seldom-told history of Black people. This introduction led to an increase in African Americans wanting to trace their family's lineage back to Africa. It also led to an increase in colleges and universities offering courses in African American history. The series provided audiences with a seldom-examined history of the lives of African people before they were taken from their homes as well as a detailed presentation of the journey through the middle passage.

Yet *Roots* limits the presentation of the slave hierarchy. Limited attention gets paid to conflict between those who live in the big house and others on the plantation. The conflict among the enslaved appears strongest between those who have known slavery for a long time and those like Kunta Kinte (LeVar Burton) who are never going to accept the bonds of slavery. This longing to be free becomes a message that resonates throughout the family and moves the narrative toward a satisfying conclusion when the descendants of Kunta Kinte work their way to freedom. This lack of intraslave conflict allows the narrative to be centered on the family and their single-minded drive toward freedom. It also allows audiences to focus on the resilience of the Black family as strong and nurturing even while in the bonds of slavery.

The convention of the slavery-narrative genre gains additional power in televisual presentations through the act of bearing witness. Much of the brutality inflicted on Black bodies is done not just to correct the actions of the offending slave but also to serve as a warning for others who may be thinking of breaking the rules. In *Roots*, we bear witness to the beating of Kunta after he is captured trying to escape. He is beaten until he agrees to respond to the slave name of Toby. During the scene, audiences are focused not only on Kunta but also on the ways in which the others react to the beating. This act of bearing witness builds a connection to the event. It connects the viewers to the emotion and affective intent as they occupy empathetic positions to those who are diegetically watching the act. The inability to help the victim is shared by viewers as well. The desire to save Kunta was one of the most powerful moments of the program and would have a very strong effect on Black audiences, as all the faces diegetically watching the moment are Black.

Roots benefited from being the first television series to present the horrors of slavery to American audiences. As such, it continues to share a strong place in the discussion of slavery in America. It continues to be rerun in syndication and serves as a mainstay in programming connected to Black History Month. The series was even remade by the History Channel in 2016. Slavery as part of U.S. history has long been avoided by the media. Audiences seem to be shocked by the brutality of it, even though the television narrative "softened" much of the violence in Haley's novel. Before the broadcast of *Roots*, "novels for television" had been scheduled to air weekly, which would allow their positive impact on the ratings to be felt over an extended period of time. The network executives were so concerned that the show would have a negative impact on ratings, they chose to air the episodes on successive nights. According to the Nielsen ratings, *Roots* was the most-watched television program in American history, with over 85 percent of American households viewing at least one episode.

Despite the success of *Roots*, network television has avoided the subject of slavery within its programming. While the vast majority of viewers believe the program's impact on popular culture was positive, some criticized the program as being used to "make White people look bad" or asked, "Why are we bringing up stuff that happened a long time ago?" Reports surfaced of verbal arguments escalating to physical conflicts about the show and some hesitance to the demands of Black students for schools to dedicate resources to teaching Black history. None of these, however, detract from the positive impact of the broadcast. The program instilled in Black families pride in overcoming obstacles since being taken from Africa. Even with all the success of *Roots*, it would take almost forty years before television would produce another slavery-narrative.

Underground

By the time *Underground* premiered on March 9, 2016, the landscape of television was very different from the one in place when *Roots* aired. The dominance of network television had been diminished as more and more people turned to cable or the internet to receive their content. The cultural landscape had also changed as America was preparing to say farewell to President Barack Obama, who was nearing the completion of his two terms as America's first Black president. America was also reacting to the presidential candidacy of Donald Trump and his promise to "Make America Great Again."

Underground was purchased by WGN as part of a plan to expand its audience by including more original content. WGN was a network reeling from the loss of its most valuable asset, the broadcast rights to Chicago Cubs baseball. The prohibitive costs of renewing the contract for Cubs baseball forced the network to pivot toward other sources of content in an effort to create a superstation on par with TBS and TNT. *Underground* focuses primarily on the lives of seven enslaved people as they plan and execute their escape from a plantation in Georgia. The story follows members of the Macon Seven as they reach freedom and return to help others. Along the way, they interact with abolitionists and historical figures like Frederick Douglass and Harriet Tubman as well as relentless slave trackers. Like *Roots*, *Underground* carried many of the conventions of the slavery-narrative. The difference with the series was the creative forces behind the narrative. *Underground* was created by Misha Green and Joe Pokaski. Green, a Black woman, came to the project with a long list of television experiences as a writer, director, and producer. One of the major criticisms of

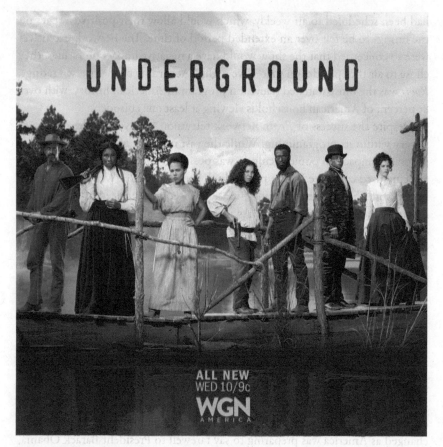

FIG. 1.1 *Underground* cast

Roots was centered on the lack of Black voices involved in the creative process. The production team for *Underground* included Black talent at almost all levels of production.

   While the narrative focus of *Roots* spent limited time exploring the hierarchy among the enslaved, *Underground* made this conflict one of the central foci of the show's narrative. This hierarchy among the enslaved makes their plan to escape difficult, as the slaves spend a great deal of time and energy fighting among themselves. The hierarchy is further complicated by the relationships that the house slaves share with the master. The master is having an "affair" with Ernestine (Amirah Vann), the head house slave, and the affair has yielded two children: Rosalee (Jurnee Smollett), a young house slave, and her brother, James (Maceo Smedley). The mistress of the house, Suzanna (Andrea Frankle), is well aware of her husband's infidelities but seems more concerned with maintaining her lifestyle than addressing his extracurriculars. As the enslaved plan their escape, they debate if they can trust the house girl, Rosalee, to keep their plan a secret. Also thrown into the mix are Cato (Alano Miller), a slave with some stature on the plantation, and Noah (Aldis Hodge), the field slave who is seen as the group's leader. The Cato/Noah conflict provides the show an opportunity to explore the ways in which slaves hold different understandings of freedom. Noah sees freedom as independence, while Cato sees freedom as acceptance. This intraslave conflict was never resolved during the two seasons that the show was in production.

The abolitionist movement was an important narrative thread and allowed the program to have a very active debate surrounding the evils of slavery. The series is more than just a slavery-narrative; it works to engage the audience regarding the history of slavery. It interweaves historical figures like Harriet Tubman, Frederick Douglass, and Patty Cannon into the storylines. It also spends time addressing the legal rights of slaves and critiques the Dred Scott decision. The show takes time to examine the practice of not allowing the enslaved to read or write as a way to control them. The ability to write proves to be very important as they seek traveling passes to help them in their escape. The dangers of enslaved reading are highlighted in the episode entitled "28," where Daniel has his eyes blinded with lye after he is caught teaching others to read.

Underground inserts itself into contemporary politics with an episode that aired in the second season titled "Minty." The episode focuses on Harriet Tubman giving a speech to a group of abolitionists. Tubman, played by Alisha Hinds, delivers a forty-five-minute monologue where she recounts her life and explains why she keeps returning to the South to help runaway slaves. The power of the episode comes from Hinds's performance as she speaks of Harriet's life without the help of flashbacks, just the power of her words. The episode takes an interesting, overtly political turn when at the end of the speech, Tubman breaks the fourth wall and looks directly into the camera and references the phrase "Make America Great Again." She says, "You gotta find what it means for you to be a soldier. Beat back those that are trying to kill everything that's good and right in the world and call it 'making it great again.' We can't just be citizens in a time of war. That would be surrender. That'd be giving up our future, and our souls. Ain't nobody gets to sit this one out, you hear me?"[2]

Underground uses the power of bearing witness not just to highlight the brutality of slavery but also as a way to call attention to the indifference of those supporting slavery. In *Roots*, the acts of bearing witness were carried out by other slaves. We get to see the action from their point of view, and we get to see their expressions. *Underground* shows us the point of view of several whites as they bear witness, and in their reactions (and inaction), they display a certain apathy toward the violence. The act of bearing witness becomes a spectacle in the episode "Grave" from the first season. To convince the community that he will represent their values in his quest to become a U.S. senator, Tom Macon (Reed Diamond), the master of Macon Plantation, has a runaway slave lynched. As the body of Sam hangs over the balcony, Macon stands on the platform that

Sam helped construct and gives a campaign speech to his fellow slave owners. The body swings behind him. The crowd's reaction to Sam's dead body is one of both celebration and indifference. They are sure that they have found the right candidate to support.

Underground was canceled after two seasons, intersecting with the politics of the day. As the show began its second season, WGN was in the process of looking for a buyer for the network. The buyer that emerged was the Sinclair Media Group. The Sinclair Media Group is a conservative media group that saw the rise of Donald Trump as an opportunity to expand its holdings. Given that Sinclair has been characterized by some as a far-right media company, the canceling of *Underground* could be seen as an attempt to stifle Black voices.[3] While the series delivered respectable ratings, there was little interest in picking up the show among other networks—especially with its estimated production cost of 4.5 million dollars per episode, a very expensive hour of syndicated television. The series did find a home at OWN, where it reruns with new interviews from the cast and creative team. There are currently no plans for OWN to produce new episodes.

The Underground Railroad

As *Underground* moved through its first season, Colson Whitehead's novel *The Underground Railroad* was on the *New York Times* best seller list and won a Pulitzer Prize. In September 2016, it was announced that Barry Jenkins would be adapting the novel with the intention of bringing the story to television. In March of the next year, it was announced that Amazon had come on board and Jenkins would not only write but also serve as the director of the ten-episode project. The addition of Amazon implied the production would have access to the resources needed to deliver high-quality content. Given the quality of Colson's book, the proven talent of Barry Jenkins as both a writer and a director, and the deep pockets of Amazon, there were high expectations surrounding the project. The casting of the lead character, Cora, would be crucial to its success. Cora appears on almost every page of the novel, and she serves as our guide through the story. Jenkins chose Thuso Mbedu for the role, an actress unfamiliar to U.S. audiences.

The Underground Railroad tells the story of Cora as she makes the decision to join fellow enslaved Caesar (Aaron Pierre) in a plan to escape from a plantation in Georgia. As they flee, the noted slave catcher Arnold Ridgeway (Joel Edgerton) and his Black assistant, Homer (Chase Dillon), are not far behind. Cora and Caesar find refuge and a degree of solace in South Carolina, which is soon interrupted by Ridgeway. Caesar is captured as Cora escapes to North Carolina. Cora spends months hiding in an attic until Ridgeway and Homer arrive to search the town, and she is captured. Instead of returning Cora to Georgia, Ridgeway drags Cora back to his home in Tennessee as he attempts

FIG. 1.2 *The Underground Railroad*

to reconcile with his dying father. During the visit to the Ridgeway home, a group of freemen led by Royal (William Jackson Harper) rescue Cora and use the Underground Railroad to send her to Indiana. In Indiana, she becomes part of Valentine Farm, a farm owned and managed by free people. Cora finds peace in the community until, once again, Ridgeway and Homer find her. Upon her capture, Ridgeway forces her to lead him to the Underground Railroad. During a struggle, Ridgeway is killed and Cora escapes into the railway tunnel.

The Underground Railroad signals from the beginning that it will be a very different type of slavery-narrative. For example, while most stories spend much of the narrative with the plantation as the primary setting, this story leaves the plantation after the first episode and only returns in the form of character flashbacks. The absence of this storytelling device allows the story to focus on the two types of Black people in the world of the story, those who are free and those who are not. *The Underground Railroad* focuses on Cora's emotional, spiritual, physical, and psychological journey. In focusing on Cora, the series excels in its ability to offer a full examination of slavery and the institutional forces that contribute to slavery's maintenance and proliferation. Medicine, politics, religion, and the law all have a role to play in the subjugation of Black people.

Cora and Caesar make their way to South Carolina and begin to build a life for themselves in a community that appears to welcome them. Their view is shattered when they are made aware that the Black women in the community are being sterilized without their knowledge, and the men are being given free "vitamins" that are making them ill. They are in the middle of a eugenics experiment.[4] Under the guise of care and concern, the community uses Black bodies for experimentation. The "vitamins" given to Black men are designed to see how long it will take for the Black body to break down. The reluctance of some Black people to take the COVID-19 vaccine may not be based on some irrational fear but from a knowledge of medicine's past indifference to (and active attacks on) the health of Black citizens.[5]

Upon fleeing South Carolina, Cora finds herself in North Carolina forced to hide in an attic while she waits for the next train on the Underground Railroad. The station master hides Cora until the train comes. As he sneaks her into town, he stops to show her the road leading into town lined with Black bodies hanging from the trees as a warning. The community believes that the Bible teaches them they are superior. Their superiority gives them the right to burn books and newspapers and the right to lynch any Black person they meet regardless of being free or enslaved. The members of the community all assemble at an outdoor building with an altar featuring a cross in the front of the building. As the crowd is worked into a frenzy by a preacher, a young Black woman is led to the stage and hanged to the applause of the community. Using the Bible as a rationale for bigotry and hatred continues in our contemporary setting.

When Cora makes her way to the Valentine Farm, the role of politics and the law are highlighted. The Valentine Farm is run by a successful group of free Blacks who have built a prosperous business harvesting their grapes and turning them into wine. Because they are in Indiana, a free state, they have rights. But those rights are only as good as the white politicians charged with their enforcement. John Valentine, the community's founder, must pay regular tribute to a local judge to make sure no surprise raids on the community occur. Valentine debates moving the community to California out of fear that their success has fostered resentment from whites, and the law may not be willing or able to protect them from potential violence. His concerns are realized as the community is attacked while they have church service. The ambush's goal is simply to kill as many people from the community as possible. The images of the attack would connect to the audience as they remember the actual Tulsa massacre, which would have its hundredth anniversary shortly after the show premiered on Amazon.

The series highlights the importance of documenting the history of Black people by Black people. As Cora travels on the Underground Railroad, she is asked to tell her story. These stories are from actual records of those who have traveled on the railroad. It ensures that the history is not lost or distorted over time. The contest over historical narrative resonates with audiences as we find ourselves in contemporary debates surrounding critical race theory (CRT). The core of the debate about CRT is not the theory but whose version of history will be taught. In this contemporary debate about history, there appears to be a desire to remove dialogue about the impact of race on the past, the present, and the future.

The process of bearing witness in *The Underground Railroad* is primarily through the eyes of Cora. We see and experience the world as she does. She is our guide. Because we have Cora as a guide, her emotional journey is intertwined with the audience. The acts of violence and brutality are seen not just as a series of individual moments; they are part of Cora's psychological trauma. We (the audience) feel the weight of incident after incident and begin to understand how the impact of slavery affects not only the body but also the mind. The series makes a powerful statement on the long-term trauma of slavery. That trauma is highlighted in a speech by the freedman Mingo (Chukwudi Iwuji) as he argues against letting Cora continue to be part of the Valentine community:

> We accomplished the impossible . . . but not everyone has the character we do. We're not all going to make it. Some of us are too far gone. Slavery has twisted their minds, an imp filled their minds with foul ideas. They have given themselves over to whiskey and its false comforts. To hopelessness and its constant devils. We've seen these ones on the plantations, on the streets of towns and cities—those who will not, cannot respect themselves. You've seen them here, receiving the gift of this place but unable to fit in. They always disappear in the night because deep in their hearts they know they are unworthy. It is too late for them.[6]

The Underground Railroad also provides a moment seldom presented in these slavery-narratives; audiences get to bear witness to the horrors of slavery as presented through the eyes of slaveholders in a way that reflects a disgust for the brutality. When the runaway slave Big Anthony is captured, he is tortured for three days. Lunch is served outdoors so that the torture can be witnessed up close. Jenkins includes the reactions of those who are witnessing the process, and it becomes one of the few times that we see repugnance from someone other than the enslaved.

The Underground Railroad offers a powerful narrative for public discourse. But it is worth noting that it hides behind the paywall of Amazon Prime. The same paywall that allows Amazon to support creative storytelling with significant financial resources also limits the audience that will have access to that programming. Because the show is behind a paywall, there seems to be less public discourse than what usually accompanies these types of narratives. The power of Whitehead's book and the powerful direction and creative energy of Barry Jenkins are clearly on display in the narrative. That power would be expanded if there was a way to increase the size of the audience. In the last few years, a number of television programs have focused on Black stories. Critically acclaimed shows such as *Lovecraft Country*, *Watchmen*, *Small Axe*, and *Queen Sugar* all require audiences to pay for access. This surcharge for quality Black stories has limited the ability of these programs to offer audiences a wider understanding of Black experiences.

Slavery-narratives are never just stories about slavery. Televisual slavery-narratives give audiences an opportunity to dialogue about the impact slavery has had on the United States in the past, debate the impact that it is having on us currently, and develop strategies to help mitigate the influence it can have on the future. Television has changed a great deal since *Roots*, and those changes have impacted the ways in which audiences engage with television. But the power of visiting this period of history has not changed. No other institution has had a more lasting and troubling impact on the United States. These narratives allow audiences to see and understand the historical resilience of Black people and the Black family. They remind us that contemporary struggles around voting rights, fair housing, inequalities in wealth distribution, criminal justice reform, educational disparity, and other social issues are rooted in and connected to the past. These visits to the past are a necessary reminder of how far we have come while demonstrating how much more remains to be done.

Notes

1 Historians credit the popularity of Stowe's novel with an awakening to the evils of slavery. The novel became a powerful tool for abolitionists in the fight against slavery and in convincing white citizens to support the Civil War.
2 *Underground*, season 2, episode 6, "Minty," directed by Anthony Hemingway, written by Misha Green, Joe Pokaski, and Tiffany Greshler, aired April 12, 2017, on WGN America.
3 Dominic Patten, "John Legend Seeks New Home for 'Underground,' Blasts 'Far-Right' Sinclair," Deadline, September 27, 2017, https://deadline.com/2017/09/ john-legend-underground-resurrection-sinclair-broadcasting-tribune-wgn-america -1202177723/.
4 The American eugenics movement had a profound effect on Black people and their relationship to the medical profession. Medical doctors carried out sterilizations on Black women without their permission under the guise of routine gynecological procedures and actively worked to "prove" that Blacks were genetically inferior.
5 During the Tuskegee Experiment, 1932–1972, hundreds of Black men suffered with untreated syphilis as the government agencies of the Public Health Service (PHS) and the Centers for Disease Control and Prevention (CDC) conducted "research" on the impact of leaving the disease untreated.
6 Colson Whitehead, *The Underground Railroad* (New York: Doubleday, 2016), 288.

2

History, Trauma, and Healing in Ava DuVernay's *13th* and *When They See Us*

•••••••••••••••••••••••

CHRISTINE ACHAM

> In accepting both the chaos of history and the fact of my total end, I was freed to truly consider how I wished to live—specifically, how do I live free in this black body? ... The greatest reward of this constant interrogation, of confrontation with the brutality of this country, is that it has freed me from ghosts and guarded me against the sheer terror of disembodiment.
> —Ta-Nehisi Coates[1]

> In America it is tradition to destroy the Black body—*it is heritage*.
> —Ta-Nehisi Coates[2]

While it was practically mandated watching for Black people, the original ABC television series *Roots* (1977) seared indelible images and sounds into my mind.

I thought that maybe I was too young to cope with brutality or, as my family often called me, too sensitive. However, my reaction to rewatching the series in my mid-twenties was about the same—it was simply painful. I wanted to and had to look away from so many of the scenes of the horrors put upon those who had come before me, those who had paved the way for my freedom. *Roots* makes it *nearly* impossible for me to make it through any film or television program set during the era of slavery, no matter how well reviewed. I am clearly not alone in this. Articles, tweets, and blog posts that call for a moratorium on slavery as a subject for media projects are easy to find. In 2016, at the height of the reemergence of visualized slave narratives, even *Ebony* magazine featured an article entitled "Films about Slavery Are Important, Even If You're Tired of Seeing Them."[3]

This seeming rejection of slave narratives is the residue of collective Black cultural trauma. In his book *Cultural Trauma: Slavery and the Formation of African American Identity*, Ron Eyerman suggests, "The 'trauma' in question is slavery, not as an institution or even experience, but as a collective memory, a form of remembrance that grounded the identity-formation of a people. There is a difference between trauma as it affects individuals and as a cultural process. As cultural process, trauma is mediated through various forms of representation and linked to the reformation of collective identity and the reworking of collective memory."[4] Slavery, personally experienced or not, has formed a collective Black identity, and African Americans—while diverse in our eventual regional, class, or political affiliations—still share a bond borne of this trauma. The representation of slavery in historical Black cultural forms, from slave songs to slave narratives, had a variety of purposes. Slave narratives for instance were used politically as a form of advocacy against slavery with sympathetic white audiences. Often these cultural acts show unity, sharing history with future generations of Black people, preserving the memory of what they had survived, and even serving as a gauge of Black people's progress within a hostile, unchanging world.

Trauma has been a continuing part of Black existence within the United States, seen with the collapse of Reconstruction, the atrocities of life during Jim Crow, the historic and continuing brutal policing of Black bodies, and the ongoing mass incarceration of Black people within the prison industrial complex. Even within a country that shows such limited regard for their existence, Black people have always found ways to cope, resist, and find joy. Through the decades, through forms of popular culture (poetry, literature, music, dance, comedy, film, and television), Black creatives have expressed a wide range of emotions and represented the multifaceted nature and history of African Americans. However, Black creatives, especially those who are interested in telling stories about African American history, must wrestle with this trauma, the ways to express it, and how to engage an audience flooded with assaults on Black life on an everyday basis.

Since the shooting death of seventeen-year-old Trayvon Martin (2012) and the widely publicized trial and acquittal of George Zimmerman, the rallying call of "Black Lives Matter" (BLM) has become a mainstay in the U.S. social, political, and cultural imagination.

The rise of BLM forced open a space within the television and streaming industry for Black stories and storytellers. While popular network television shows such as Shonda Rhimes's *Scandal* (2012–2018) and *How to Get Away with Murder* (2014–2020), Issa Rae's *Insecure* (2016–2021), and Donald Glover's *Atlanta* (2016–2022) gained momentum during the rise of BLM, a series like Misha Green's antebellum period piece *Underground* (2016–2017), while critically acclaimed, was unable to find a wide viewership. Was it because of the show's material and its connection to the painful roots of Black life in the United States?

Cell phone cameras, surveillance footage, and often reluctantly released police body cam and dashcam footage have continued to fuel protests across the country. This was especially evident in the mass uprisings following the horrific death of George Floyd on May 25, 2020. These eight minutes and forty-six seconds seem to have awakened mainstream America to what has been the reality of Black life in this country since slavery. But how long will this impetus to understand and address systemic racism, implicit bias, and white privilege really last? So much of Black history in the United States is enmeshed in the reality of Black trauma, yet to ignore this history puts Black society in jeopardy.

As an artist, Ava DuVernay has produced a wide-ranging body of work, much of which asks both Black society and mainstream audiences to confront the trauma that is Black life in this country. From independent theatrical releases such as *Middle of Nowhere* (2012), the Academy Award–nominated films *Selma* (2014) and *13th* (2016), and the miniseries *When They See Us* (2019), her work shows a distinct drive toward social justice activism through expanding the public's knowledge of often ignored or distorted Black history. Through her nonprofit company ARRAY, DuVernay supports the production and distribution of films of people of color and women, providing mentorships and grants. ARRAY also produces a variety of panels and programming around issues of social justice. In 2019, for example, she livestreamed an event on the National Day of Racial Healing that combined both performances and conversations with a variety of politicians, activists, and engaged celebrities. Far from dismissing Black trauma, DuVernay uses her projects to challenge the very structures that perpetuate the damage to Black bodies in this country. This chapter analyzes Ava DuVernay's Netflix programs *13th* (2016) and *When They See Us* (2019) as well as the paratext *Oprah Winfrey Presents: When They See Us Now* (2019) to explore questions of Black trauma and televisual/streaming representation. How can Black storytellers use television to explore Black history at this time of heightened mainstream engagement with Black lives? How can viewers contend with Black history when so much of it is intertwined with violence, criminalization, trauma, and death?

13th: Slavery to the Prison Industrial Complex

Much of Black history is unknown to the wider U.S. public, left out of history books by a country unable—or more likely, unwilling—to truly grasp the inequities that its systems have created. In the late 1990s, Angela Davis gave talks across the country about the prison industrial complex. She later formalized her research into a book called *Are Prisons Obsolete?* which was published in 2003. Davis suggests, "Despite the important gains of antiracist social movements over the last half century, racism hides from view within institutional structures, and its most reliable refuge is the prison system."[5] Released in 2016, Ava DuVernay's film *13th* is a visual representation of Davis's book, furthering the argument by drawing in the contemporary connections to prison privatization, police brutality, and the rise of BLM.[6] I make this very simple point to note that issues related to mass incarceration / the prison industrial complex and its impact on the Black community have been critically discussed for over two decades. Yet there has been little mainstream conversation about a system that has disproportionately destroyed the lives of so many Black people.[7]

Visualization of a social issue through mass media makes it more legible for a mainstream audience, and the publicity created by media products can often push society to engage with these problems. While *13th* had a short theatrical run to make it Academy Award–eligible, most of the viewership of the documentary was on the Netflix streaming service. Indeed, on June 16, 2020, during the height of the BLM protests, Netflix reported that the documentary had a 466 percent increase in viewership from the previous three weeks.[8] The film provided context and knowledge for millions seeking answers to questions about Blackness and police brutality during this turbulent time.[9] Additionally, Netflix made the documentary available on YouTube and for community and educational screenings. Lisa Mishimura, Netflix's vice president of original documentary programs, stated, "We have been overwhelmed and inspired by the response to *13th* from people of all ages. Communities across the country are feeling the full weight of this particularly divisive moment in time. And, while some are capitalizing on this fear, we are especially inspired by the next generation, who are able to acknowledge the complex system they have inherited while simultaneously vowing to change it. Like DuVernay, they understand that we must come face to face with our past before we can fix our future."[10]

Whether this was a true commitment to social justice by Netflix or simply a publicity ploy, the importance lies in DuVernay's usage of the platform to interrogate the historical roots of the most devastating source of Black cultural trauma since slavery and, in essence, the systemic and deliberate continuation of slavery. By mapping out the roots and ramifications of the trauma of mass incarceration of Black people, *13th* encourages the reformation of collective cultural identity among those who may have disparate views about the myths of Black criminality. This collective can empower proactive change.

The title *13th* comes from the Thirteenth Amendment of the U.S. Constitution, which states, "Neither slavery nor involuntary servitude, except as a punishment for crime whereof the party shall have been duly convicted, shall exist within the United States, or any place subject to their jurisdiction." That clause, "except as a punishment for crime whereof the party shall have been duly convicted," provided the loophole to continue to use Black people as free labor for this country. Early in the documentary, historical black-and-white images of the freed give way to numerous images of Black people, including young Black children dressed in prison garb, working in fields and on railroad tracks. The voice overs of selected scholars discuss how during the post–Civil War era the myth of Black criminality evolved. Black men were therefore arrested for minor or nonexistent offenses so that they could be physically used to rebuild the Southern economy.

The documentary further discusses how representations of Black men in popular culture confirmed this so-called impetus to criminality and highlights the centrality of D. W. Griffith's film *Birth of a Nation* (1915) in this process. At the time, the film's images reverberated throughout the country leading to the rise of the KKK and the lynching of numerous Black people. It is relevant that DuVernay addresses *Birth of a Nation*, as it is a foundational text in American film history. Even with his racist history, D. W. Griffith is identified by many universities and in many books as the father of American cinema—often without appropriate context. Griffith used technology to define race and rewrite history in a way that had not been seen before. DuVernay's *13th* reminds the audience that these were not simply images for entertainment but ones that had a visceral impact on the lives of Black people. This image of Black criminality would never subside and led to trauma for generations of Black people within the prison system. *13th* allows DuVernay to use this same technology to expose the myths, the system, and to advocate for change.

The documentary further connects how Black people became pawns within the prison industrial complex. Victories won during the civil rights movement, the Civil Rights Act, and the Voting Rights Act were all used to suggest that these new freedoms for Black people led to an increase in crime, requiring the government to step in to curb these "crime waves." Starting in the 1970s, this "overreach" by the government led to mass incarcerations impacting Black and brown people ever since. DuVernay traces the rise in mass incarceration, increased federal spending on prisons and policing, and the influence of corporate "for-profit" lobbying through the presidencies of Richard Nixon, Ronald Reagan, and Bill Clinton.[11] She demonstrates the increasing ways in which each used the rhetoric of being "tough on crime" to appeal to voters while simultaneously criminalizing addiction, unevenly targeting poor people for their use of crack versus the wealthy and their use of cocaine. Thus, Black and brown people continue to be fed into the for-profit prison system.

13th argues that you can't talk about police brutality without understanding the history of the prison industrial complex. This very infrastructure has led to the problems we have today with law enforcement overreach and police brutality. The Clinton presidency and Federal Crime Bill of 1994 expanded the prison system and increased the number of police on the street. These policies were the arm of the "tough on crime" rhetoric born into a country that historically believed in Black criminality. Thus, *13th* connects this history to the numerous Black people who are killed with impunity by the police, the rise of BLM, and the importance of protest and advocacy.

Through editing, a poignant moment near the end of *13th* shows two young Black people debating the need to see images of violence and murder done to Black people by the police. The young man identified as Cory Greene, formerly incarcerated activist and cofounder of Holla, states, "For many of us whose families lived through this, who are extensions of this kind of oppression, we don't need to see pictures to understand what's going on. It's really to . . . speak to the masses who have been ignoring this for the majority of their life. But I also think there is trouble of just showing—Black bodies as dead bodies, too. Too much of anything becomes unhealthy, unuseful." The documentary then cuts to a young woman, who responds, "I think they need to be seen, if the family is OK with it. It wasn't until things were made visual in the civil rights movement, that we really saw folks coming out and being shocked into movement." This is the divide I see when discussing programs such as *13th* and *When They See Us* with my students. There is a desire by many to engage, while others are traumatized, weary, overwhelmed, and at times paralyzed by seeing the constant destruction of Black bodies.

Through the years, using technology and imagery, Black people have protested the destruction of Black bodies: the image of Slave Gordon, lynching photographs, the photos of Emmett Till, the footage of civil rights protesters assaulted by police. All these images had a role in forwarding the movement for Black freedom and equality. *13th* keeps within this tradition of using imagery for advocacy. What comes near the end of the documentary is a series of cell phone, dashcam, and public camera footage that captured the assaults and murders of Black people by the police. Each video is inscribed with the words "with permission of (victim name's) family." The audience sees the murders of Oscar Grant, Eric Garner, Tamir Rice, Sam Du Bose, Freddie Gray, Jason Harrison, Laquan McDonald, Eric Courtney Harris, and Philando Castile. At the end, a whiteboard, with the names of many others who died at the hands of police is animated onto the screen.

The final credit montage of the film works to draw together the protests of the civil rights movement with BLM. It begins with the images of Black joy, everyday pictures of Black families, fathers, and mothers with their children; Black firemen; Black people dating, living their lives, as the refrain "Freedom, Freedom Come, Hold On, Won't Be Long" plays. This montage ends with a series of images from BLM marches and one from the civil rights era. This final image dissolves into an image of a raised fist. DuVernay calls together these different generations who share a collective cultural identity into a movement for the humanity of Black people. This very desire for Black humanity led Raymond Santana, one of the Central Park Five, to reach out to DuVernay to tell their story, which was briefly featured in *13th*. After seeing DuVernay's film *Selma*, Santana tweeted to her, "What's your next film gonna be on?? #thecentral park five #cp5 #centralpark5 maybe???? #wishfulthinking #fingerscrossed." DuVernay direct messaged him back, and there began the five-year journey through the production and release of *When They See Us*.

When They See Us: The Paradox of Hypervisibility and Invisibility

> "Dirty Nigger" or simply Look! A Negro!
> I came into the world anxious to uncover
> the meaning of things, my soul desirous
> to be at the origin of the world, and here I
> am an object among other objects.
> —Frantz Fanon, 1952[12]

> I am invisible, understand, simply because
> people refuse to see me. . . . It is as though I
> have been surrounded by mirrors of hard,
> distorting glass. When they approach
> me they see only my surroundings, or
> figments of their imagination—indeed,
> everything and anything except me.
> —Ralph Ellison, 1952[13]

The epigraphs from Fanon and Ellison describe the binary of Black existence in this country, seen as objects whose skin color makes one hypervisible while at the same time something that has been rendered invisible or unknowable because of the dehumanizing power of racism. These epigraphs also speak to the title of DuVernay's four-part miniseries *When They See Us*, suggesting that while the race of the Central Park Five marked them as guilty, these five young boys were unseen as people by the NYPD, the justice system, and the many people across the country who assumed their guilt due to their race. The title speaks to the objective of humanizing these five young Black teenagers: Kevin Richardson, Raymond Santana, Antron McCray, Yusef Salaam, and Korey Wise.

When They See Us is the embodiment of *13th*. It puts real faces on the facts of the documentary. In 1989, these five boys were arrested, charged, and found guilty of the assault and/or gang rape of Trisha Meili, a white jogger in Central Park. Interrogated for hours—mostly without parental supervision, even though four were under the age of sixteen—the boys were coerced by the police into making videotaped false confessions. These confessions, while inconsistent, sealed their fates.

Two weeks after the attack on Meili, then real estate developer Donald Trump paid $85,000 for full-page advertisements in four of the major New York newspapers. These advertisements bore the headline "BRING BACK THE DEATH PENALTY. BRING BACK OUR POLICE!" He described his feelings about the case: "It's more than anger. . . . It's hatred, and I want society to hate them."[14] Trump's rhetoric had an impact on the case, influencing public beliefs. Although the boys recanted, their confessions were still used against them during their trials. They were all found guilty and spent between six and thirteen years in prison. When given the opportunity for parole, each continued to proclaim their innocence. While four were considered juveniles and were sentenced to youth corrections facilities, the eldest, Korey Wise, was tried as an adult and spent all thirteen years in adult prisons. In 2002, the young men were finally exonerated of the crime after Matias Reyes, a serial rapist, confessed and his DNA confirmed his role in the crime.

When They See Us, which premiered on Netflix on May 31, 2019, rewrites the public history of the case from the perspective of the boys and their families. It also draws attention to a story that was lost over the years. Many young people were unaware of the injustices of the case and the damage done to these Black lives. DuVernay tells their story over four episodes. The first image of part 1 reveals a pair of young Black hands tossing a ball between them in a room flooded by the bright light of the sun. Later identified as Antron McCray, the boy is called out of his room by his father, and they eat and talk over the sports section. The scene cuts to Kevin Richardson, walking down the street, excitedly talking to his sister about his musical accomplishments that day. Light seeps into the dark corridor where Korey Wise talks to his girlfriend; the close-up of the two reveals the soft light on the couple's faces as they tease each other. The daylight is slowly fading, and Raymond Santana checks himself out in the window of a car, hanging out and joking with his friends. And framed against the setting sun, Yusef Salaam makes plans with a friend. This opening scene marks them as five innocent, young Black boys simply enjoying their lives.

As Public Enemy's "Fight the Power" plays on a boombox, an overhead shot shows the group as they enter the park. The audience can recognize the boys within the group, Kevin entering the park a bit later. At the first sign of violence, when a man is struck in the face, the boys flee the scene. As the police descend upon the park, the aesthetic changes. The park is lit just by the streetlights, and the use of a handheld camera adds to the confusion of the chase. Kevin is caught. The policeman takes his helmet and slams it into the boy's face as Antron, hiding in a bush, witnesses the act. By starting the episode in the morning with the boys, instead of with the jogger at night, DuVernay shifts the focus to the other victims of the night of April 19, 1989. The episode presents each boy as an individual with a distinct personality and relationships with family and friends—the very ordinariness of their lives. The sudden and brutal end to this pre-title sequence indicates the stark direction the story will take.

As the episode progresses and the boys become the focal point of the investigation, the audience learns more about their families. Raymond's father needs to go to work and leaves his son in the custody of his mother, who does not speak English. Antron's father and mother ask him what he has been up to that night, and he explains. But when providing the police with the same explanation, they still take him into the precinct. The narrative cuts rapidly between the interrogations of the boys as the police cajole and manipulate both children and parents. The audience witnesses what will lead to their imprisonment and the destruction of these families. The episode ends as the boys are led out of the police station in handcuffs, their faces lit only by the flashes from the cameras and the lights of the police cars. As the camera focuses on each boy, a flashback takes us to the beginning of the episode, to the beautifully lit shots when they were carefree and with family and friends. By immediately involving the audience in the lives of the boys and their families, DuVernay humanizes individuals who have been demonized as a group. By creating this level of empathy and engagement at the very beginning of the series, each episode, while necessary viewing, becomes more and more painful to watch. Part 2 focuses on the interrogations, false confessions, and eventual trials and convictions of the five boys. Part 3 follows the lives of the four boys sent to juvenile facilities, their difficulties both there and upon release. Part 4 of the series is harrowing and exposes some of Korey Wise's horrific experiences in a variety of adult facilities.[15] As an activist filmmaker, DuVernay places the audience in the traumatizing position of bearing witness to the injustice placed on these Black bodies.

When They See Us was a critical and commercial success for Netflix. Although the platform is notoriously silent about its actual viewership, on June 12, 2019, Netflix reported on Twitter that the show "has been the most-watched series on Netflix in the U.S. every day since it premiered on May 31st."[16] Ava DuVernay later reported that Netflix informed her that by June 25, 2019, over 23 million accounts had watched the miniseries.[17] In June 2020, Reuters reported that the series viewership had increased by 83 percent in the wake of the murder of George Floyd.[18] The reach of the platform is undeniable.

A simple perusal of one thread on Twitter reveals a snapshot of the reactions to the series. A woman tweets, "This series is a must watch especially for those of us who weren't alive during the trial of the central park five and maybe even more ignorant. We must not forget our history, and we must fight injustice wherever we find it." Other examples of tweets include these: "This movie broke me can't even watch it again." "I still can't bring myself to watch this." "Way too traumatizing. It was almost too good." "I don't have the strength to watch this movie man smh." "Only got through one episode. That was enough for me."[19] There is inherent trauma in so many aspects of Black history, made more indelible by this visual medium. These images and stories have the potential to galvanize or paralyze members of the community it seeks to inspire. After viewing the mini-series, the audience is given the opportunity to have a firsthand glimpse into the contemporary lives of the "Central Park Five," as Oprah Winfrey hosted a one-hour special that featured the five men as well as the actors who portrayed them in the film. Considering the moderator, structure, and initial content of the special, *Oprah Winfrey Presents: When They See Us Now* sought to be a healing text, a way of processing the trauma that both the men and the viewing audience had experienced.

Oprah Winfrey Presents: When They See Us Now: Uncontainable Trauma

Released on Netflix and on the Oprah Winfrey Network (OWN) on June 12, 2019, less than two weeks after the miniseries premiered on Netflix, *Oprah Winfrey Presents: When They See Us Now (WTSUN)*. Akin to *The Oprah Winfrey Show* (1986–2011), which hosted celebrities, covered social issues, and focused on self-help and personal improvement, *WTSUN* is a coping text, a therapeutic space structured to provide healing for the audience, actors, and victims. Winfrey's traditional role of confidant, expert, and "therapist" places her in a position to facilitate this healing.

The one-hour program is divided into two segments. The first discusses the experiences of the actors, DuVernay, and the goals of the miniseries. The second half is a conversation with whom Winfrey calls the "real life innocent men once known as the Central Park Five." DuVernay wants people to "know them and say their names," a clear nod to BLM, connecting the case to the ongoing movement. Winfrey announces, "From this day forward, we call them the Exonerated Five."[20] She then inserts the new name into the conversation, in essence attempting to normalize the change, rewriting inaccurate public history, and reconstructing collective memory of the case.

The second half of the special intends to be therapeutic. The questions Winfrey asks are designed to elicit both their stories and their feelings about them. She wants to see their pain and be the person who supportively listens. However, in keeping with her brand, she also wants an uplifting conclusion. The final question posed is "What gives you hope?" Sarah Henstra argues, "As a talk show host and interviewer, Oprah is anything but a passive cipher for her guests' 'truth.' On the contrary, she determines the structure and emphasis of their stories even as she solicits those stories with her questions; she meets—and very often trumps—their conclusions with her own."[21]

Yet the deep trauma these men carry disrupts the structure of the Oprah interview. This becomes most evident in a conversation she has with Antron McCray and his response to her question to all the men, "How were you able to hold on to your sanity?" Salaam is the first to respond and speaks about hope and the power of meditation. However, McCray's wounds are open. Winfrey

FIG. 2.1 Distressed actors

repeatedly attempts and fails to guide McCray toward change or a positive outlook. Their following dialogue illustrates this struggle:

MCCRAY: I'm damaged. I know it, but I just try to keep myself busy. The system broke a lot of things in me that can't be fixed.

WINFREY: Do you feel broken?

MCCRAY: Yes, ma'am. My wife asked me to go see a therapist. But I keep refusing.

WINFREY: Why?

MCCRAY: I keep myself busy. I work out. I ride my motorcycle and go see Ray. He lives five minutes away from me. . . . But I'm struggling.

WINFREY: But wouldn't going to therapy offer you a kind of real freedom and a kind of peace? Don't you yearn for that? Or, do you yearn for that?

MCCRAY: No ma'am.

WINFREY: You don't? . . . So we get to see in the film that beautiful scene where Michael K. (plays McCray's father) is in the bed and is being put down by his son, grown son. Did you ever have reconciliation with your father? Did you ever forgive him—for convincing you to lie?

MCCRAY: No, ma'am. Like I said before he's a coward. I have six kids. Four boys, two girls. I couldn't imagine doing that to my son. He allowed them to mush me, push me in my chest. (sniffling) No ma'am.

WINFREY: No.

MCCRAY: I hate him. My life is ruined. (sniffles)

(Image cuts to the young actors in the audience, who are visibly crying.)

Winfrey later suggests to McCray that the recognition brought to him by the release of the miniseries has brought him redemption. But for McCray, there is no internal peace. He responds that his mother passed away. The money won from the lawsuit could not save her, nor could it make up for the time lost with her during incarceration. At the end of the program, Salaam gestures to the other four to hold hands, and they raise their hands in victory. However, the memory of McCray is the image that remains, Black trauma that cannot be resolved.

Conclusion

In the age of BLM, the rise and ramifications of white fragility continue. The ease at which Black history can be erased or rewritten has been exacerbated by social media and executive orders. There are numerous examples. In September 2020, then president Donald Trump attacked diversity training and critical race theory as divisive to American culture. He then signed an executive order banning racial sensitivity training by federal agencies. As Trump explained, "I ended it because it's racist. I ended it because a lot of people were complaining that they were asked to do things that were absolutely insane, that it was a radical revolution that was taking place in our military, in our schools, all over the place. . . . We were paying people hundreds of thousands of dollars to teach very bad ideas and frankly, very sick ideas. And really, they were teaching people to hate our country, and I'm not going to allow that to happen."[22] This was government-sanctioned backlash against minimal attempts to address America's false history and systemic racism. The events of January 6, 2021, and the insurrection at the U.S. Capitol were the culmination of the same presidency that fanned the flames of racism.

While the Biden administration recognized the Tulsa race riot and made Juneteenth a federal holiday, many more Republican legislators, educators, and elements of the right-wing media continue to follow Trump's lead and fight against critical race theory (CRT) in schools and federal institutions. In 2021, Republicans in states across the U.S. introduced bills that would ban the teaching of CRT in schools. In May 2021, a Republican-sponsored bill that would ban teaching CRT in any federal institution was introduced to Congress. Bills that limit or ban CRT in schools have been passed in several states, including Oklahoma, North Carolina, Tennessee, Florida, and Texas.

Black life in this country was borne out of trauma, and the fight and struggle continue. Yet racial exhaustion is real. Ava DuVernay's *13th* and *When They See Us* reengage collective Black memory and fuel political action. Struggling with and embracing the history of these images and the experience of trauma is a necessary part of a Black activist's agenda. As Ta-Nehisi Coates argues, "All our phrasing—race relations, racial chasm, racial justice, racial profiling, white privilege, even white supremacy—serves to obscure that racism is a visceral

FIG. 2.2 "Exonerated Five"

experience, that it dislodges brains, blocks airways, rips muscle, extracts organs, cracks bones, breaks teeth. You must never look away from this."[23]

Notes

1 Ta-Nehisi Coates, *Beyond the World and Me* (New York: One World, 2015), 16–17.

2 Coates, 201.

3 Matthew Allen, "Films about Slavery Are Important, Even If You're Tired of Seeing Them," *Ebony*, June 3, 2016, https://www.ebony.com/entertainment/slavery-films -important/.

4 Ron Eyerman, *Cultural Trauma: Slavery and the Formation of African American Identity* (Cambridge: Cambridge University Press, 2003), 1.

5 Angela Y. Davis, *Are Prisons Obsolete?* (New York: Seven Stories, 2003), 120.

6 DuVernay also draws from the *New York Times* best selling book by Michelle Alexander, *The New Jim Crow: Mass Incarceration in the Age of Colorblindness* (New York: New Press, 2010).

7 When I say mainstream conversation, I refer, for example, to the way apartheid was part of general knowledge in America in the 1980s.

8 Emma Nolan, "'13th' Netflix Documentary Viewers Surge by 466 Percent in Three Weeks," *Newsweek*, June 17, 2020, https://www.newsweek.com/13th-netflix-youtube-documentary-watch-ava-duvernay-race-movies-1511535.

9 Nolan.

10 Ellen Gray, "Netflix Allows More Groups to Show Oscar-Nominated 13th," *Philadelphia Inquirer*, February 14, 2017, https://www.inquirer.com/philly/blogs/entertainment/television/Netflix-Oscar-nominee-13th-Ava-DuVernay-public-viewings.html.

11 American Legislative Exchange Council (ALEC), a political lobbying group of politicians and corporations, wrote bills such as Florida's Stand Your Ground and SB1070. These bills increased prison sentences, in turn adding to the profits of ALEC corporations that, for instance, provide phone services, health care, and food services to prisons or profit off low-cost prison labor in the creation of their goods.

12 Frantz Fanon, *Black Skin White Masks* (New York: Grove, 2008), 89.

13 Ralph Ellison, *Invisible Man* (New York: Signet, 1952), 1.

14 Jim Dwyer, "The True Story of How a City Brutalized the Central Park Five," *New York Times*, May 30. https://www.nytimes.com/2019/05/30/arts/television/when-they-see-us-real-story.html.

15 DuVernay, in consultation with Wise, did not show the complete brutality of Korey's existence in prison.

16 Todd Spangler, "Netflix Says 'When They See Us' Has Been Most-Watched Show since Premiere," *Variety*, June 12, 2019, https://variety.com/2019/digital/news/netflix-when-they-see-us-most-watched-show-premiere-1203241480/.

17 Rick Porter, "Ava DuVernay's 'When They See Us' Seen by 23 Million, Netflix Says," *Hollywood Reporter*, June 25, 2019, https://www.hollywoodreporter.com/tv/tv-news/ava-duvernays-they-see-us-seen-by-23-million-netflix-says-1221069/.

18 Nolan, "'13th' Netflix Documentary."

19 @Jameca2011, "Only the real ones know 100," Twitter, July 20, 2021, 3:29 p.m., https://twitter.com/Jameca2011/status/1417612721961439232.

20 While describing their position as exonerated is appropriate, I believe the name "Exonerated Five" creates another object, not five unique individuals.

21 Sarah Henstra, "The Politics of Talk: The Oprah Interview as Narrative," *Studies in Popular Culture* 30, no. 2 (Spring 2008): 59, https://www.jstor.org/stable/23416125.

22 Cady Lang, "President Trump Has Attacked Critical Race Theory. Here's What to Know about the Intellectual Movement," *Time Magazine*, September 29, 2020, https://time.com/5891138/critical-race-theory-explained/.

23 Coates, *Beyond the World*, 13.

3

Thinking about *Watchmen* with Jonathan W. Gray, Rebecca A. Wanzo, and Kristen Warner

• •

MICHAEL BOYCE GILLESPIE

> There are people who believe the
> world is fair and good, that it's all
> lollipops and rainbows. . . . We don't
> do lollipops and rainbows. We know
> those are pretty colors that just hide what
> the world really is: black and white.
> —Angela Abar (Regina King), *Watchmen*

This roundtable with Kristen Warner, Rebecca A. Wanzo, and Jonathan W. Gray was organized to talk with scholars about *Watchmen* (HBO, 2019) and the issues of medium, genre, fandom, and African American history that shaped this rich series.[1] Created by Damon Lindelof, the HBO series elaborates extensively on the famed twelve-issue comic-book series of the same name, written by Alan Moore and drawn by Dave Gibbons (1986–1987).

The comic is set in the 1985 of an alternate timeline, one where the heroes/vigilantes of the past have been outlawed and only government-affiliated heroes remain legal. With the suspension of the Twenty-Second Amendment, Nixon is president for life, and the escalation of the Cold War has put the world on the brink of World War III, a nuclear holocaust. When one of the retired heroes is murdered, the subsequent mystery sets in motion a critique of the social order and its mythologies of superheroes. Instead of virtuous resonances, the comic series brutally proposes that superheroes are not immune to the systemic flaws of the social order but rather that they manifest these failings particularly as they relate to issues of power. Brilliantly dense, the comic is a metatextual exercise that exquisitely refuses to perpetuate the fantasy of clear divisions between good and evil. Its unsentimental rendering and critique of a world painfully familiar defy the simple explanation of a "dystopic" genre.

The HBO series *Watchmen* presents itself as a disobedient adaptation that modifies, extends, and redirects the world-making of the source. Located in the continuity of the comic but not determined by it, the series is set thirty-four years after the events of the comic. It elaborates on its source not as a sequel, reboot, or even translation but rather as an adaptation that substitutes speculation and deviation in place of fidelity. Importantly, the Tulsa Race Massacre of 1921 acts as the historical and ideological trigger that sets the series in motion.

Across nine episodes, the series generates a storyline of a world yet again on the brink but with an inflection of restitution that augments the original comic's despairing social critique. As a result of redevising the consequences of the original comic, the *Watchmen* series offers some of the most consequential television of the century, particularly with regard to its concentration on history, culture, and race. I hope this conversation might be of use for the many *Watchmen* conversations to come.

FIG. 3.1 *Watchmen* Tulsa Race Massacre of 1921

MICHAEL BOYCE GILLESPIE: What do you find significant about the ways that *Watchmen* remediates American history?

REBECCA A. WANZO: Various moments in history have had a profound influence on the development of U.S. superhero comics: World War II, the Cold War, the civil rights movement, 9/11. But in the case of the emplotment of the civil rights movement in comics, the inclusion of Black heroes elided the issue of white supremacy as a villain, often choosing tokenism or allegory. *Watchmen*, by opening with the Tulsa Race Massacre, makes Black trauma central to its origin stories and those of its superheroes, thus rewriting the inspiration for the desire for superheroes.

In a well-known Green Lantern / Green Arrow comic from the 1970s, an African American man asked the Green Lantern why he wasn't helping the Black man, speaking to the excessive brutality Black people had experienced in the U.S. history of white supremacy and anti-blackness.[2] Superheroes occasionally have dealt with racists and with other instances of discrimination (the Black Panther, for example, once fought the Klan), but failures of the nation are treated as missteps and not as a foundational villainy masked by the flag and myths of American exceptionalism. *Watchmen* imagines a redemptive narrative for superhero origins, both by writing a Black man into the origin story and by making state-ignored (and state-generated) white supremacy the enemy.

GILLESPIE: I've been thinking about the "Fight the Power: Black Superheroes on Film" series at the Brooklyn Academy of Music back in 2018. It included an extraordinary range of work that concluded with the release of Ryan Coogler's *Black Panther* (2018).[3] Each film in the series enacted a fantastical conceit of race and (super)heroism but crucially also posed distinct tensions between exceptionalism and ambivalence.

These tensions were historically and generically grounded throughout. Furthermore, the films in the series offered varying and potent definitional logics of heroism and villainy. The BAM series has informed some of the ways that I identified with elements of *Watchmen*. In *Watchmen*, there is a great deal of nuanced historiographic conjuring around these issues. It avoids the prescriptive "It's time for this week's history lesson" shtick of *black-ish* [ABC, 2014–2022]. It also avoids the shenanigans of *American Gods* [Starz, 2017–2021], where the Black and brown characters and storylines of Mr. Nancy [Orlando Jones], Bilquis [Yetide Badaki], Jinn [Mousa Kraish], and Mr. Ibis [Delmore Barnes] often offer the most compelling moments of the show, yet only complement the show's primary (and weaker) focalization.

Watchmen's opening sequence in the very first episode ["It's Summer and We're Running Out of Ice"] sets the historiographic tone for the entire series. Its seamless pivot from cultural mythology (in terms of Bass Reeves, U.S. marshal and suspected model for the Lone Ranger) to early cinema and black cinema spectatorship to the historical erasures of American/white-supremacist violence was flawless and startling. The show's expanded writing of a history across temporalities and locations (galactic or otherwise) underscored how speculative fiction as "a genre of inventing other possibilities" often concentrates on measuring the conditions of the present through an excavation of the remains of yesterday and tomorrow.[4] This is evident throughout the series. For example, the way the show's "Victims of Racial Violence Act" ("Redfordations") draws on historical debates of reparations and Ta-Nehisi Coates's essay "The Case for Reparations" gave me a great deal of speculative joy.[5] I know the series has been spoken of as a remix, but "reprioritizing" feels closer to how I'm thinking.

WANZO: I think "speculative joy" is a wonderful articulation of what many of us felt watching it. The dystopian quotidian that is so common in the black fantastic does not foreclose the possibilities for joy—the heroic reimaginings emerge from it. There has been a lot of discussion recently about Black trauma being overrepresented in popular culture. Yet as *Watchmen* shows, we have not even begun to scratch the surface of this history. Here, the speculative becomes the grounds for a pleasurable affective trajectory that also avoids the traps of uplift narratives that too often cheapen Black history.

GILLESPIE: **Were there any elements of *Watchmen* that you found compelling with regard to speculative fiction, film history, allegory, culture, and/or conceptions of the nation?**

KRISTEN WARNER: The opening scene inside the movie theater with the focus on the Black boy and his mother at the piano. They watch, wait, and worry as the screen centers Bass Reeves saving white people. "Trust in the law" was an unforgettable moment for me as a Black audience member and also as a scholar. I think that scene was compelling because that specific imagery is so rarely seen in the collective mediated history. It centered and set the course of this story around not just blackness but a historical moment of blackness that is not celebrated enough.[6]

JONATHAN W. GRAY: I recently wrote on how successfully *Watchmen* places the horrors of white supremacy at the center of its story by making it as dangerous to the polity as the Cold War was in the 1970s and 1980s for the original comic. It is a delicious irony that Alan Moore and Dave Gibbons largely ignored race, because it's now clear that the politics of the Cold War unintentionally submerged an embrace of what can now be understood as ethnic nationalism across the globe.[7] Today, the extent to which white supremacy's toxicity has corroded the nation's possibilities ever since the Civil War ostensibly ended de jure discrimination is clear. The series masterfully toggles back and forth from the end of World War I to 2019. Its comic form allows for the manipulation of time through retroactive continuity, flashbacks, and flash-forwards, but I've never seen a television series or film manipulate these elements of time and scope to such great effect.

WARNER: Watching that cold open, complete with the continuing action of the Tulsa Race Riot and with the central character of Angela Abar / Sister Night [Regina King] placed in the middle as the origin tale, it felt like a very potent attempt at televisual remediation. And then it just kept on happening—like microdosing racialized remediation across nine episodes of storytelling. For me, the dosing is absolutely an advance because achieving that kind of specificity in an urtext that has to carefully maintain its structural integrity while also attending to and arguing its established thesis is goddamn hard. We don't have enough examples of such splendid success on this scale.

GILLESPIE: What do you find consequential about a series so centralized around race and the myth of the superhero? How might this relate to the way some comics have remediated genre and history with an emphasis on race and culture—for example, *Genius*; *Truth: Red, White, & Black*; *Destroyer*; *Infidel*; *Black*; *American Carnage*; *Kindred*; *Bitter Root*; *Harriet Tubman: Demon Slayer*; *The Silence of Our Friends*; the *March* series; *Bayou*; and *King: A Comics Biography*?

WANZO: As you note with this list, creators have been reimagining the myths of the superhero through the Black experience for some time. People have objected to racebending and to racism becoming the subject of comic-book storylines. Some fans are much more comfortable with the allegorical representations common in comics that don't require confrontation with the realities of discrimination.

But I think this is a profoundly "playing in the dark" iteration of the Black superhero, not by recasting superheroes through Black experience but by saying that a racialized nationalism is important to the foundations of vigilantism, heroism, and alienated citizenship at the core of this myth. That's why the Hooded Justice origin reveal is so brilliant. The absence of such origin stories in the Golden Age of Comics makes visible the problem of the impossibility of such heroes.[8] Of course, a superhero with a hacked-off noose around his neck could be a Black man who, having escaped white-supremacist violence, is carrying the markers of his origin story.

WARNER: To Wanzo's point, audiences who are entirely loyal to the superhero-franchise genre seem to feel most comfortable with the "happened to be" racialized bodies who subsume those parts, but only within reason.

And I'll never forget that even that "racially transcendent $4 billion man" (at the time because of his box office success) Will Smith couldn't be even remotely considered for Captain America. So it can be OK (within reason) to have a Black or brown and/or woman as . . . hero/heroine/superhero as long as that difference is primarily signified by the body. Yes, we can have a couple of quips that test well with notions of "girl power and empowerment"—hey, colonizer!—and memeable dialogue and visual signifiers that illustrate an attention to "the culture," but the centrality of blackness/otherness is never explicit. It's not just that Hooded Justice, the body of the diegetic television show [*American Hero Story*], has been whitewashed. It's that the rationale for that choice, even as it connects to the real story of Will Reeves [Louis Gossett Jr.], becomes laid out and then further exploited as a site of racial disruption.

It's not just that Reeves is hooded with a rope around his neck as a consequence of a lynching attempt by his white-supremacist police colleagues. No, the story stretches into an inverse minstrelsy with him wearing white makeup and believing that he's finally been seen. The visibility of his Black invisibility put on display in such a tragic manner is the apex of the series that pivots the story toward its finale. Blackness is truly centered here in a way I'd never seen accomplished before.

GRAY: To build on Kristen's point, superheroes must "happen to be" Black because comic-book heroism is so often connected to—as the Superman radio serial from the 1940s would have it—truth, justice, and the American way. But American ideology has often constructed blackness in general, and African American demands for full citizenship in particular, as a threat. Until now, a vigilante dedicated not to reforming a broken system (Captain America, Batman) or avenging its depredations (Punisher, Daredevil) but to a wholesale redefinition of what it means to be a citizen has always been a step too far. Superhero comics can confront this reality only through metaphor, as the X-Men comics demonstrate.[9] It's unsurprising that Black bodies, which carry a history that calls American exceptionalism into question and which the series so expertly unpacks, can occupy space at the center of the narrative only when they uphold the ideology.

WARNER: The fetish/disavowal of Reeves's Black body by others as well as by himself throws into sharp relief the rational and irrational reasons for why we can't have Black superheroes, or more to the point, why Black superheroes must happen to be Black. There's a historical lens placed on that story in episode 6 ["This Extraordinary Being"] that, unlike a more recent Black superhero film that was immensely successful, enables the tale to become more than simply signifiers and a fictional locale.[10] Instead, the story becomes about the stakes of the bodily difference as a trauma and a haunting. The complex dystopia of the images and the narrative that serve to produce Reeves's (and Angela's) superheroism proves far more pessimistic and discomforting than audiences have been socialized to navigate within this genre.

GILLESPIE: I adored the "pessimistic and discomforting" nature of Reeves, his personification of the acute engagement of the series with the mythology of the comic and its inattention to race. I think it's extraordinary how the series treats the comic itself as a show bible and builds from there. Victor LaValle's *The Ballad of Black Tom* (2016) and *Destroyer* (2017) serve as essential precedents for my thinking about the HBO series. The former offers an engagement with H. P. Lovecraft's anti-black legacy, and the latter stages a fantastic blending of classic and quotidian horror.

    Watchmen does a comparable thing in not treating the source material, its inspiration, as sacred. Complete fidelity to the source work is never the most engaging or satisfying approach to adaptation. As a result, the series opens the comic up for consequential refabulations of culture and politics.

WANZO: I also think LaValle's work invites thinking about two ways that black revision is at play in the series. Just as I can never read *Jane Eyre* again without thinking of *Wide Sargasso Sea*, so does *Black Tom* transform Lovecraft's "The Horror at

FIG. 3.2 Sister Night

Red Hook" for me forever. Similarly, viewers will always look at Hooded Justice differently. It changes the audience's relationship to the original text—whereas *Destroyer* is less about changing the original text than claiming Frankenstein as a Western cultural mythology to which Black people can have equal access.

GILLESPIE: I've been waiting forever for a screen adaptation of Frank Miller and Dave Gibbons's *Give Me Liberty: An American Dream* [1990], because the character of Martha Washington has been my favorite Black comic hero. Then there was Regina King as Sister Night. With King's significant run of great roles in mind [*The Boondocks* (Cartoon Network / HBO Max, 2005–2014), *Southland* (TNT, 2009–2013), *American Crime* (ABC, 2015–2017), *The Leftovers* (HBO, 2014–2017), *Seven Seconds* (Netflix, 2018), *If Beale Street Could Talk* (Barry Jenkins, 2018)], how does she challenge the classical models of star/celebrity studies?

GRAY: King charts a new model for stardom, but that's largely due to the fact that Hollywood has no model for Black women. You could say that Michael B. Jordan is following/updating a path laid for him by Will Smith and Denzel Washington by moving from a critically acclaimed TV show to eventually become a box office champion, but there seems to be no consistent or guaranteed formula for Black women in Hollywood.

WANZO: She has demonstrated how television has been a site for some of the best and most complex work for women in Hollywood over the last fifteen years or so, particularly women over forty. Older Hollywood stars have long found an afterlife on television; as Mary Desjardins argues, they negotiate the differences between film and television models of stardom, glamour, and approachability.[11] King might be read as part of a genealogy of African American stars like Hazel Scott, who saw possibilities for representation in television that were not available to her in Hollywood film.[12]

While King has been working since she was a teenager, she has done her best work in the last decade. It's not a coincidence that shows like *Southland*, *Seven Seconds*, *American Crime*, and *Watchmen* have had diverse writing rooms. That television has been a site for King to become a star in her forties, in ways long denied her as a Black woman given the conventional preferences for white ingenues, is a tribute to the medium as a place where some of the most interesting and inclusive storytelling is happening in U.S. corporate media. Mia Mask has discussed the models of charisma for Black women's stardom—the sexual charisma of Pam Grier, the comedic charisma of Whoopi Goldberg, the multicultural-beauty charisma of Halle Berry.[13] King's case is interesting for the fact that she does not function in relation to any single model.

WARNER: I would add that her directing television while also acting may have enabled her to be more selective about the kinds of projects she wanted to build toward in her career. If she's earning consistent money directing television, then that allows her to decline parts she might otherwise have to take to pay the bills. Also, it certainly puts her in a place where she spends consistent time with white male showrunners and thus can establish a rapport absolutely necessary for the kinds of work she wants to do.

It takes time to go from being Brenda Jenkins in *227* and a voice actor for *The Boondocks* to transitioning to a more dramatic actor in *Southland* to being able to carry a large part in the *American Crime* ensemble. And then, to be able to move to *The Leftovers* to play a character who wasn't written as race blind (though I don't necessarily buy that story) but became a heavy character—well, that required time, and training, and money quite frankly. By the time King gets to *If Beale Street Could Talk* and *Watchmen*, all the stuff she worked for came together. I attribute her success as much to her directing as a longevity plan for surviving—in an industry that expires Black women actors as part of its franchise—as I do to her skill set as an actress.

GILLESPIE: Post-*Lost*, Damon Lindelof's television work has thrived in the cable television format, with his cocreator and showrunner role with *The Leftovers* along with his creator and showrunner role with *Watchmen*. Are there any distinctive narrative and structural tropes about the series that interest you? What about the writers?

WANZO: Indeed, he has thrived post-*Lost*! It was Kristen who convinced me to give *The Leftovers* a try after my disappointment with the infamous (for some) ending of that show. Sean O'Sullivan pushes against the idea of "satisfaction" in serial narrative, arguing that dissatisfaction is inherent to serial narrative—not only in the constant, pleasurable anticipation of resolution but in the end.[14] However, *Lost* invited the audience to read various threads as essential to understanding character- and world-building and to believe that the resolution to these threads was important to closure—that's what mythology shows do.

GRAY: I think Lindelof deserves credit for self-awareness and possessing the flexibility to listen to detractors, both in the academy and in the industry. Lindelof has mocked the all-white *Lost* writing room on several podcasts, noting that although *Lost* told some good stories featuring people of color, he'd never attempt to do such a thing today.[15]

WARNER: You're welcome, Wanzo! I did not watch *Lost*, but I understand the weight of getting it right that seems to burden Lindelof since that show's end. I believe that burden absolutely informs how he has made television post-*Lost*. The move to cable/premium television serves a couple purposes for him—he can make shorter seasons that seem to allow him to concentrate more fully on the goals and breaks and revelations and closures he wants to deliver in eight to ten episodes a year. And the "freedom" away from broadcast certainly grants him the ability to keep focused on what he has tasked himself to complete. But even with that, he focuses on similar themes of origins, family, religion, and the law.

Seasons 2 and 3 of *The Leftovers* are such a wonder because the questions he asks around those themes result in an absurd and affecting kind of pathos and melos. It is just compelling television. Then he uses that formula in *Watchmen* again, and even within the scope of a different genre (for the most part), the results are stunning.

WANZO: *The Leftovers* established at the outset, as Tom Perrotta's novel did, that the hole in our knowledge was something the characters and audience must live with, and the core emotional arcs of the characters were about the trauma of this mystery and loss in itself. Similarly, *Watchmen* establishes a discordant world at the outset that requires you to accept certain truths about the world even as they will never explain all the details that led to it.

To a certain extent, speculative fictions often do this with world-building, but just as *The Leftovers* used the mystery of a rapture-like event to get at fundamental questions about dealing with loss, *Watchmen* uses narrative gaps to get at fundamental questions about what it means to place Black people at the center of normative stories about heroism and moral binaries that have governed nationalist fantasies in the United States.

GILLESPIE: There has been a lot of commentary about *Watchmen* being definitively pro-cop or too political / not political enough and its perceived failure to address certain aspects of history. There's a certain irony about criticism of a series devoted to an alternate timeline of American history by people who seem to live in an alternate timeline where Stuart Hall never existed and questions of representation never progressed beyond the 1970s. Any thoughts about the criticism?

GRAY: I think that many critics treat Black characters—and indeed, Black people—as ciphers with no real interiority. There are hundreds of Black people that willingly engage with the criminal justice system as officers and prosecutors out of a sincere desire to improve it from within. They may wildly overestimate their capacity to transform an entrenched bureaucracy, but that desire is real. There is in fact nothing incongruous about African Americans attempting to reform the United States through demonstrations of patriotism. While it may be appropriate to dismiss these people politically by calling them cops, a failure to grapple with their motives impoverishes art. If every mainstream text were to be evaluated based on how it advances notions of, for example, posthuman Afropolitan existence, then most artistic output will be found wanting.

WANZO: We never seem to get beyond positive and negative binaries, do we? But that is also indicative of how rarely people read media criticism from scholars. Scholars such as Hall and Herman Gray and Racquel Gates, and some of the work by the scholars in this conversation, address this. Yet there is a permanent disconnect between the complexity and genealogies of that scholarship and the belief that some representations are perpetually bad and others perpetually good. That's a longer conversation about what it takes for work to cross over to be influential in the public sphere.

The "too political" claim is so ridiculous that if anyone has read even a single page of Alan Moore then it's not worth discussing, but the "pro-cop" critique should be debated: Moore's *Watchmen* was not only about the questionable pleasure in romantic narratives of superhero violence but about state violence in general. However, I think in the end it is an alternative history that can't easily be mapped onto seeing the Black cops as functioning the way Black cops have been utilized in realist fictions. At the same time, the show does fail to interrogate imperialism and the Vietnam War. Criticisms of the show's failure to address imperialism and treatment of Lady Trieu are right on.[16]

WARNER: "But that is also indicative of how rarely people read media criticism from scholars." Amen, Wanzo! Part of what I found so compelling about the series was noting how difficult and time-consuming it was to complicate the characterizations of Reeves, Angela Abar, and Jon / Cal / Dr. Manhattan [Yahya Abdul-Mateen II].[17] There came a point when positive/negative would no longer be sufficient to answer the questions about their representation.

There were times when I wrongly assumed that the show was taking the easy way out with Angela's representation because there are moments I read her early on as an instance of blind casting—the practice of casting actors for parts where race isn't specifically mentioned in the description of the characters. Then there were moments where the toil of her development paid off when she tells Jon to wake up. Cal/Jon's character is written smartly and transgressively, especially with regard to how it plays with the color-blind impetus of a white man [Jon] taking on the body of a Black man [Cal] because that's what Angela wants to look at. I knew Cal felt odd at the beginning of the series; that was a correct read. But it must have been a much more fun performance for Yahya once you consider just how he had to imagine this character (a Black man playing a white man who doesn't realize he's a white man until a literal block is removed from his memory). If someone with only baseline or lay knowledge of positive/negative stereotyping watched the show, the analysis would be thin.

GILLESPIE: I can't engage with the pro-cop criticism for the simple fact that it disallows for ambiguity and ambivalence with its tacit and strict binaries of positive (heroism) and negative (villainy). Overall, the show thrives on muddling that binary, and thankfully, no character in the show meets the sociological/ethical demands placed on these categories by some critics. The cop critique suggests that Angela Abar essentially remains the same throughout. Is she really just a cop by the close of the series? How can a show that suggests that cops are historically in collusion with white supremacists be read as pro-cop?

For me, critiques that have been made of the series in terms of its treatment of Vietnam and imperialism do not acknowledge that Vietnam has a very particular function in its narrative arc: as an element of the show's intertext and to develop Angela, Cal, and to a lesser but still vital extent, Lady Trieu [Hong Chau]. I understand those critics who wanted the show to engage more deeply with the history of Vietnam, but I question whether the show must, or even could, do so in any way equivalent to the show's radical regard for American / African American history.

Lindelof's own regrets about Lady Trieu and the decision to keep the series at nine episodes should be kept in mind with regard to some of the criticism devoted to the character's development.[18] I say that not as a casual dismissal of concerns about marginalization, white supremacy, and media. Admittedly, I am trying to reconcile my own skepticism concerning the representation/image debates, the mythic efficacies of representation, and their implied political ends.[19] Of course, the bigger issue for me is the weak conceptualization of representation in some criticism of the show and of media more generally.

WARNER: I honestly think that Stuart Hall and the Birmingham School of cultural criticism would have had something to say about this pro-cop/anti-cop question.[20] While I've read really persuasive analysis arguing that the show reinforces the power of the state, I would counter: it may, but I think the series finds itself much more comfortable in the space of ambivalence. It refuses to be simply about good and evil. What's more, I believe that it's truly the reading strategy and framework that you as a viewer enter into with *Watchmen* that defines how you translate that. I am weary of overdetermined yet perfectly argued assessments of televisual representation that do not take the medium and its commercial nature into account.

GILLESPIE: **What are your thoughts about Damon Lindelof's contention that *Watchmen* is "an expensive bit of fanfiction"? How does the series pose new ideas about adaptation and comic-book / graphic-novel adaptation more precisely?**

WARNER: The thing I like about Lindelof is that, at least as far as I can determine from his work on *The Leftovers*, he's good about adhering to the source material—but when he's completed that task and is allowed to play in the world built by that material, that's when he shines. Seasons 2 and 3 of *Leftovers* are more interesting and perplexing and frustrating by far than season 1. Similarly, I think the way Lindelof approached *Watchmen*, with such reverence but also with an eye for what's missing, allowed him to make a really successful piece of fan fiction. For me, fan fiction can be about correcting authorial errors but also be about picking up where a show left off or taking note of an unaddressed part of the story or character.

WANZO: *Watchmen* does two things that are very standard in fan fiction: it continues a story beyond the existing material, and it thematically reimagines the conceptual center to address a different set of politics. Comics writers do this with long-standing characters all the time: a well-known example is Mark Millar's *Red Son*, which imagines that Kal-El landed in the USSR instead of Smallville. So I'm hesitant to make a claim that *Watchmen* poses new ideas about comic adaptation.[21] I think it's important to be careful about making claims about the radical newness of something when most cultural productions are shaped by one or more long genealogies.

WARNER: When Lindelof describes reevaluating *Watchmen* and looking for some holes he could dig into, that's the quintessential notion of fan fiction at work. Fan fiction often gets treated with disdain, so his description is self-deprecating when it need not be. Fan fiction is generative writing and often illustrates how closely audiences do watch texts—so closely at times that they can spot the inconsistencies and the undeveloped material. So in his mind, it may represent a deficit, but it's really good generative material informed by a great source.

GILLESPIE: ***Watchmen* was an elaborate reading process. Over the course of the series, parallel narratives intersected, crossed, and integrated. Does the seriality of the series distinguish it from classical television narration? Might the series demonstrate a transtextual or multitextual model of comic-book narrativity? Formally speaking, what were some of your favorite things?**

WANZO: I've been noticing an increased play with time on television series to varied success. For decades, there have been shows with the occasional *Rashomon*-inspired episode, or other episodes that move back and forth in time in some way. But now a number of series have made temporal play a standard way of serial storytelling.

Manipulations of time have been done very successfully on Lindelof's shows before. One of the best episodes of *Lost* was "The Constant" [season 4, episode 5], and similarly, *Watchmen*'s "A God Walks into Abar" [episode 8] turns on romantic love. There's something about its tweaking of that theme (in relation to Dr. Manhattan simultaneously experiencing past, present, and future) that becomes an elegant meditation on race and genre. Both the pleasure and the disappointment of genre are, often, in its very predictability. And blackness, not just as theme but as narrative trajectory in drama, presupposes tragedy or uplift or other black narrative conventions.

Through the love plot, there's also a hint of an indictment of narrative expectations of blackness: Dr. Manhattan says he falls in love with her at this moment after years together through her heroism, because for him that was always going to happen, she was always going to be that. And even without seeing what it is that Angela does as a god on earth, she was presented as exceptionally heroic and self-sacrificing.

I know a number of people were looking for a second season. But I felt that the story of Angela becoming what she already embodied was the important arc. When she begins to step on the water (with that clear Christ reference), it's easy to imagine what she will be; it works because her character already represents an ideal for so many viewers. Unfortunately, people often ignore the present of Black subjectivity by focusing on its utopian futurity.

GILLESPIE: You're right, it's a rare pleasure to see blackness narrativized as a formal and temporal principle in this way. "This Extraordinary Being" [episode 6], which features Angela's overdose on Nostalgia pills, was remarkable in this sense, with its blend of embodied memory and epigenetic memory. And for me, too, "A God Walks into Abar," with its multiple and simultaneous temporalities, was a highlight. There's a lot of mise-en-scène labor in orchestrating Angela and Cal's growing intimacy without showing his face. I was thrilled with how the blocked and canted framings of the camera accented the cycling of their romance, from beginning to end. The scene beautifully illustrates the nonlinearity of the series narrative in general.

WARNER: I hadn't read the graphic novel previously, only seen the film [*Watchmen* (Zack Snyder, 2009)] and remembered just a few moments. But I know Lindelof's style, and that was what helped keep me grounded while watching. It's a difficult show in those first couple of episodes. It's not just that action is happening from the start, or that the characters aren't clearly laid out, but that there's a whole lot happening and overarching connections between the past and the present that you must attend to as a viewer.

Even as the opening seems to want to appear to be a procedural whodunnit, *Watchmen* lends you that crutch only long enough to get your bearings; then, it's jetting past you and constantly laying the groundwork for wherever it is headed. This makes it different from a classical television show as it's neither "least objectionable programming" nor unambiguous in its storytelling.[22] I would also add that, unlike other series that purport to be edgy and want to claim prestige by making their audiences feel smart about really obvious stuff, *Watchmen* doesn't seem to offer that generosity. And yet, when you catch what it's up to, it's so enjoyable to watch as it reveals itself.

Notes

1 This conversation took place in early 2020 following the conclusion of *Watchmen* in December 2019. It was originally published as "Thinking about Watchmen: A Roundtable," *Film Quarterly* 73, no. 4 (Summer 2020): 50–60.

Jonathan W. Gray is an associate professor of English at the CUNY Graduate Center and John Jay College. He is the author of *Civil Rights in the White Literary Imagination* (2012) and is currently working on the book project *Illustrating the Race:*

Representing Blackness in American Comics. He co-edited the essay collection *Disability in Comics and Graphic Novels* (2016) and served as the founding editor of the *Journal of Comics and Culture.* Professor Gray's work has appeared in *Keywords for Comics Studies, Film Quarterly, The New Republic, Entertainment Weekly, Medium,* and *Salon.*

Rebecca Wanzo is a professor and chair of the Department of Women, Gender, and Sexuality Studies at Washington University in St. Louis. She is the author of *The Suffering Will Not Be Televised: African American Women and Sentimental Political Storytelling* (2009) and *The Content of Our Caricature: African American Comic Art and Political Belonging* (2020). Her research interests include African American literature and culture, feminist theory, cultural studies, and graphic storytelling. She has published in venues such as *American Literature, Camera Obscura, differences, Signs, Women and Performance,* and numerous edited collections. She has also written for media outlets such as *CNN,* the *Los Angeles Review of Books,* and *Huffington Post* and the comic book *Bitch Planet.*

Kristen Warner is an associate professor in the Department of Performing and Media Arts at Cornell University. She is the author of *The Cultural Politics of Colorblind TV Casting* (Routledge, 2015). Kristen's research interests are centered on the juxtaposition of racial representation and its place within the film and television industries as it concerns issues of labor and employment. Warner's work can be found in academic journals, a host of anthologies, and online platforms like the *Los Angeles Review of Books* and *Film Quarterly.*

2   Denny O'Neil (writer) and Neal Adams (artist), "No Evil Shall Escape My Sight!," *Green Lantern,* no. 76 (April 1970).

3   Programmed by Ashley Clark, the series ran February 2–18, 2018, and included *Sweet Sweetback's Baadasssss Song* (Melvin Van Peebles, 1971), *The Harder They Come* (Perry Henzell, 1972), *The Spook Who Sat by the Door* (Ivan Dixon, 1973), *Yeleen* (Souleymane Cissé, 1987), *Foxy Brown* (Jack Hill, 1974), *Brother from Another Planet* (John Sayles, 1984), *Candyman* (Bernard Rose, 1992), *Strange Days* (Kathryn Bigelow, 1995), *Spawn* (Mark A. Z. Dippé, 1997), *Blade* (Stephen Norrington, 1998), and *Attack the Block* (Joe Cornish, 2011).

4   Aimee Bahng, *Migrant Futures: Decolonizing Speculation in Financial Times* (Durham, N.C.: Duke University Press, 2017), 8. Bahng importantly notes, "Speculation is not exclusively interested in predicting the future but is equally compelled to explore different accounts of history. It calls for a disruption of teleological ordering of the past, present, and future and foregrounds the processes of narrating the past (history) and the future (science)" (8).

5   Ta-Nehisi Coates, "The Case for Reparations," *Atlantic,* June 2014, http://www.theatlantic.com/magazine/archive/2014/06/the-case-for-reparations/361631/.

6   My thinking on this scene and its implications are drawn from Clyde Taylor, "Black Silence and the Politics of Representation," in *Oscar Micheaux and His Circle: African-American Filmmaking and Race Cinema of the Silent Era,* ed. Charles Musser, Jane M. Gaines, and Pearl Bowser (Bloomington: Indiana University Press, 2016), 3–10. Taylor's article explores race films around the time of the Tulsa race riot and examines how those films were undermined by Hollywood ultimately reducing blackness to a peripheral shadow economy that could be exploited. In *Watchmen,* by contrast, the opening sequence centers the Black subject as the dominant viewer gathered around a black cinematic text.

7   See Jonathan W. Gray, "*Watchmen* after the End of History: Race, Redemption, and the End of the World," *ASAP/J,* February 3, 2020, http://www.asapjournal.com/watchmen-after-the-end-of-history-race-redemption-and-the-end-of-the-world-jonathan-w-gray/.

8   The Golden Age of Comics is commonly understood as spanning a period from the late 1930s to the mid-1950s. This period roughly corresponds with the time from the release of the first issue of the *Superman* comic (1938) up to the self-regulation of comic content with the formation of the Comics Code Authority (1954).

9   The current X-Men reboot takes this to its logical conclusion by having the mutants become citizens of a new nation where they use their powers to make that nation the most prosperous on earth. The mutants have essentially been given their own Wakanda.

10 See the discussion of *Black Panther* in *Film Quarterly*'s online *Quorum*: Racquel Gates and Kristen Warner, "Wakanda Forever: The Pleasures, the Politics, and the Problems," *Quorum*, March 9, 2018, https://filmquarterly.org/2018/03/09/wakanda -forever-the-pleasures-the-politics-and-the-problems/.

11 Mary Desjardins, *Recycled Stars: Female Film Stardom in the Age of Television and Video* (Durham, N.C.: Duke University Press, 2015).

12 Desjardins, 38.

13 Mia Mask, *Divas on Screen: Black Women in American Film* (Urbana: University of Illinois Press, 2009).

14 Sean O'Sullivan. "Serials and Satisfaction," *Romanticism and Victorianism on the Net*, no. 63 (April 2013), https://ronjournal.org/articles/n63/serials-and-satisfaction/.

15 See DJ BenHaMeen and Tatiana King Jones, "Who Watches the Watchmayne Feat. Damon Lindelof," *For All Nerds*, October 23, 2019, podcast, 90:00, https://podbay .fm/podcast/632843709/e/1571850110; and Chris Ryan and Andy Greenwald, "Damon Lindelof on the World-Building of 'Watchmen,'" *The Watch*, December 9, 2019, podcast, 74:00, https://podbay.fm/podcast/1111739567/e/1575930268.

16 Viet Thanh Nguyen, "How 'Watchmen's' Misunderstanding of Vietnam Under-cuts Its Vision of Racism," *Washington Post*, December 18, 2019, http://www .washingtonpost.com/outlook/2019/12/18/how-watchmens-misunderstanding -vietnam-undercuts-its-vision-racism/.

17 In *Watchmen*, the first version of Jon Osterman / Dr. Manhattan is a white man. But once Angela Abar chooses a different body for him so they can be together, Jon is sub-sumed into the body of Cal (Abdul-Mateen II), a Black man. This is how the second Dr. Manhattan becomes "Black" within the text; it is Cal's body on the floor that Abar tells to wake up.

18 Damon Lindelof has said,

> The original plan was to do 10 [episodes]. And, then, I think around the time that we had written the scripts for four and five, and understanding what episode six ["This Extraordinary Being"] was going to be . . . that we were closer to the ending than we were to the beginning. Six didn't feel like a midpoint. It felt like, we now know everything that we need to know to move into the endgame. . . . If there are any regrets, it's that we didn't get to dimensionalize Lady Trieu as much as we did in the writer's room. . . . Especially given . . . the magnitude of [Hong Chau's] performance. . . . It was one of those things where we got into the endgame of the season, and it felt like we were moving back too much, between episode seven and eight. We talked about Lady Trieu's childhood, how she became who she was. But, a lot of her backstory got shorthanded between what Bian is saying to Angela[,] and [what] Lady Trieu is saying to Angela in episode seven.

Adam Chitwood, "Damon Lindelof Explains Why 'Watchmen' Was Shortened to 9 Episodes Instead of the Original 10," *Collider*, December 17, 2019, https://collider .com/why-watchmen-was-9-episodes-instead-of-10/.

19   Shawn Shimpach is insightful on the importance of *Watchmen*: "Here's a show deeply
     and at length imagining, pondering, and delving into a complex history of nation and
     race and justice, among the very few that have done so like this. So, maybe let's get
     into that instead of immediately looking for 'what else' or 'what about.' Let's bring at
     least one margin to the center for a minute and look at that before claiming this is a
     failure because it didn't bring more or all to the center, by itself, all at once." Shawn
     Shimpach, personal communication with author, March 14, 2020.
20   See Stuart Hall, Chas Critcher, Tony Jefferson, John Clarke, and Brian Roberts, *Polic-
     ing the Crisis: Mugging, the State, and Law and Order* (1978; repr., London: Macmil-
     lan International Higher Education, 2013).
21   *Superman: Red Son* was recently adapted as an animated film (Sam Liu, 2020).
22   "Least objectionable programming" was a television network policy established
     in the 1960s that prioritized providing content that would be found objectionable
     by the least number of its potential viewers as a means of maintaining viewership and
     courting advertisers.

4

From Sitcom Girl to
Drama Queen

● ●

Soul Food's Showrunner
Examines Her Role in Creating
TV's First Successful Black-
Themed Drama

FELICIA D. HENDERSON

Before *Power* surged, before *Empire* sang, before *Greenleaf* rejoiced, *Soul Food* cooked.

—Greg Braxton, *Los Angeles Times*

It is a peculiar sensation, this double consciousness, this sense of always looking at one's self through the eyes of others.... One ever feels his two-ness, an American, a Negro; two souls, two thoughts, two un-reconciled strivings; two warring ideals in one dark body, whose dogged strength alone keeps it from being torn asunder.

—W. E. B. Du Bois, *The Souls of Black Folk*

For over twenty years, I have written, produced, and directed television comedies and dramas for broadcast, basic, and premium cable and streamers. The first half of my career was spent writing Black and Black-themed family-oriented situation comedies (sitcoms). I purposely differentiate "Black sitcoms" and "Black-themed sitcoms." Black sitcoms are shows that employ a Black lead actor, but the show's content is culturally, purposely nonspecific in order to attract a mainstream, predominantly White audience (*Family Matters, The Fresh Prince of Bel-Air*). Black-themed sitcoms are ones in which the characters and content are culturally and racially specific (*Moesha, Everybody Hates Chris*).

Being employed on the writing staffs of *Family Matters* (1989–1998), *Moesha* (1996–2001), *The Fresh Prince of Bel-Air* (1990–1996), and *Everybody Hates Chris* (2005–2009) was immensely rewarding. I was well compensated to gather in a conference room with other writers, where we bested one another's jokes to make episodes funny, relevant, and buzzworthy. Essentially, I was paid to laugh for ten to twelve hours (sometimes more) per day. Of course, this is an oversimplification of the job's description, but it is also the essence of it. I was content with rising through the writing staff ranks—from writing trainee to coproducer—for the first seven years of my career. Eventually, however, my ambition led to a desire to broaden the scope of my writing career. I wanted to write adult comedies such as *Seinfeld* (1989–1998) and *Frasier* (1993–2004). I pressed my literary agent to pursue such opportunities. But after months of waiting for meetings that never materialized, I shared my frustration. My agent insisted that he was "pushing to get me in the room" when staffing opportunities came to his attention. But he was often told by showrunners that they simply did not need my "voice."[1] "What voice is that?" I remember asking my White, male agent with a fair amount of indignation—the voice of an experienced comedy writer whose career began in the prestigious Warner Bros. Television Writers' Workshop and who has compelling life experiences to share? Or was it the voice of a woman with an MBA in corporate finance who had worked on Wall Street and built homes for Habitat for Humanity that was of no interest?

In my career as a television writer, it was my first experience with being knowingly placed in the proverbial box. I was a Black woman who wrote Black family sitcoms, and a deductive holding pattern was being imposed on my career. It was inconceivable to White showrunners that I could relate to and write about a stand-up comedian with quirky friends who hung out at his apartment—*Seinfeld*. What could I bring to the table on a comedy series about a college-educated man with a bright, anxious brother and working-class father who had put his sons through college only to witness them become snobs—*Frasier*?

I was wrestling with the double consciousness W. E. B. Du Bois first lamented over a century ago—the internal conflict emerging from knowing the cultural experiences of the Black community while simultaneously understanding and navigating the connection to my mainstream education and life experiences. As a student, I was often the only person or one of a few people of color in my classrooms. The same was true of the breakrooms where I lunched as a working adult. Like other upwardly mobile people of color, I was shaped by my two-ness. Yet in the late 1990s, showrunners of mainstream comedy series gave little thought to how intimate my knowledge of their lives was, whether I was ever given the opportunity to write about them or not.

In order to break down the walls of the Black sitcom writer box, I needed to recreate myself. I returned to UCLA in pursuit of a second advanced degree, an MFA in screenwriting. Credentialed and armed with a feature film screen-play that won UCLA's screenwriting contest, I was able to transition to televi-sion drama writing just as sitcoms were disappearing from network television schedules and one-hour dramas were being scheduled in more and more prime-time slots. Fortuitously, my transition was aided by Paramount Television and the Showtime Network forming a partnership to adapt the hit film *Soul Food* (1997) into a one-hour television family drama. It would be the second adapta-tion of the story about three adult sisters (Teri, Maxine, and "Bird") living in Chicago's southside and struggling to adjust to the death of the family's matri-arch. The first adaptation was a sitcom for FOX Broadcasting Company (FOX) that failed to make the network's 1999 broadcast schedule.

Ironically, it was Paramount Television's vice president of comedy develop-ment, Rose Catherine Pinkney, my longtime champion, who recommended me for my first drama series assignment. After meeting with Paramount's drama executives, I met with the executive music producers of the film, Tracey Edmonds and her husband, Kenneth "Babyface" Edmonds. Then I met with and was approved by George Tillman Jr., the writer-director of the film. Finally, a meeting was set with Showtime's Jerry Offsay, the president of entertainment, and Pearlena Igbokwe, the vice president of drama series development (cur-rently the chairwoman of Universal Studios Group).

"Why should I hire a sitcom writer to create this important drama?" asked Offsay. I nervously quipped, "Because the show is about three sisters, and I've got five of them. Obviously, I will never run out of material." Everyone chuckled warmly, and then the hard questions followed. Offsay asked if I was aware of the previous Black dramas that had failed. Did I have an opinion about why they failed? If so, had I a plan for ensuring a different outcome for *Soul Food*? The questions were disconcerting. If all writers had the winning formula, every series would be a hit. That said, I had completed preliminary research on TV dramas such as the James Earl Jones–led *Under One Roof* (1995) and Steven Bochco's *City of Angels* (2000) and told them so. I had also studied shows like the secret agent adventure *I Spy* (1965–1968), historically significant for casting Bill Cosby as the first Black colead on a network drama (NBC).[2] Ultimately, I did not con-sider *I Spy* in my creative analysis because it was not doing the work that *Soul Food* would be. This show and shows like it represent studio and network deci-sions to cast physically diverse actors as a sign of progress toward inclusion for viewers searching for representation. However, as Kristen J. Warner points out in her analysis of contemporary image-making and what she terms "Plastic Representation"—a combination of synthetic elements put together and shaped to look like meaningful imagery but that can only approximate depth and substance because ultimately it is hollow and cannot survive close scrutiny—such overdetermining of Black images as the marker of societal progress or regression makes any image acceptable on its face, obliterating context and sidelining any consideration of depth.[3] In other words, rendering cultural, ethnic, and racial difference invisible ensures a show's acceptability for a mainstream audience that may consider physical difference palatable but a deeper exploration and representation of difference an intrusion.

In my meeting with Showtime, Offsay was asking that I opine about why Black-themed drama series had not attracted viewers. In 1999, shows that embraced what Herman Gray calls pluralist or separate but equal discourses on the Black experience—Black characters tackling the same problems mainstream America tackled—had not earned impressive ratings.[4] In this regard, *Under One Roof* and *City of Angels* shared a twofold commonality that impeded their success. Both were exceptionally reverential in their depictions of culturally specific Blackness, and both lacked a sense of humor.

Understandably, the showrunners / executive producers of *Under One Roof* and *City of Angels* were committed to illustrating nearly perfect Black characters. Since the 1970s, Black-themed sitcoms had been plentiful. But there had never been a successful Black-themed drama. Unlike mainstream shows that presented endless opportunities to depict a variety of White characters, the lack of opportunities for Black characters burdened the creators of the aforementioned shows with presenting proud, perfect, model citizens. Early Black-themed dramas were also burdened with offsetting television's historical depiction of Black characters. *Amos 'n' Andy* (1951–1953)—with its dim-witted, naïve Amos and conniving and lazy Andy—was a powerful signifier of American racial attitudes in the first half of the twentieth century. More offensive depictions of Black people had an even longer history in film and radio. So much so, some eighty-five years after the release of *Birth of a Nation* (1915) and nearly fifty years after *Amos 'n' Andy* debuted on CBS, the first Black-themed dramas overrepresented flawless Black characters as a counter-hegemonic response to a century of offensive portrayals of Black people.

With *City of Angels*, this issue was compounded by two factors. First, the characters were Black doctors and nurses, which added a layer of profession-based rarefication. Second, Steven Bochco, an Emmy Award–winning series creator (*Hill Street Blues* [1981–1987], *L.A. Law* [1986–1994], *NYPD Blue* [1993–2005]), was a non-Black showrunner creating a series about Black doctors working at a predominantly Black hospital. Although director Paris Barclay, who cocreated the series, was Black and the leads of the show were Black (including Blair Underwood, Vivica Fox, and Viola Davis), Bochco, the head writer and the most esteemed voice behind the camera, was not. Many elements rang false for Black viewers, including the use of gospel music to score tension-filled hospital scenes and Blair Underwood's character's attachment to surgical caps made of African kente cloth to signify the depth of his cultural commitment.

Under One Roof and *City of Angels* both aired for one season before being canceled due to low ratings. What resulted from their inability to attract viewer attention was the false narrative perpetuated by studios and networks—neither mainstream audiences nor Black viewers were interested in watching Black characters in shows that explored their lives. When dramas starring White characters failed, networks and studios did not halt the creation of new dramas starring White characters. However, when a Black drama failed, the cancellation was painted with a broad brush that generalized the failure. Decision-makers reasoned that even Black people did not want to see Blacks in dramas, as opposed to the possibility that Black viewers were not drawn to specific characters that lacked authenticity or were so devoid of frailties that they were neither entertaining nor compelling.

I shared my point of view with the Showtime executives as unapologetically as possible. I did not want to represent three Black sisters from the southside of Chicago through the gaze of the White, male president of the cable channel, so I was forthright when describing how I intended to depict *Soul Food*'s Joseph sisters. Shortly after the Showtime meeting, I was hired to develop *Soul Food* for a television audience. I would be creating my first drama series. "She came into the room and pitched herself. . . . The decision was made based on who she was, how she spoke about family and how she had a clear understanding from her own personal life of relationships between siblings and family members," Offsay would later say when asked about hiring me.[5]

The process of discovering how I would fashion the series began. It was important to create three-dimensional characters that were flawed. Well-crafted dramatic conflict was essential to compelling storytelling. And there had to be humor. No matter how dark the despair, there is always a place for tone-appropriate comedy. Given my comedy background, finding that tone was a challenge I relished.

The Last Laugh: A Career in Transition and Reinvention

> I don't think I've ever left Felicia's office without confidence. . . . I'd walk into her office insecure, doubtful. But I always left confident. She understood that many of her cast and crew had never worked with a woman showrunner before let alone a Black woman showrunner.[6]
>
> —Rockmond Dunbar, *Soul Food*'s "Kenny"

I developed *Soul Food* for television and was the series showrunner, head writer, and occasional director for the first three of its five seasons. My philosophy was that there would be no perfect characters and the series would include a fair amount of character-driven humor. The film was written and directed by George Tillman Jr. and loosely based on his Milwaukee, Wisconsin, family. "*Soul Food* will find particular resonance with those of us who happened to be the favored grandchild, and as children were the center of attention of a large extended family forever coming and going in a big old house," was how the *Los Angeles Times* described the film upon its theatrical release.[7] It was a critical and popular success. Families like my large, multi-generational one saw the film multiple times because it reminded us of our own families. Landing the assignment to adapt the film for television was the highlight of my career.

However, the honeymoon period was short-lived. It ended when Tillman Jr. read the first draft of my pilot script. He believed I had strayed too far from his original vision. He was put off by the additional layers I added to characters in my effort to make them more three-dimensional, to weave in more flaws and more opportunities for conflict. I explained that there is a significant difference between feature films and series television. A feature film's story begins and ends in roughly two hours. Therefore, it can survive a lack of narrative depth and character exploration. But a series needs both if it is to air for many seasons.

The conflict with Tillman Jr. did not resolve amicably and represented the first of many instances in which I had to take a firm stand regarding my vision for the show. I respect him as a filmmaker, and I am a fan of his work. I told him that I understood his desire to protect the characters that he created, characters largely based on his family members. But I hoped that he could see that they were my family now, as well, and I would do my best to take good care of them. I discovered that Tillman Jr.'s concern was partially motivated by the fact that I had strictly been a sitcom writer before being hired to develop his film into a television series. He had read my feature film. But in his opinion, going from winning a writing contest to creating an actual TV show was quite a distance to travel. He also assumed that he would have more input and authority in my decision-making process. As a writer-director who had only worked in feature films, he was unfamiliar with television production culture. Interacting with a writer who had a great deal of authority and autonomy was challenging for a director who had made a living in the feature film world—an environment where writers are summarily dismissed and replaced, with or without cause, by producers and directors. Today, with more and more A-list film directors and actors producing television series, feature film culture is creeping into television's content creation environment. Historically, in television, the showrunner / head writer has been the most powerful voice in production, and this was so on *Soul Food*. Tillman Jr. was an executive producer of the show. But he was not the writer or director, which would have given him more power on the series. Along with my writing staff, I shaped the direction of the series, season after season, and Tillman Jr. and his producing partner receded into the background. Unfortunately, it would take two decades, a plan to celebrate the twentieth anniversary of the show's premiere, and a meeting between Tillman Jr. and me to discuss a reboot of the series for the two of us to reconcile and develop a new relationship.

Soul Food was the first drama series I executive produced. The experience continues to shape my sensibilities and approach to the responsibility of being the head writer and showrunner. As a showrunner, I am hired to craft the on-screen narratives of the series, and I do not believe it is possible to do that by committee. Although television production is a collaborative endeavor (one of the reasons I enjoy it most), there is a difference between collaboration and groupthink. I am always open to collaboration. Meaningful creative input can emerge from anywhere, and encouraging others to share their ideas further invests them in the success of the show. At the same time, I also subscribe to the notion that a series most benefits from a strong point of view and creative vision that is then negotiated with other stakeholders. Ultimately, *Soul Food*'s groundbreaking success is attributable to several factors, including a singular creative voice from its showrunner.

Leading a Horse to Water: Instituting Comedy Writers' Room Rules in Drama Series Writers' Rooms

Implementing specific workflow processes commonly found in sitcom writing rooms, a commitment to telling the stories of multifaceted characters full of contradiction and conflicts, and embracing tonally appropriate humor were the keys to *Soul Food*'s success. The writing staff remained in Los Angeles, and I traveled to Toronto, Ontario, where the show would be produced. In the beginning, I was on set for approximately twelve hours. To keep the writing staff engaged and their writing specific, each visited Toronto to physically see the sets and spend time with the cast. For the less experienced writers, it also afforded them the opportunity to be exposed to the day-to-day tasks of running a show. I had never written on the staff of a drama series, let alone run one. So Showtime insisted that a veteran drama showrunner also join the staff. (They had also suggested that a veteran drama writer supervise me while I wrote the pilot. However, my agent, armed with my absolute agreement, managed to convince them to back down.) I was allowed to write the pilot script and the second episode on my own. Based on those scripts, twenty episodes of the series were ordered. The financial investment was significant. Kevin Arkadie—who had made a name for himself working with David Milch on *NYPD Blue* (1993–2005), with Sean Ryan on *The Shield* (2002–2008), and on creating *New York Undercover* (1994–1999) under Dick Wolf's banner—was hired as an executive producer to co-run *Soul Food*. I would be the second in command (co-executive producer). He managed the writers and story-breaking process in Los Angeles, while I

SHOWTIME © 2004 Showtime Networks Inc. All rights reserved. SOULFOOD© Twentieth Century Fox. © 2004 Paramount Pictures All rights reserved.

FIG. 4.1 From Sitcom Girl to Drama Queen

produced the show in Toronto. There were many one-on-one meetings between Kevin and the writers to develop the stories they would eventually write. Often, I felt left out or uninformed. Finally, I asked how I was supposed to stay abreast of our progress if there was no writers' room, where all the writers gathered together to discuss every episode, to which he quipped, "Writers' room? That's what you do on comedies, Sitcom Girl." Today, it is common for drama series to have daily writers' room meetings where the entire writing staff breaks stories together, but this was not the case when *Soul Food* was produced. In 2000, and since the 1950s, the writers' room had been the revered and protected workspace of comedy shows.[8] Conversely, the common practices on drama series included a writer meeting with the executive producer / head writer to discuss the assigned episode's story.

I insisted we change the system. Every writer needed to know what every other writer was writing while they were writing it. They needed to be in dialogue with one another. What if one had a question about what was in the next script? Also, the writers' room space encourages an interest in the whole season's episodes, not just the one a writer is writing. Writers could also bring challenges to the table when a script concern arose and reap the benefit of the fresh ears of other talented writers. "All right, Sitcom Girl. Let's try it," said Arkadie. I also implemented bringing completed first drafts to the writers' room table so the staff could read them aloud to offer feedback to the writer for the next draft of the script. This was also something I had often done on comedy staffs.

From my first drama to my 2022 one (a young adult genre drama for Netflix called *First Kill*), I employ a writers' room. My first speech to the writing staff is always the same. I explain that it is a safe place where no idea is too big or small, too wild or ridiculous. It is a place where you do not have to laugh at the showrunner's jokes or praise ideas when they are bad (I have worked in such rooms, and it is not a rewarding experience). I assure them that I have only hired "killers," so there is nothing to prove. The writers' room is where the most rewarding part of the creative process occurs, where creativity in storytelling is the most unencumbered—before executives give feedback on which they hope you will agree, before actors are not sure the words are the right ones, before directors shape your ideas into theirs, and before a line producer informs you that the show cannot afford to produce what is on the page.

In one of the early *Soul Food* writers' room meetings, I shared that we would not attempt to make up for every racist or poorly drawn Black character that had ever appeared in film and television. We would not attempt to depict every Black person. We would not attempt to avoid criticism. We would pursue honest and messy portrayals of the Black experience. As people do in real life, our characters will make mistakes. Some will be apologetic, others will not. But all will be three-dimensional. I believe that characters can do anything, and I believe that viewers will go on the journey with those characters as long as the story explains why they make the decisions they make. We will write our characters into unique situations. They will say things that Black characters have never said on television. I jokingly assured the Black writers that I did not want characters who were "a credit to their race." To the non-Black writers, I jokingly promised that they would not be called racist for writing a Black character who is a criminal—and our characters will laugh, and they will make us laugh.

The Ties That Bind: Finding Family Away from Home

Paramount Television chose to produce the show in Toronto to take advantage of the country's new production tax incentives. It was a livable but foreign country where neither the actors nor I had ever worked. Relocating led to a familial bond between the cast members and a strong commitment to the show. In 2020, while conducting interviews in support of the show's twentieth anniversary, actresses Malinda Williams (youngest sister Tracy "Bird") and Vanessa Williams (middle sister Maxine "Max") shared their experience. Malinda stated that she wanted to be truthful in her work: "Truthful about depicting life, not just Black lives, but lives. These are things that happen to people, not just Black people. Yes, there are nuances to Black life; however, these were universal stories that we were telling. It gave us an opportunity as Black actors." Vanessa added, "as Black people to be fully human in a way that I had never had an opportunity to do before.... It set a precedence for us and for Black excellence."[9]

In speaking about my role as the showrunner, Rockmond Dunbar (middle sister Max's husband, "Kenny"), added, "She always had a decision to make, and she made it.... She stuck with it. She was strong about it. Those are the things that gave you the confidence needed in order to perform it."[10] After reading the *Forbes* article from which these quotes were taken, for the first time, I realized how much I was part of the familial bond that the cast shared. My showrunning style was and continues to be part mother hen. If the actors felt insecure about a scene, for any reason, it was my job to instill the confidence they needed to perform the scene well. I had an open-door policy with an expiration date, we often joked. Any cast member was welcome to meet with me to discuss any concerns with the script up to twenty-four hours before we shot the material in question. This policy required that completed scripts be delivered well ahead of schedule and, with few exceptions, they were. I welcomed their input when they wanted to experiment and took the time to discuss the material when they were unsure about it. Although I could not be on set when every scene was shot, I was always there if a scene was being shot with which an actor had expressed concern. I did not always accommodate requests for changes in the script, but I was always willing to explain my thinking, why I believed the character's actions were best for the long-term story arc of the character, and the long-term appeal of the show.

A Good Director Is Hard to Find: Creating Opportunities for Women to Helm and Other Leadership Challenges

Women direct 25% of dramas now. . . .
Back in the Soul Food days, it was under
5%. It's come a long way. Actors would
primarily say to me, "You're the first
woman director I've ever had." That's
rare now.
—Bethany Rooney, director

Since the show was based on the relationships and lives of three adult sisters, it was important to hire women directors and directors of color. Ultimately, such directors also brought impressive levels of commitment to excellence, as many of them were getting an opportunity that would not otherwise have been afforded them. When the line producer, the producer responsible for managing the crew and finances on the show, told me it would be difficult to find qualified women, I balked. Too often, I had heard White showrunners claim they desired more diverse staffs but simply could not find qualified candidates. I knew candidates existed, and we would find them if we were committed to the search. We were shooting twenty episodes per season. It was unfathomable that some of those episodes would not be directed by women. I called every woman showrunner I knew, every woman agent I knew, and the Directors Guild of America to share my plan. Soon, we were booking women directors and were astounded to know that *Soul Food* alone contributed to a 50 percent rise in the number of women directors hired to direct one-hour dramas in prime-time television. In recent years, women showrunners such as Melissa Rosenberg (*Jessica Jones*, 2015–2019) and Ava DuVernay (*Queen Sugar*, 2016–2022) have shown similar commitment to furthering the careers of women directors by hiring women directors exclusively.

The most significant and possibly least pleasant task was the ongoing battle for an adequate budget. I was forced to engage with the studio on a weekly, episodic, and season-to-season basis regarding the budget. Often, it was the most difficult and most frustrating of my responsibilities. Each season the ratings increased, the popular press engaged with the show, and the show won awards and was nominated for an Emmy Award in the first season. And yet, each season, Paramount Studios threatened to cancel the series. The claim was that because the studio had not been able to make a lucrative deal to air the series internationally (with European countries), the show was deeply unprofitable. I often was made to feel that there was no show worth less than the one that I had created. Measuring with this limited rubric, Paramount TV had a difficult time determining how the show about three Black sisters from Chicago could be profitable for them if the show had no European value. According to Timothy

Havens in his work on how Black television travels globally, "Globalization has helped narrow the diversity of portrayals or eliminated them altogether. . . . In large part, African American characters and cultural allusions are most frequently used to attract young male demographic across multiple racial and national boundaries."[11] While Paramount TV's concerns about the lack of global interest in Black women characters may have had merit, it also demonstrated narrow thinking in terms of where the studio should have searched for the show's value. Additionally, while they struggled to support the show during its entire run, Showtime praised the show and shared internal ratings research about its relevance for the premium cable outlet. When new episodes of the show were airing, subscriptions increased. When the show was not airing, subscriptions decreased.

Given the institutional challenges, *Soul Food*'s success was heavily dependent on how well it was produced. I felt a great deal of pressure to make sure that the studio could never complain about the quality of the series. I also knew that a crew that felt respected by the showrunner would be a content crew that would go beyond its stated responsibilities for the good of the show. I learned every crew member's name, spent one hour per week visiting various departments, listening as department heads explained what they did and the integral role the department played in a successful production. With the help of the guitar-playing cinematographer, I created the Soul Food Band. On most Friday nights after the show wrapped for the day, I bought pizza for the crew and the Soul Food Band would jam on the show's nightclub set.

My leadership style was based on a commitment to being sensitive to how challenging change can be for many people. Most of the predominantly White crew had never seen a woman showrunner. Most had never experienced working for a Black person. Most of the men had never worked with a woman director, as well. I also endeavored to invest the crew in the show's success. I reminded each department head that I had never run a drama before and asked that they speak up if they thought I was making a mistake. I told them that I believed good ideas could come from anywhere, and I did not want them to be reticent to share story ideas that they would like to see tackled. I employed similar language when a woman director was scheduled to direct. I reminded the cinematographer, the crew's leader, that the woman director would probably be nervous because women do not get many chances. While supremely qualified for the job, she would still be hyperaware and possibly nervous about the significance of her presence. She would also be aware of how the quality of her work would impact the women directors who followed her.

To be clear, there were times when my inclusive management style was not successful. A crew member was fired after using the N-word when he learned that I expected every department to be diverse. My first production designer, a British White male, resigned rather than listen to me share one more unwanted opinion about *his* department's work. In moments like these, I was reminded that being a showrunner is akin to being the CEO of a company with 200–300 employees. You are tasked with protecting, building, and increasing the value of your assets (the television show you are running). Additionally, if the company has trouble of any kind, viewership wanes, or a cast member regularly refuses to leave the dressing room, ultimately it is the showrunner's responsibility to right the ship—while continuing to manage the show's investors (the studio and network) and all other department heads (editors, music composer, hair and makeup departments, costume designer, etc.).

Soul Food's Popular Impact: Toward a Critical Future

> "Soul Food" represents the beginning steps of trying to answer the question: How do you deal with the new African-American reality on television? . . . It's not dealing with stereotypes and the way (white people) think things are. It just shows the great potential of African-American drama on television.[12]
> —Ron Simon, curator, Museum of Television and Radio

Soul Food aired on Showtime for seventy-four episodes over five seasons. It was the first Black-themed drama to be an unqualified success. During the show's second season, the *New York Times* declared, "Simply by having survived, whether or not it manages to attract the critical attention it deserves, the show has beaten the odds against black dramas."[13] The series was a significant part of Showtime's schedule in its fourth and fifth seasons. So much so that when Paramount TV again threatened to stop producing it, Showtime substantially contributed to the budget to guarantee its production through season five. According to Offsay, the show "tremendously enhanced our business over the ten years that I was there. Our audience doubled in large part due to *Soul Food* and its sibling shows."[14] At the end of the fifth season, the *Washington Post* bemoaned the loss of the seven-time NAACP Image Award winner that presented a "realistic, frank and, at times, funny look into love lives and relationships of a family from Chicago's southside."[15]

The fan base was committed to supporting the show, as well. Fans held *Soul Food* viewing parties, and the show's official website amassed over ten thousand hits daily.[16] For three of its five seasons, it was Showtime's highest-rated series among all women. Showtime set up regular fan call-in events that were the most popular among all its series. Letters addressed to cast members arrived steadily, and the phone lines at Showtime's New York headquarters were overwhelmed after each week's episode aired. On one occasion, after I spoke on a panel at the

FIG. 4.2 Left to right: Boris Kodjoe, Nicole Ari Parker, Tracey Edmonds, Darrin Henson, Aaron Meeks, Malinda Williams, Vanessa Williams, Felicia D. Henderson (not pictured: Rockmond Dunbar)

National Association of Black Journalists, a teary-eyed woman approached me, apologized for crying, thanked me for the show, and then shared her story.

After ten years of estrangement, her only sister called on a Wednesday and asked, "Are you watching *Soul Food*?" That night, they stayed on the telephone while watching the show together and agreed to do so every week. At another event, a couple approached me to say that until *Soul Food*, they had never seen a Black couple make love on television.

Showtime's marketing department often called on the cast to make appearances at cable system sales events and flew them all over the country to attend them. The show's publicists booked me on a steady stream of speaking engagements with Black professional organizations, women's organizations, colleges, and surprisingly, NBC's Black Leadership Council's quarterly gathering. Def Jam Recordings, the most successful hip-hop record label in music history, produced a *Soul Food* soundtrack CD that featured many of its top artists.

Fifteen years after the show was canceled, the cast is frequently asked, through social media, about whether there will be a reboot of the show. In a recent internet search, I discovered five articles in the popular press addressing rumors of a *Soul Food* reboot. While working as a consulting producer on

Empire (2015–2020), the show's creator shared that he used *Soul Food* as an example of a successful Black drama when pitching *Empire* to networks.

After creating a successful, Black-themed drama, I easily found employment as a co-executive producer on mainstream dramas such as *Gossip Girl* (2007–2012) and *Fringe* (2008–2013). However, in the two seasons following *Soul Food*'s cancellation, I confidently pitched new iterations of Black family dramas without success. I struggled to understand why networks were uninterested in Black family dramas from the only television writer who had ever created a successful one. When I attended a Black Filmmaker Foundation (BFF) conference where Les Moonves, the former chief executive officer of CBS, served as the keynote speaker, someone in the audience of approximately four hundred asked him why networks still were not buying Black dramas after *Soul Food* had proven that Black dramas work.[17] Moonves quickly responded that in his opinion, *Soul Food* had not proven anything. It would not work on network television because network television had restrictions on nudity and language. He then asked for the next question.

His response demonstrated that mainstream networks had not adjusted their belief systems. In the mid-2000s, *Soul Food*'s success had not normalized the creative and business value of Black family dramas. It was easy for Moonves to engage in what Havens calls the "carrier discourse of industry lore, a discourse that is parasitic. . . . Seizing only those elements and insights that are useful for institutional goals and discarding all else."[18] In other words, Moonves was writing off a successful show as a fluke because it presented a reality contrary to ongoing, stale beliefs about Blacks and Black families. It was more acceptable to attribute *Soul Food*'s success to its use of partial nudity and occasional foul language than it was for him to defend CBS's long history of being the least diverse network.

It would be nearly a decade after the last *Soul Food* episode aired before the new wave of mainstream dramas starring Black leads became ratings successes. Series such as Shonda Rhimes's *Scandal* (2012–2018) and *How to Get Away with Murder* (2014–2020) and Black-themed family dramas like *Empire* (2015–2020), which became one of the biggest hits in FOX's history, were among television's most buzzworthy shows. It's worth noting that Rhimes did not get the opportunity to create a series that starred Black women until the impressive success of *Grey's Anatomy* (2005–), whose central character is a White, female doctor surrounded by a "color-blind" cast. The television landscape now includes many Black-themed family dramas—OWN's *Queen Sugar* (2016–2022), FOX's *Our Kind of People* (2021–2022), multiple *Power* (2014–2020) spinoffs on Starz, Epix's *Godfather of Harlem* (2019–), and Starz's *BMF* (2021–).

However, it is imperative that neither the number of Black-themed series nor mainstream shows starring Black actors be automatically accepted as a significant move toward parity. Despite the impressive rise of Black-themed dramas and Blacks in a variety of other dramas, *Soul Food* has suffered the TV history version of the Matilda Effect.[19] Exegetic, historical, and industrial analyses of the show's pioneering role in TV drama history in general, and Black-themed dramas, specifically, remain absent from media and creative industries studies. Until media scholars begin to include the history of Black-themed TV dramas, critical considerations in the study of television history are incomplete. Without such scholarly study, Black representation and diverse representations, in general, continue to be defined by the practice of counting the number of Black and Brown faces, seeing an increase in those numbers, and calling it progress. As Warner states, "The problem with such a line of thinking is that quantifiable difference alone often overdetermines the benchmarks of progress and obscures the multifaceted challenges inherent in booking roles as well as securing work on writing staffs, directing gigs, or even reaching executive gatekeeper status—thus privileging the visible (actors) over all other cinematic and televisual functions."[20] Simply put, privileging the visible reinforces the stagnation in the analytical progress of the invisible. We will continue to experience the cyclical waves of popularity that come along every ten to fifteen years or so, when for yet another fleeting moment, Black is the new Black on mainstream television.

Notes

1 The term *voice* is often used to describe the writing sensibilities or specific point of view that a writer appears to have based on samples of one's screenwriting.

2 Cicely Tyson had actually already starred in *East Side West Side* (1963–1964) and was the first Black actor to star in a drama series, but it was an anthology; therefore, she wasn't in every episode. This allows Bill Cosby to be described as the first series regular in a drama series. Diahann Carroll is often cited as the first Black woman to star in a half-hour series (*Julia*, 1968–1971). However, Hattie McDaniel, Louise Beavers, and Ethel Waters (who all played the title character), came a decade before her in *Beulah* (1950–1953). These women are often ignored, particularly by the Black media, because Beulah was a stereotypical Black maid, and therefore not a role Black media typically celebrates.

3 Kristen J. Warner, "In the Time of Plastic Representation," *Film Quarterly* 71, no. 2 (Winter 2017), https://filmquarterly.org/2017/12/04/in-the-time-of-plastic-representation/.

4 Herman Gray, *Watching Race: Television and the Struggle for Blackness* (Minneapolis: University of Minnesota Press, 1995), 87–91.

5 Cheryl Robinson, "Showtime's Multiple NAACP Image Award-Winning Series 'Soul Food' Celebrates 20th Anniversary," *Forbes*, May 28, 2020, accessed October 15, 2021, https://www.forbes.com/sites/cherylrobinson/2020/06/28/showtimes-naacp-image-award-winning-series-soul-food-celebrates-20th-anniversary/?sh=3e1f580d164e.

6 Robinson.

7 Kevin Thomas, "'Soul Food' Stirs Hearts with Life's Ups, Downs," *Los Angeles Times*, September 26, 1997, accessed November 10, 2021, https://www.latimes.com/archives/la-xpm-1997-sep-26-ca-36184-story.html.

8 Sid Cesar's iconic comedy/variety show *Your Show of Shows* (1951–1954) employed one of the most celebrated writers' rooms in television history and is responsible for

the myth-building idea regarding superior creative television comedy as a product of the collaborative work space in which comedy is created.

9   Robinson, "Showtime's Multiple NAACP."

10 Robinson.

11 Timothy Havens, *Black Television Travels: African American Media around the Globe* (New York: New York University Press, 2013), 2.

12 "No Black Dramas Left on Television," Today, May 24, 2004, accessed November 16, 2021, https://www.today.com/popculture/no-black-dramas-left-television-wbna5054030.

13 K. A. Dilday, "A Black Drama Beats the Cliches, and the Odds," *New York Times*, May 24, 2001, 25.

14 Dilday, 25.

15 Oveta Wiggins, "Last Call for Soul Food," *Washington Post*, May 26, 2004, accessed November 16, 2021, https://www.washingtonpost.com/archive/lifestyle/2004/05/26/last-call-for-soul-food/553430d0-cd31-4b88-aab8-1cfdefed6b63/.

16 "No Black Dramas."

17 The Black Filmmaker Foundation (BFF) was founded by film producer Warrington Hudlin (older brother of Reginald Hudlin). It was created to nurture Black filmmakers and was the largest and most prestigious media arts nonprofit organization from the 1980s to the early 2000s. HBO, NBC, and other media conglomerates sponsored its invitation-only weekend conference attended by a Black who's who of Hollywood.

18 Havens, *Black Television Travels*, 4.

19 The Matilda effect is a bias against acknowledging the achievements of women scientists whose work is denied, ignored, dropped from the record, and/or often attributed to a male. This phenomenon was first described by suffragist and abolitionist Matilda Joslyn Gage in her essay "Woman as Inventor."

20 Warner, "In the Time."

Part II

Attending Black
• •

Part II
Attending Black

5

Gaming as Trayvon

• •

#BlackLivesMatter Machinima
and the Queer Metagames of
Black Death

TREAANDREA M. RUSSWORM

In addition to concerns about exhibition, authorship, and representation, the
fight for racial justice has been central to how we understand Black participation in complex media industries like film and television. The born-digital
movement #BlackLivesMatter has increasingly drawn our attention to the
fact that Black civic participation, activism, and organizing cannot be thought
about without also contending with digital media—the social, cultural, and
procedural logics of digital platforms (Twitter, Facebook, and Instagram) as
well as the digital distribution practices of new media corporate titans (Netflix,
Amazon, and Hulu). While Black media scholars might not hesitate to explore
how a film like *Black Panther*, a TV series like *black-ish*, a cable TV series like
Watchmen, or a Netflix Original show like *Marvel's Luke Cage* relate to dominant discursive threads in Black media studies, video games routinely remain
missing from similar critical conversations about Black audiences, production,
and media savviness. And yet the large community of Black gamers, players, and
game spectators have much to contribute to our leading discussions about digitality and the political solvency of Black media. As such, this chapter explores
how the hashtag #BlackLivesMatter surfaces in the media production, public

play practices, and affective lives of Black gamers in an attempt to foreground this blind spot in Black media studies. What can "watching while Black" even mean without thinking about how digital avatars, DIY culture, and the police state converge in an always online—and often always *gaming*—public sphere?

When actively navigating what it means to watch, create, and play while Black under regimes of white supremacy and global anti-Blackness, an international cadre of Black gamers, players, and game spectators have long-participated in the cultural trend of using video games to create media that are both related to and independent of the original product. Although using games for original storytelling is a long-standing cultural practice, in game studies the term *machinima* (a portmanteau of the words *machine* and *cinema*) is used to describe some of the ways in which people use video game footage to create other media, such as episodic web series, short films, and even animated feature films. As a participatory form, machinima are often composed of many elements at once: gameplay, voice-over narration, music, and other types of media (like film and television clips, photography, and documentary footage). Machinima usually find their distributary home on platforms like YouTube where content creators can engage with active spectators.

For aspiring creative media producers who also happen to avidly play video games, machinima is often appealing as an affordable production option because projects can be created without hiring actors (there are in-game characters that can be appropriated for that) or using real props and sets (digital photorealistic interiors of in-game spaces may be used instead). In fact, entire scenes may be staged using comprehensive digital replicas of city skylines and game-rendered city streets that are replete with stoplights, traffic, and passersby. In this way, machinima refers to the DIY practice of appropriating anything that appears in a single title or taking background art, characters, sound effects, and mise-en-scène from multiple games and editing them together to create an entirely new work.

As a form of sampling and creative innovation, machinima has much in common with hip-hop as a cultural practice and art form. This particular hybrid media form relies on the signs and symbols (game assets) of game worlds, and the resulting project is also always extradiegetic media. Consider, for example, Black-authored machinima that remixes and repurposes an assemblage of gamic content in order to pay tribute to Black victims of police violence. One video, which was posted to YouTube by Brown Girls Gaming less than a month after Derek Chauvin murdered George Floyd, "SIMS 4 #BLACKLIVESMATTER Rally" was filmed exclusively using the popular life simulation game, *The Sims 4* (Maxis, 2014).[1] The three-minute video begins with animated sequencing of a richly rendered cityscape: a bridge, a skyline, cars commuting. These establishing shots are slowly alternated with still and motioned imagery of digital Black men and women being thrown to the ground, slammed against police cruisers, held in handcuffs, and forcibly detained. Close-up shots of their faces capture consternation, resignation, despair. These images of Black people in custody transition to depictions of marches and rallies and more Black people walking, protesting, inaudibly chanting, fists raised high in the air.

The accoutrement of protest is also on full display: Trayvon Martin posters, "Hands Up Don't Shoot" sweat shirts, #BlackLivesMatter gear, including digital reproductions of lists that contain the names of real victims of police violence. A young girl who appears directly involved in the organizing of this virtual #BlackLivesMatter rally sits at a table cluttered with pamphlets, water bottles, burning candles; she adorns a "Young, Gifted, and Black" T-shirt and "Melanin Poppin" earrings. Many of the protesters pose together in matching attire, heads down, fists clenched; others stand with posters at their side and COVID-19 facemasks partially obscuring their faces—a representation of the real-life protesting that took place around the world in the summer of 2020 (see figure 5.1). The video ends with the words "Stand for something or fall for anything," and then with each name displayed singularly for a few moments on-screen: "ERIC GARNER. BREONNA TAYLOR. ELIJAH MCCLAIN. FREDDIE GRAY. MICHELLE CUSSEAUX. STEPHON CLARK. PHILANDO CASTILLE. TANISHA ANDERSON. GEORGE FLOYD."

Of particular note here is the music track, a sultry King Sis neosoul single, that provides the video's only audible sound ("Living for weekends, wishing I could take a break from this world"/ "I wanna be free, finally, finally"). The music's rhythm is accentuated by the coordinated movements of the digital protesters, who appear to walk in slow motion to the beat, their hips sashaying and synchronizing together in unison as they dance-march with their picket signs. The game's visual style further underscores the highly stylized nature of this formal protest. The thematic focus on systemic violence and racism and the

FIG. 5.1 *The Sims 4* #BlackLivesMatter rally, Brown Girls Gaming

all-too-common affective register of public mourning that risks codifying and potentially spectacularizing Black death contrasts with the cheerful and bright animated canvas from which this project was drawn. The project's appropriation of this particular game—*The Sims 4*, which is often described as a suburban, capitalist utopia—contrasts almost nonsensically, then, with the motion-captured footage and in-game screenshots that depict Black people protesting the dystopian machine of systemic violence. Anyone familiar with *The Sims* franchise will be keenly aware that most of what we see in this production—from the expansive and subtle range of skin tones of the digital Black avatars to the hairstyles, unique clothing, props like burning police cars, custom dance-like movements, Black Power fist gestures, and other animations—were all created by Black players, designers, and hackers whose creation of custom content productively blurs the lines between utopia and dystopia, playing and grieving, and leisure and labor. At the time this machinima was created, you could not adequately depict Black people at all in the game, and you especially could not animate any symbolic rituals of political protest in any of the commercially sanctioned or "vanilla" copies of games from this best-selling franchise.

There are evident and uneasy tensions—ready contradictions—between form and cultural context that make #BlackLivesMatter machinima difficult to classify. Is this creation "play," a music video, or an amateur animation with low-budget aesthetics? Is the production superficial "hashtag activism"? What does it mean to stage and then film a #BlackLivesMatter "rally" in a video game and post it to YouTube? How do we make sense of the various distantiations, the visual and affective discontinuity between the signifying political project at hand and the creative compromises inherent in repurposing digital media and computer code? How does the existence of such work complicate our understanding of what it means to play in the dystopian logics of white supremacist capitalist America?

Metagaming #BlackLivesMatter

Perhaps it comes as no surprise that representing #BlackLivesMatter in a video game that by default deprioritizes Blackness and Black player experiences is no easy task. Through a steadfast "technological inheritance steeped in white power structures of history, fantasy, and imagination," false assumptions about who plays games have defined the technological and cultural ascension of the video game industry since the 1970s.[2] Since its inception, the industry has adhered closely to "hobbyist traditions" like mainstream science fiction and literature and "western ideologies of play" that are "predicated exclusively upon white experience with technology."[3] In one of the first examinations of race and the video game industry, Anna Everett argued that anxieties about Blackness factored heavily into contemporary game characterizations and that the "racial problematic" predictably coagulated around "moral panics about gaming's potential dangers."[4] In thinking about how games were designed mostly by white men and marketed almost exclusively to men and boys in the 1980s and 1990s, Everett knew that the "high-tech blackface" and "orientalism" readily apparent in popular games like *Ready 2 Rumble* (Midway Games, 1999) were never intended for her. As she reflects in *Digital Diaspora: A Race for Cyberspace*, "I am acutely aware that my mature, black, and female body is marked and thus marginalized as a shadow consumer in the gaming industry's multibillion-dollar marketplace."[5]

Indeed, throughout gaming history, the industry has proliferated and profiteered racist caricatures, essentialized narrative conceits, and maintained exclusionary hiring practices that have been further exacerbated by the targeted harassment campaigns directed at Black players who publicly play or discuss games on social media. Although it is now a media industry that generates more revenue per year than the film, television, and music industries combined, the video game industry's problems with race and representation are also rooted in the industry's overlapping histories of computation, technology, and information. As a media industry that is also a computing industry, then, the medium is further imbricated in what Alondra Nelson has succinctly argued about "politics of the future" billed as "novel paradigms for understanding technology" that yet and still ultimately and continually "smack of old racial ideologies."[6]

Exclusionary practices that are hardwired into game design history and culture offer another way to understand why Black identities at play so often seem to distantiate from the lusory task at hand—both for the players who have to labor in their play against the machine logics designed to exclude them and for the spectating audiences that view these moments in prerendered videos on YouTube or live on Twitch. In addition to some of the discontinuities we can note in *The Sims 4* #BlackLivesMatter machinima, there are also ready disputations between games as a site of unfettered play and games as tools of indoctrination that reinscribe the types of disciplinary systemic negation that would understandably preclude "play" for Black and nonwhite folks. Black gamers must uniquely labor to find any respite, pleasure, or freedom of being and imagination that "play" typically engenders given that the mainstream video game industry's successes have been so routinely predicated on criminalizing, vilifying, or denying our existence.

On the one hand, these types of contradictions are evident at the textual level of games as play spaces when, for example, a Black player tries to create themselves in *The Sims 4* but cannot because the default game assets did not fully imagine Black bodies. On the other hand, when games are used as mediascapes, the discontinuities are further amplified when the same player sets out to use the game as a media tool of protest but first has to create or otherwise seek out custom content and programming to enable and enliven this type of goal-driven play. Both of these types of play ambitions clearly work against the intended use of the game. Yet are terms like "game" and "play" even applicable to thinking about the production of #BlackLivesMatter machinima when the whole idea of Black play has always been cast as an implausible or unimportant goal of the medium?

Are there any important differences between playing a game as it was intended, playing a game in spite of how it offends and excludes, and *playing with* a game? This latter possibility, of *playing with* games, as Peter Krapp explains in *Noise Channels: Glitch and Error in Digital Culture*, is often a participatory expectation of the medium as a whole. Krapp clarifies, "Whereas [playing a game] teaches one the game through navigating the game's commands and controls, [playing with a game] opens it up to critical and self-aware exploration. Like learning to swim, gaming means learning to learn and initiates us into training systems, but like learning to read, it does not stop at a literal obedience to the letter."[7] In departing from that "literal obedience" to games as hegemonic "training systems," Black players who endeavor to work with and against the confines of the exclusionary practices of the medium do so in ways that expand beyond any easy definitions of play. The uninviting but modifiable gamespace becomes a catalyst for more imaginatively and less literally exploring Black subjectivity's relationship to systems in general. This work requires the constant type of critical self-awareness that depends on the active cultivation of emergent technological, media, and civic literacies.

If machinima is the form and by-product of playing out-of-bounds, then machinima also engender additional ways to understand the critically reflexive process of playing with and against systemic and digitized proxies of oppression. In game studies, discussions about "critical play," "serious play," and "transformative play"—design goals and play practices—share some commonalities with media discourses on resistant and oppositional Black spectatorship.[8] Relatedly, the concept "metagaming" is another way to productively think about what we see in #BlackLivesMatter machinima as players and spectators resist and reconfigure dominant messaging. As envisioned by Stephanie Boluk and Patrick LeMieux, metagaming is a discursive mode of play that includes all the play done within and outside of a system in ways that may break, expose, and subvert such systems. As they elaborate, "Metagaming functions as a broad discourse, a way of playing, thinking, and making that transforms autonomous and abstract pieces of software into games and turns players into game designers. Metagames reveal the alternative histories of play that always exist outside the dates, dollars, and demographic data that so often define videogames."[9] As players who have always existed "outside" the defining attributes of the medium, Black gamers, modders, and machinima producers take metagaming even further than some of the most common examples of playing with systems, such as writing alternate storylines by creating fan fiction or speedrunning a game by exploiting its glitches. This can be perilous work, as gaming against the system in ways that "stray further from the [ideological standard of the medium] are not as easily tolerated."[10]

To return to the example of the "SIMS 4 #BLACKLIVESMATTER Rally," the horrifying and chronically repetitious reality of Black death in the United States literally has no place or time in the game if one plays with an obedience to the commercially released training system. It is only when Black players metagame in critical disobedience to the system that representing Blackness and a wider range of lived experiences becomes even imaginable and speculatively possible. Since this machinima was shared on YouTube, we can also note how it resonates with viewers, the vast majority of whom also play *The Sims*. This stylish music video turned protest rally appears spatially and temporally unintelligible and staged in the game as a diegetic event, where the characters in this particular neighborhood were imagined as "marching down to City Hall in solidarity with Black Lives Matter." The description for the video speaks extradiegetically, however, to implore its spectators to action, challenging, "Stand for something or fall for anything." In responding through the comments, the international audience of viewers registers a range of responses, including solidarity ("America you in our prayers"—from South Africa), emotionality ("My heart dropped when the littler girl put up her fist"), a reflexive awareness of social media troll culture ("o dislikes = o racist [*sic*] watched this video!"), direct appeals for more Black-authored mods and content ("Sooooo where u get all this blm cc? I neeeeeeed it"), and reflections about the personal impact of police brutality ("[I lost] my cousin this year and every body jest [*sic*] dying"). Such responses reveal that just as Brown Girls Gaming uses a range of technical and creative tools to simulate the consequences of Black death in this utopian paradise, so too does the audience participate in a complex spectatorial process that brings an urgent political articulation, collective mourning, and technological training to the ludic frame.

Gaming Trayvon vs. Gaming Systemic Racism

Black players have not been alone in making the connection between #BlackLivesMatter and diffuse notions of play. For example, the professionally produced interactive virtual reality experience *One Dark Night*, which debuted at South by Southwest in 2015, invites you to "play" as a witness on the night Trayvon Martin was killed by George Zimmerman. Developer Emblematic Group worked with forensic specialists to create a reanimation of the murder that was "produced exclusively from real recordings of 911 calls, witness trial testimony, and architectural drawings that provide the exact layout of both interiors and exteriors of the condo complex."[11] It uses reconstructed audio in order to establish that "Zimmerman cocked his gun just before he gave chase."[12]

Unlike machinima, where playing the game may occur as part of the production process of creating a video that is intended to be viewed and not played, *One Dark Night* asks you to essentially play as a roaming omniscient spectator who maintains a 360-degree view of key events. From a first-person perspective, you as the camera are outside in the dark viewing Zimmerman pacing frantically around; you listen to the actual 911 call that he makes before and during his pursuit; you hear and view residents of one apartment making their own 911 calls; you watch and listen from a different apartment as another witness calls to report Trayvon's agonized screams and the gunshots you both hear.

One Dark Night is currently listed on Steam, the leading distribution platform for downloading digital games, as a "simulation game," a categorization that seems to belie both logic and form. The peculiar categorization of this work as a simulation game invites players into the diegesis of the murder scene as a game space. Yet other than the controllable rotating camera, no other mechanics (like altering time, automating actions, or manipulating numerical representations—characteristic features of the simulation games genre) exist. Since the work appeared well after the July 13, 2013, acquittal, the intentions here seem to be to use VR's adjacency to the games industry to evidentially exonerate an unarmed Black teenager in the court of American public opinion. *One Dark Night* uses tools of computation, like the "cleaned" and enhanced audio files and omniscient point of view, to turn computational authority into the type of expert testimony or objective spatial-temporal location from which to comprehend the experiential reality of Black death.

Even if we set aside the ethical implications of distributing Black death as its own simulation game, *One Dark Night* lacks any awareness of the impossibility of creating impartiality or objectivity in the greater American social scene. The comments on Steam unsurprisingly confirm the futility of persuading mainstream gamers that anything untoward happened that night, as many commenters directly challenge the gamic presentation of legal objectivity. Most of the gamers on Steam seem to see the fight for racial justice as inherently incompatible with the project's investments in objective representation. For example, one poster suggests that Emblematic Group tampered with—rather than enhanced—the scene's audio files: "[They edited] voice audio out of context to make Zimmerman out to be a racist. The experience is clearly based on an agenda with hints of BLM propaganda." Additionally, labeling this material as a game seemed to enrage players—but not for the same reasons I would hesitate to call this a game.

Distributing this project as a game subverts player expectations that are predicated on a long tradition of first-person shooter games (like *Resident Evil 5*) where much of the gamic action thrill relies on killing Black and other racially marginalized persons. So while I would hesitate to call this a game strictly because of the ethical implications of inviting people to play with Black death, many commenters seemed to want to protect the idea of a game from a political project that ideologically offends them. Another poster espouses that the game is "completely biased against George Zimmerman and completely in the camp for Trayvon Martin, there is no objectivity. Also this is not a game."

Among gamers who used Steam to access this production, the single most common complaint is that the project errored irrevocably by not allowing you to play as Zimmerman. Emblematic Group's refusal to let players "simmer the Zimmer"—play as George Zimmerman as he murdered Trayvon—was received as a game-breaking failure ("F#CK social justice" / "the gameplay was pretty bad, couldn't even play as Zimzam"). By making players maintain a tertiary perspective that is independent of either person at the scene, the metagame this production stages asks gamers to critically deduce that the legal verdict was wrong. Yet as this chorus of toxic discord makes clear, reenacting Black death with the goal of persuading American viewers to even play at objectively valuing Black life quickly succumbs to the thorny politics of recognition that I have critiqued elsewhere as unsustainable.[13] Attempts to force the recognition of Black humanity by creating an empathetic response through depictions of Black suffering nearly always fail and, importantly, risk further compounding a broken system that is itself an automated simulation with predictable ends.[14]

Although arguably more aesthetically polished than the kind of #BlackLivesMatter machinima posted on YouTube, *One Dark Night* is not an anomaly when it comes to a concerted effort to use video games to remediate Black death. For example, predating *One Dark Night*, immediately after Zimmerman's acquittal, Black players hopped onto their computers and game consoles to mix the processes of mourning, witnessing, and systemic critique with gameplay in novel ways. Most notably, in addition to *The Sims*, Black players have consistently used other commercial game environments like the *Grand Theft Auto* franchise (*GTA*; Rockstar Games, 1997–2013) to protest exclusionary and punitive systems in ways that are consistent with what scholars Arturo Cortez, Ashieda McKoy, and Jose Ramon Lizarraga theorize as "Blacktivism," an Afrofuturist speculative practice.[15]

In fact, for over a decade a wide range of *GTA*-generated #BlackLivesMatter machinima has been uploaded to YouTube, but this content can be particularly difficult to find because of how YouTube's machine-learning ranking system deprioritizes material it deems less likely to garner views. Then too, unlike most videos that when viewed are paired with likeminded suggestions, *GTA* #BlackLivesMatter viewed machinima often gets coupled with suggestions for what appears to be white supremacist and ultraconservative propaganda that ultimately sympathizes with the murderers. Despite these "algorithms of oppression" (to use Safiya Noble's phrase[16]), the dynamic range of *GTA*-created #BlackLivesMatter machinima includes tributes and gamic memorializations of Black victims of police brutality that often remediate real footage and photographs of the victims with game-rendered content; reenactment videos (i.e., playing as Trayvon Martin or playing as Mike Brown) that attempt to digitally recreate the victims' final moments; and other videos that combine the act of reenacting and witnessing Black death with creative departures from any lived reality as the works shift to depict alternate retaliatory endings for the murders.

Additionally, several purely fictionalized productions thematically address systemic violence in short machinima films and creative episodic web series.

Some of these works are filmed by single players who metagame their engagements with the games while other productions are filmed with casts and crews of players who provide voice acting, writing, and direction. These intentional media makers seem to have a range of ambitions when producing and sharing such content, but perhaps the most common motivation for making the productions is fatigue and frustration with the judicial system's chronic and repeated failures.

One compelling work in this archive of *GTA* #BlackLivesMatter machinima is the project "GTA 4 TRAYVON MARTIN [HD]," which was posted three days after the Zimmerman verdict on July 16, 2013, by kassanTv.[17] With 181,000 views, it appears to have garnered the most viewers of any work of this kind. The eleven-minute and twenty-second machinima begins as a typical reenactment project with one player representing Trayvon and another playing as Zimmerman chasing him through the darkly rendered streets. This attempt at literalization simulates its own reenactment of the 911 calls (remediated with what sound like snippets of the actual calls), and it inserts some imagined internal dialogue from both Trayvon and Zimmerman as the chase and altercation ensue.

Even in these opening moments as the game engine is being metagamed to recreate these events, there are moments when the game's system proves noncompliant, not entirely suitable for the task at hand, and so jarring discontinuities and distantiations proliferate. For instance, the person/avatar playing as Trayvon appears much older than the teenager and is wearing a jacket and tie, not a hoodie. Before the chase, he is also seen trying to purchase Skittles in what appears to be a bar, probably because this location was the only interior space available in the game that could be recuperated to stand in for a convenience store. Perhaps due in part to the evident noncompliance of the game machine to literally represent the murder, a competing creative vision for that night and its aftermath unfolds just moments after we see the "realistic" attempts at reenactment. The remainder of the machinima becomes a more speculative enterprise as it abandons any commitment to portraying the experiential reality of Black death's proximity to the machine logics of systemic racism.

This departure from the real begins after the on-screen shooting occurs, as a cut to a title screen announces, "What Really Happened." This break in the action is followed by the digital Trayvon noncompliantly running around in circles—appearing to glitch even—with a quick fade to a GIF of the teenager being robed by a white Jesus, captioned with "Trayvon's New Hoodie" (figure 5.2). Hence after Black death appears as a glitch in this machine, Trayvon is depicted as being neither here nor there as he is compassionately received by the Christian deity in the nongame asset form of a meme. This moment shifts back to the crime scene where now Trayvon's body is surrounded by all the media crew's player avatars on-screen. A group of seven men, who call for help, discuss the injustice of what has transpired and generally speak in an increasingly escalating chorus of competing sounds and dialogue. Instead of representing

FIG. 5.2 "Trayvon's New Hoodie," kassanTv

Trayvon dying alone in the dark, these guardians congregate around him, forming a semicircle of protective digital bodies.

"GTA 4 TRAYVON MARTIN [HD]" continues by metagaming the official game and systemic racism as complicit training systems. The next scene includes the funeral, where the player-spectators are all in suits, firing their guns into the air, commemorating Trayvon as a fallen hero. After this short scene, the on-screen action shifts to the day of the verdict and the same posse waits outside the in-game courthouse as they impatiently await the verdict that spawned the #BlackLivesMatter movement. After another title screen, "Text Message Said He 'Not' Guilty," the crowd of armed spectators immediately opens fire on the courthouse and turns their attention to the car transporting Zimmerman. The players use Molotov cocktails, an array of fully automatic weapons, rocket launchers—all the excessive mechanisms of force that are widely available in *GTA*'s system, a system carefully designed to spectacularize American violence. With Zimmerman dead and a corrective vision of justice instated, the men tour the city in a highspeed motorcade featuring a custom pulsating rap soundtrack ("You killed Trayvon, nigga you is racist"), a visually compelling set of alternating camera angles, and live cross-cutting using developer Rockstar's in-game "cinematic mode." In terms of its content, style, and speculative vision of retributory justice, the work has more in common with a Blaxploitation film than its original "source material" game and a chronic failure of justice.

The distantiations that emerge from metagaming Black death, in this case, draw our attention to a few ways in which systems can be both deployed and critiqued in nonliteral spaces like play. The process of gaming the system by playing as Trayvon both traffics in and exploits the prohibitive systemic game design logics of the *GTA* franchise—a franchise that, as a whole, has advanced representations of Blackness as criminal and deviant and Black masculinity as nihilistically ensnared in gang violence. The machinima not only further spectacularizes these programmatic logics but also encodes its own riffs and breaks from these structuring norms as it does the work of speculating and simulating an alternate reality. The work of collective grieving combined with the work and play of machinima production speculatively creates a new—alternate—reality that digitally seals a Black victim of systemic violence into its own complex process of protective and affective looping.

The work that combines grieving, protecting, and avenging is only speculatively plausible in this liminal time-space continuum. Then too, the game's formal system, with its imperfect options for manipulating Black digital bodies through time and space, gives way to a competing creative process of world-visioning that uses sonic and visual remediation and extradiegetic storytelling to disrupt the all-too-familiar simulation of Black death. At the spectatorial level, the process of viewing the machinima mirrors the queer temporality of Black death that has persisted before and since this murder. The queerness of this temporality is evinced not only in the chronic repetitions of state-sanctioned violence but also in the indexicality of the digital grief process with its timestamps and comments that are notably marked and unbound by any logical passage of time. Nine years after this video was first uploaded, spectators of kassanTv's prolific Black-themed machinima channel continue to view and return to this particular video whenever there is another publicly mourned and processed Black death. Indeed, this machinima has become a site for collective grievance whenever the cyclical, simulative nature of Black death is reconfirmed, usually documented by other videographic works, like cell phone recordings, that have also gone viral.

Playing with systems in this way makes the creators vulnerable to the obligatory disciplinary techniques of the toxic feedback loops masked as public discourse dominating the digital era. That is, although the majority of the 687 comments simply repeat the statement "R.I.P. Trayvon," there are also comments left by posters who espouse white-supremacist ideologies that criminalize and vilify Trayvon as they argue Zimmerman only did what was necessary. Such outbursts are jarring reminders that in a now digitized public sphere where the simulacra of Black death have primacy, the nonliteral work of speculating or playing beyond the brokenness of dominant systems will always take place in spaces that are an extension of the same structures that police, deny, and annihilate any important visionary dissension.

Conclusion: The Racially Queer Politics of Playing While Black

As a process and as a form, #BlackLivesMatter machinima affectively contends with the virality and inhumanity of Black death on its own digitized terms. The works may help us think about the relationship between simulative systems and lived experiences that have overlapping histories of repetition and spectacle, proceduralism and performativity. This does not, however, entirely absolve the works from what Ashleigh Greene Wade and others have critiqued as the retraumatizing practice of reproducing imagery of Black suffering and death. As Wade critiques, recycling videos and images of Black suffering on social media has the potential to undermine the transformative and world-making capacities of "viral Blackness" and digital tools like the hashtag #BlackLivesMatter that have rich potential to bridge our on- and offline modes of being.[18] Following Sylvia Wynter and other posthumanist thinkers, Wade argues that digital ephemera and tools are no longer inseparable from us; our use of technology creates different modalities of critiquing and refining the "virtual-physical assemblages" that have become the body that may now be understood as a human-machine interface.

As we can note in videos like *The Sims 4* #BlackLivesMatter rally and kassanTv's speculative attempt at playing as Trayvon Martin, some of the more interesting #BlackLivesMatter machinima produced experiment with connecting grief and protest, on the one hand, and the body and representations of the physical world, on the other hand, in ways that veer beyond the circulation of Black suffering. As metagames, Black-authored machinima, like other examples of viral Blackness, use "images, hashtags, and embodiment to de-center colonized languages and the relationships of those languages to knowledge production."[19] While I stop short of arguing that machinima is further evidence of our changed status as posthuman, perhaps viral Black interventions and technological remediations that are skilled at manipulating the languages of image, code, and virality are the types of subversions that will come to matter most in a heavily mediated world. Perhaps the experientially and digitally trained Black subject who speaks fluently in the language of these things stands the best chance to subvert the persistent simulations of destruction and systems of oppression that continue to devalue Black life and ingenuity.

Notes

1 Brown Girls Gaming, "SIMS 4 #BLACKLIVESMATTER Rally," YouTube video, 2020, 3:33, https://www.youtube.com/watch?v=OfCd6VTcwiU. The channel was later renamed Sprinkle of Gaming.
2 Raiford Guins, "May I Invade Your Space? Black Technocultural Production, Ephemera, and Video Game Culture," in *AfroGEEKS: Beyond the Digital Divide*, ed. Anna Everett and Amber J. Wallace (Santa Barbara, CA: Center for Black Studies Research, 2007), 114.
3 Guins, 114.
4 Anna Everett, *Digital Diaspora: A Race for Cyberspace* (Albany: SUNY Press, 2009), 111.
5 Everett, 111.
6 Alondra Nelson, "Introduction: Future Texts," *Social Text* 20, no. 2 (Summer 2002): 1.

7 Peter Krapp, *Noise Channels: Glitch and Error in Digital Culture* (Minneapolis: University of Minnesota Press, 2011), 77.

8 See Katie Salen and Eric Zimmerman, *Rules of Play: Game Design Fundamentals* (Cambridge, Mass.: MIT Press, 2003); Mary Flanagan, *Critical Play: Radical Game Design* (Cambridge, Mass.: MIT Press, 2009).

9 Stephanie Boluk and Patrick LeMieux, *Metagaming: Playing, Competing, Spectating, Cheating, Trading, Making, and Breaking Videogames* (Minneapolis: University of Minnesota Press, 2017), 9.

10 Boluk and LeMieux, 284.

11 "About this Game," Steam page for *One Dark Night*, Emblematic Group, 2015, https://store.steampowered.com/app/460510/One_Dark_Night/.

12 *One Dark Night*.

13 TreaAndrea M. Russworm, *Blackness Is Burning: Civil Rights, Popular Culture, and the Problem of Recognition* (Detroit: Wayne State University Press, 2016).

14 See TreaAndrea M. Russworm, "Dystopian Blackness and the Limits of Racial Empathy," in *Gaming Representation: Race, Gender, and Sexuality in Video Games*, ed. Jennifer Malkowski and TreaAndrea M. Russworm (Bloomington: Indiana University Press, 2017).

15 See Arturo Cortez et al., "The Future of Young Blacktivism: Aesthetics and Practices of Speculative Activism in Video Game Play." *Journal of Future Studies* 26, no. 3 (2022): 53–70. The authors examined livestreaming sessions of *The Sims 4* and *Grand Theft Auto V* and defined Blacktivism as a speculative play practice that includes hacking, glitching, collective farming and grinding, spawning and respawning, and firewalling. While their article was published after my chapter was already in production, I concur with Cortez et al. on many points, especially about the complicated and speculative nature of Black play cultures. My approach in this chapter, however, is to closely examine #BlackLivesMatter machinima as a unique media practice and art form that needs to be considered in the broader contexts of gaming history and of the Black media-making, spectatorship, and reception practices that are the focus of this edited collection. Other distinctions between my approach here and Cortez et al. include the earlier historical arch for these types of play practices that I demarcate in my consideration of representations of Trayvon Martin in *Grand Theft Auto IV*.

16 See Safiya Umoja Noble, *Algorithms of Oppression: How Search Engines Reinforce Racism* (New York: New York University Press, 2018).

17 kassanTv, "GTA 4 TRAYVON MARTIN [HD]," 2013, YouTube video, 11:20, https://www.youtube.com/watch?v=700Txj1DDPA.

18 Ashleigh Greene Wade, "'New Genres of Being Human': World Making through Viral Blackness," *The Black Scholar* 47, no. 3 (Fall 2017): 33-43; Jessica Marie Johnson and Mark Anthony Neal, "Introduction: Wild Seed in the Machine," *The Black Scholar* 47, no. 3 (Fall 2017): 38.

19 Wade, "'New Genres,'" 40.

6

"Trying to Find Relief"

• •

Seeing Black Women through
the Lens of Mental Health and
Wellness in *Being Mary Jane*
and *Insecure*

NGHANA LEWIS

When *Essence* magazine featured Mara Brock Akil, Issa Rae, Shonda Rhimes, Debbie Allen, and Ava DuVernay on the cover of its May 2015 "game chang-ers" edition, neither Brock Akil nor Rae had inked the deals that would catapult them to mogul status in the realms of on-demand and streaming media.[1] The impressive cult following Rae amassed over the two-year run of her YouTube series *The Misadventures of Awkward Black Girl*[2] grew to an audience of millions after the 2016 debut of *Insecure* (2016–2021) on HBO.[3] And while *Girlfriends* (2000–2008), *The Game* (2006–2015), and *Being Mary Jane* (2014–2019) scored substantial ratings consistently over their series runs on UPN, CW, and BET,[4] Brock Akil herself acknowledged that her 2020 deal with Netflix to stream *Girlfriends* and *The Game* and to develop new screenplays and other creative projects gave her and other black women, who have always been at the center of her creative vision, a level of "validation" that she did not experience while writing, producing, and creating for broadcast television. "Way back in the day," she explained during an interview on *The Breakfast Club*, "I'm like, hey, can we get on Netflix, can we get on Apple, can we . . . get to these places, and nobody was feeling it, and I didn't understand it."[5]

In an interview with Trevor Noah on *The Daily Show*, Rae expressed sentiments similar to Brock Akil's in recalling her battles to secure creative spaces in which to foreground black women's stories, to now calling shots as writer, creator, producer, and new-talent developer as a result of her 2021 five-year, 40 million dollar contract with WarnerMedia:[6] "That's what was the frustration about not seeing [black women] on television for so long, because I was surrounded by these women who occupied so many different spaces, and I wasn't seeing that reflected on television. And it was just, like, 'but this is my life, this is their life, this is my mom's friend's life, so what is the problem, where is the disconnect? . . . Where are these women that I know so well?'"[7] It may seem odd to open this chapter by relating Brock Akil's and Rae's past struggles in an industry where both women are currently dominating and experiencing both financial and creative success. But because Brock Akil's and Rae's struggles to cultivate and express their artistic visions so closely mirror some of the struggles at the center of their protagonists' developments, I find it useful to play out some of the implications of their use of television and digital media to engage issues of black women's mental health and wellness by "seeing" Brock Akil and Rae against the backdrop of an industry that has historically given little to no relief to black women's lived experiences as human beings and as artists.

The frustration, confusion, and disconnect Brock Akil and Rae experience as a result of working in an industry that renders black women largely invisible echoes some of what Alice Walker said decades ago about black women artists of her mother's and grandmother's times: "They were creators who lived lives of spiritual waste, because they were so rich in spirituality—which is the basis of Art—that the strain of enduring their unused and unwanted talent drove them insane."[8] Frustration, fatigue, confusion, disconnect, insanity, and other tropes of mental health have long been part of the language black women have known and spoken precisely because these tropes have served as media for black women to express and negotiate the effects of their exclusion, marginalization, silencing, isolation, and erasure in spaces both social and creative, personal and professional. Because this language is so familiar and integral to the lived experiences of black women, discourses of mental health and wellness have also, less frequently, been the subject of sustained critical examination, whether in real or fictive world contexts. Trudier Harris and Melissa Harris-Perry attribute this phenomenon to cultural beliefs about black women and popular cultural representations of black women, which belie their realities and complexities and often do not consider broader questions of mental health and wellness. These include questions of quality of life, outlook on life, productivity, access to care, and quality of care.

As Harris explains, black women "have been viewed as balm bearers, the ones who held a people together against assaults from outside as well as from within the community. They were towers of strength against the degradation of slavery. They were towers of strength against the abuse of husbands and the demands of children. They were towers of strength in taking care of their families—usually through domestic work. And they formed the pillars that supported the black churches that in turn demanded a tremendous strength from them."[9] Alluding to classic critiques of the strong black woman trope and drawing from self-reported data in health studies conducted between 1995 and 2005, Harris-Perry points to correlations between black women reporting beliefs about their self-worth, families, and communities that align with the strong black woman trope and those characterizing their quality of health and satisfaction with their lives as substantially lower in comparison with their male and white counterparts.[10] She writes, "While black women are happy that their families love them, they are heavily burdened by their family members, and this burden substantially reduces their overall life satisfaction. Together these results underscore the popular critiques of the strong black woman that point to the deep personal costs black women bear as they try to meet the needs of others."[11]

By examining the relief Brock Akil and Rae give to black women's lived experiences through narratives that unearth, display, and interrogate issues of black women's mental health and wellness, this chapter contributes to the growing body of research focused on the influence black women producers, creators, writers, and directors are currently having in Hollywood.[12] Pauletta "Mary Jane Paul" Patterson (Gabrielle Union) of Being Mary Jane and Issa Dee (Issa Rae) and Molly Carter (Yvonne Orji) of Insecure are characters defined, in part and to varying degrees, by their financial stability, ambition, and intelligence. In each, we also glimpse the wear of these qualities on the characters' personal relationships, professional development, and emotional health. Narrative arcs in Being Mary Jane and Insecure center their protagonists' vulnerabilities and insecurities, especially in their endeavors to experience sustainable interpersonal relationships and fulfilling professional careers. Over time, the characters' emotional stabilities—and, by extension, professional-personal health and wellness—are facilitated through the characters' deliberate embrace of fear, awkwardness, discomfort in being alone, risk-taking, and opportunities for self-reflection and growth that come from social isolation, distancing, and (re)connecting. By providing viewing audiences multiple vantage points from which to see their characters' strengths and vulnerabilities and corresponding growths in mental health and wellness, I argue that Brock Akil and Rae demonstrate black women's tremendous capacity to seek balance and find relief through rounded narratives of self-definition, expression, and fulfillment.

Seeing Mental Health and Wellness

The first seasons of Being Mary Jane and Insecure incorporate numerous visual and dialogic referents to the strong black woman that clarify how the confluence of race and gender works to constitute, facilitate, organize, and sustain under-standing of the spaces that the lead characters of each series occupy and the deliberate and unapologetic intent of each series to tell black women's stories. In the pilot to *Being Mary Jane*, for example, typewriter sounds and inscription facilitate audience interpretation of the opening scene by attending to the fact that "42% of black women have never been married" and establishing that *Being Mary Jane* reflects "one black woman's story" among many. The strong black woman analog and related tropes of black female representation resurface in every subsequent episode of season 1—as, for example, when Kara (Lisa Vidal), Mary Jane's producer and close friend, accuses Mary Jane of always going "to mad" as opposed "to reason"; Mary Jane reminds Kara that they "made a pact," about not crying at work, there are to be "no tears in the office"; and Niecy (Raven Goodwin), Mary Jane's dark-complexioned, heavyset, teenage-mother niece, candidly acknowledges her belief that the daughter she conceived with a Filipino man will have an "easier life" and "be pretty" because she has "light skin and good hair."[13]

In *Insecure*, the first episode of season 1 serves a similar purpose. As Issa intro-duces herself to youth participants of We Got Y'all, the not-for-profit organiza-tion where she works, Issa is framed against artwork featuring Harriet Tubman. The youth barrage her with invasive, raciogendered[14] questions: "Why you talk like a white girl?" "What's up with your hair?" "Why ain't you married?" A cut-away shot later presents Issa halfheartedly listening to Frieda (Lisa Joyce) recite statistics about an at-risk school as she anxiously imagines herself as a statistic. Frieda relates facts about black women: "Educated black women are highly unlikely to get married, the more education they have. On the bright side, many black women are work-focused and find happiness in their careers." More than simply invoke their historicity, however, *Being Mary Jane* and *Insecure* engage the strong black woman and other conventional discourses of black woman-hood to pursue unfamiliar and underexplored questions of black women's men-tal health and wellness and to sketch narratives of black women's experiences that are intricately tied to mental health challenges and triumphs.

Accepting the *Black Girls Rock!* "Shot Caller" Award in 2013, Brock Akil boldly pronounced her intent to use the screen as a vehicle for putting black women on display. "We deserve to have our picture up," Brock Akil declared, "because we need to see ourselves. When we see ourselves," she continued, "we are reminded of our existence, our humanity, and that we are worth rooting for. We are worth pro-tecting. And we are worth loving."[15] Reflecting on the advantages her scripts afford audiences to engage with interrelated discourses of race, gender, and sexuality, Rae described the "double-consciousness that we all inhabit. . . . People of color," she observed, "are vocalizing what they want to see and . . . making it clear [that] *we're tired of not seeing us on-screen*" (emphasis in original).[16] Few concepts more powerfully and ambitiously render black women visible, while simultaneously underscoring their complexity, than mental health and wellness.

While linked and often analyzed in relation to mental illness, disease, and disorder, mental health and wellness is not the absence of psychopathology, cognitive dissonance, and affective dysfunction.[17] It is the presence of something affirmative. But because no standard for measuring, diagnosing, and studying its presence exists, mental health and wellness remains a largely understudied area of medical research and, in this arena, has especially gotten short shrift in relationship to black women.[18] The need for a language that speaks to and for the particularities of black women's experiences with mental health and wellness is traceable in the archives of the National Black Women's Health Project (known now as the National Black Women's Health Imperative), the first non-profit organization established with the specific mission of advancing the health and wellness of black women and girls nearly four decades ago. Byllye Avery recounts the impetus for founding the organization by recalling her frustration, first, at finding scant resources that said anything about black women's health and, second, at discovering that the limited books that had been written on the subject "didn't put [information] into a format that made sense."[19] A 2017 compilation of essays by black female scholars in the field of mental health finds little progress in the development of psychological and theoretical approaches for defining and addressing "the complex realities and daily experiences" of black women in relation to mental health and wellness.[20]

As a consequence, black women have, over time, necessarily developed discursive frameworks for translating their experiences with life challenges; conscious pursuit of mental, physical, and spiritual balance; and overall state of physical and social well-being—the core tenets of mental health and wellness.[21] This is done in much the same way that Barbara Christian and Beverly Smith, long ago, described black women artists using language to survive assaults, both actual and figurative, on their very existence: "In the stories we create, in riddles and proverbs, in the play with language," Christian explained, black women "speculate about the nature of life through pithy language that unmask(s) the power relations of their world."[22] In the process, Smith concluded, black women "necessarily deal with health."[23] Brock Akil's and Rae's interest in using the lens of mental health and wellness to give relief to the roundedness of black women's experiences is made apparent by the multiple ways in which the language of mental health and wellness establishes, drives, and sustains character development throughout season 1 of both *Being Mary Jane* and *Insecure*.

Seeing Mary Jane

In the opening shots of *Being Mary Jane*, we observe her dressed down, relaxed, and baking a cake at two o'clock in the morning. The doorbell rings, Mary Jane looks at the time, and she approaches the door with a bat-in-hand. André (Omari Hardwick), standing on the other side of the door but clearly able to view and speak with Mary Jane through the glass, beckons, "Look, babe, I—I

FIG. 6.1 Mary Jane with hose on André

know I haven't called you in a minute, but, I—I need to see you. I need to come inside. I gotta get on the other side! Can you let me in?" The double-entendre in André's request sets in motion a transformation in Mary Jane's demeanor and attire, as she prepares to let him inside the house—and her. Parallel cuts demonstrate the sex Mary Jane and André subsequently engage in, which takes place in multiple locations and positions over multiple hours. However, a third meaning soon extends from André's request to "see" Mary Jane, when, on the heels of their extended sex session, she discovers André is married and summarily proceeds to throw him out of her house.

"How do you forget about a wife?" she asks incredulously, dousing him with a high-pressure water hose. As he stumbles half-naked and wet to his car, André questions whether Mary Jane is "crazy." The scene cuts rapidly from Mary Jane sardonically inviting André to drive into the tree down the street from her house to the statistic about marriage rates among black women to Mary Jane reposting notes with inspirational quotes on the windows of her glass house. We see Mary Jane in workout clothes, taking off for a morning run, and then we see her strutting to her garage and driving off in a luxury sedan. She dons a black half-leather sheath dress, bright-yellow jacket, and platform stilettos. Within the span of roughly eight minutes, diegetic and nondiegetic sound works with dialogue, action, and imagery to cohere a narrative around the concept of "being Mary Jane." It disrupts normative codes of behavior associated with the strong black woman and other stock characterizations of black womanhood to give way to a more complex representation of what being Mary Jane embodies. Within this eight-minute span, the audience witnesses the markings of mental health and wellness through Mary Jane's recreational and sexual activities, affirmations, response to André's seduction and duplicity, and structured preparation, focus, and routine relative to her physical conditioning and profession.[24] We see Mary Jane attend to primal needs. We watch her prioritize physical fitness. We observe a dialectical relationship emerge between the pithy words of uplift and encouragement that Mary Jane covers the walls of her house with and the righteousness with which she confronts André's infidelity. Within seconds of André asking Mary Jane if she is crazy for throwing him out of her house, a dog barks, enacting a metaphorical relationship between André and the dog. This invites the audience to turn André's question about Mary Jane's mental stability on him and see justification in Mary Jane's actions, in light of our awareness of André's dissembling.

The soundtrack of Mary J. Blige's "My Life," Rihanna's "Birthday Cake" (featuring Chris Brown), and Nicki Minaj's "Fly" (featuring Rihanna) threads the sequence of events from the opening shots to Mary Jane's departure for work and intimates a connection between these artists' well-documented challenges in romantic relationships and Mary Jane's situation.[25] In contrast to Nsenga K. Burton's contention that Mary Jane's glass house masks a war raging within the character that belies an outward appearance of perfection, the opening sequence makes clear Mary Jane has nothing to hide, even in the extremely vulnerable position in which her relationship with André puts her.[26] Transparency around these vulnerabilities only fortifies as season 1 progresses.

The interworking of sound and movement in several scenes throughout season 1 adds dimension to dialogue, enabling audiences to hear and see the outward channeling of Mary Jane's thoughts and feelings in response to being vulnerable and put in vulnerable situations. This effect works doubly to critique the strong black woman trope, even as its elements are signified, and to heighten audience's awareness of Mary Jane's protection of her mental health and wellness from within actual and metaphoric spaces of introspection. We witness this dynamic at play when André presents Mary Jane with an engagement ring. He claims to have tried to "pray [her] away" and insists he will leave his wife and marry Mary Jane. He declares, "We're not put on this earth to suffer, so we need to surrender." André's use of the plural pronoun "we" assumes not only that he can speak for Mary Jane but also that he knows how Mary Jane feels in and about their situation. The temptation to "surrender" is not elided, as the nondiegetic sound of Mary Jane's heartbeat over André's speech implies. She is, at least, open to being convinced that giving in to the moment—and André—will serve her best. The temptation is reinforced by the symbolic drop of a single tear from Mary Jane's eyes and the fast-motion presentation of proof that André purchased the engagement ring well before Mary Jane learned he was married. However, the proposal is cast against three self-deprecating revelations that Mary Jane vocalizes: "Every second that I am standing here reminds me of how desperate I am to be sleeping with another woman's husband"; "We just screwed in the gym—that's not love"; and "All you do is make me cry." Mary

Jane's unwillingness to suppress these truths gives André no relief and checks him back into her reality. In the end, André is left hanging as Mary Jane walks out.

The difficulty of the decision to walk away from what she clearly desires is not lost on the audience as we see Mary Jane pause at the door and sit in momentary silence once she enters her car. However, the diegetic sound of music playing on the radio—"I gotta stay, true true / get it game, true true / all our friends with it, true true"[27]—combined with the close-up from which the audience sees Mary Jane begin to smile in response to the words of the song gives relief to the apparent affirmation she derives from her decision to leave. This sense of relief extends visually and is amplified in the next scene, alternating between establishing, medium, and close-up shots to symbolically move the audience through Mary Jane's physical actions. She squats from her kitchen to her living room with a cup of yogurt in hand, leg lifts while brushing her teeth, and pliés while completing a crossword puzzle. A thought-speech-action trope infused with Mary Jane's self-doubt (emotional), self-awareness (mental), and self-motivation (physical) emerges. This trope is repeated, with slight revision, in every episode of season 1 and across the five seasons that comprise the series. The pattern created by the repetition deepens the audience's understanding of Mary Jane's mental health and wellness. Every health-impacting behavior of Mary Jane enacts a corresponding image of her consciously pursuing wellness, even when the audience knows she is angry, unhappy, uncomfortable, or dissatisfied. This pattern, thus, exacts a more nuanced appreciation of Mary Jane's capacity to confront and cope with challenges that arise in both her personal and professional lives. It also maps onto storylines that develop Issa's and Molly's characters throughout season 1 of *Insecure*, with some noteworthy variations in techniques.

Seeing Issa and Molly

Whereas nondiegetic sound largely facilitates calling out Mary Jane's thought processes, Issa's voice often serves as both a diegetic call and diegetic response in recurring scenes that feature her rapping. Functioning both as dramatic aside to Issa's customarily awkward public self-presentation and sonic break in uneasy interpersonal communications, Issa's raps are, put simply, her outlet for mental and emotional release. As she explains in the first episode, "I used to keep a journal to vent; now I just write raps." While they usually manifest when Issa is alone, the rap scenes do not connote any sense of latent schizophrenia, psychosis, dissociation, or other mental health disorder in Issa. Rather, they serve consistently to build Issa's self-reflective and regenerative capacities. The rap scenes often give way to comic relief or pathos (for both Issa and the audience).

Collectively, the rap scenes undergird and clarify the thematic interplay between identity formation and mental health and wellness for Issa as a black woman and protagonist of *Insecure*. For example, Issa lyrically assaults and dismisses Sarah (Sujata Choudhury) for congratulating her on the success of the beach trip Issa organized for the youth at We Got Y'all—this after having originally doubted Issa could pull off the event. These scenes also enable the audience to witness Issa reckoning with the hurt her actions cause others. We get this as she stares at herself in the mirror in the aftermath of Lawrence (Jay Ellis) finding out that she slept with Daniel (Y'lan Noel). Conversations between Issa and Molly serve as entry points into the same dynamics at play in the development of Molly's character, *Insecure*'s second protagonist.

The dialogue that initiates the audience into the dynamics of Issa and Molly's relationship is reminiscent of the exchange between Mary Jane and the women to whom Mary Jane confesses that she collected and froze David's sperm in the third episode of *Being Mary Jane*. Audiences first encounter Issa and Molly casually situated and raw in an Ethiopian restaurant. Both their body and verbal language leave no room for mistaking the women as anything other than comfortable in each other's spaces. The environment cultivated by their rapport is welcoming, free from judgment, and mutually enjoyable. This framework of support gives rise to Molly laying bare to Issa the full extent—and pain—of her struggle to cultivate and maintain romantic relationships: "It's like it doesn't matter what I do, Issa. If I'm into them, then I'm too smothering. If I take my time and try to give them space, 'Oh, I didn't think you were into me.' Fine. Sex right away. Lose interest. Wait to have sex. Lose interest. If I don't have sex at all—motherfucker, no! I'm a grown-ass woman. I did not sign up for that bullshit." In an effort to allay some of Molly's apparent anguish and, simultaneously, sustain the conversation around the subject Molly raises, Issa bluntly responds, "I think your pussy's broken."

The declaration lightens the mood as the discussion of factors that may be contributing to Molly's troubled relationships extends to Molly's physical body and the psychosomatic effects of her vagina having had "enough."[28] Explicit invocation of the physical body clearly sounds in and, thus, by extension, prompts consideration of familiar, interlocking discourses of black female sexuality and pleasure, or what Carmel Ohman artfully terms "Black feminist pussy theory."[29] But because the assessment extends beyond the restaurant to structural narrative arcs in season 1 that result in the demise of Issa and Lawrence's five-year relationship as well as Molly's entry into formal therapy, the declaration reframes these familiar discourses as co-constitutive with larger questions of black women's mental health and wellness that are central to *Insecure*'s storytelling goals.

The scenes bringing Issa's troubled relationship with Lawrence into relief find Issa complaining to Molly that she and Lawrence "don't do anything" and that their relationship lacks "excitement." She bemoans always having to be the one to "see shit so clearly. You know, I love him," she concedes, "but it's hard to carry the emotional weight and the financial weight, like, those are heavy as fuck." More than just bitching, Issa's and Molly's conversations enable us to locate the roots of Issa's frustration in events that form part of the backstory of *Insecure*

FIG. 6.2 Molly and Issa sharing

and amount to Lawrence having forgotten to attend to the basics in sustaining a mutually beneficial and supportive relationship. Because he performs poorly in a job interview, the latest neglectfulness, the dialogue reveals, finds Lawrence thinking nothing of failing to prioritize what Issa wants to do on her birthday and assuming she will be OK with staying home and watching a movie. Diegetic overlay of the television sound subliminally directs Issa to "stop making excuses and do it." Sighing and texting Daniel "I miss you, too," establishes that Issa is not OK with the situation. And ultimately, this foreshadows her infidelity with Daniel. Without faulting or exonerating her, the narrative arc around Issa's infidelity bends toward a symbolic expression of her own feelings of "brokenness." "You were just an itch I needed to scratch," she later tells Daniel. By casting Issa's decision to sleep with Daniel as a direct response to her feeling emotionally and physically neglected by Lawrence, the audience sees how the metaphor of the "broken pussy" applies as much to Issa as it does to Molly.[30] Almost simultaneously, the audience also witnesses Issa wrestling with the consequences of her actions for her relationship with Lawrence.

"Lawrence, it's me," she raps over the bridge to the nondiegetic sound of Moses Sumney's "Plastic": "I hate me, too. But three days? Can we just talk? I'll do whatever it takes, just call me. I'm sorry. I miss you. Please call me back. I love you." The soundtrack's rhythm invokes a mood that extends to Issa's quavering voice and torn emotions, as a rapid succession of establishing shots locate her alone with reminders of Lawrence in every room of their apartment: the living room, the bedroom, the kitchen, and the bathroom. The scene closes with Issa lying in a fetal position on the sofa that was supposed to represent her and Lawrence's renewed commitment to their relationship. The revised repetition of this image of Issa at the close of season 1 recalls and signifies on the metaphor of brokenness that opened the season. The audience witnesses Issa come to terms with the finality of her and Lawrence's breakup. However, the camera does not castigate Issa; rather, we see her break down crying and fold into a fetal position as Molly strokes her head. The image connotes reckoning with, not regret over, loss. The implications for Issa's growth in mental health and wellness are not lost on the audience, as Issa's raw, emotional release recalls the raw, physical release she sought (and that the audience knows she needed) by having sex with Daniel.

For Molly, reckoning with "brokenness" translates into pursuing direct modes of care in coordinated scenes. The first scene constitutes a moment of clarity for Molly as she confesses to Issa, "My pussy *is* broken, and I need to take better care of her." This acknowledgment results in Molly and Issa discussing "fancy day" and the importance of taking time to engage in "maintenance" care. The second scene finds Molly randomly running into Crystal (Yakira Chambers)—a mutual friend of hers and Issa's from college—and, during catch-up talk, learning Crystal has been seeing a therapist. While Molly initially stereotypically assumes something must be wrong with Crystal and mocks the "centeredness" Crystal describes feeling as a result of therapy, Molly ultimately enters therapy. This action is foreshadowed by a series of concessions Molly makes that directly draw from discourses of mental health and wellness and build her capacity for introspection.

Molly goes from balking at Issa's suggestion that "talking through some shit with someone isn't the worst idea," to acknowledging to Jared (Langston Kerman) that her relationship expectations are often "unrealistic." In the process, she confronts just how impoverished her language is for not only articulating to Jared how she feels about him but also for clarifying what she wants for herself:

MOLLY: When it came to us, I shoulda just lowered my standards.
JARED: What?
MOLLY: Wait, no, I didn't mean it like that. I meant, like, I can meet you at your level. Not that it's, like, a lower level, but, it's just. . . . Shit, Jared, you were just different than what I thought. . . . OK. Look. I can't hang my life on trying to fake the perfect guy, so, I shoulda just learned to be happy with you. Shit, I'm still not saying it right.

The attempt at reconciliation ends with Jared telling Molly that he is tired and closing the door in her face, a response that initially drives Molly to cope with Jared's rejection by consciously pursuing detached sexual activity. "Are you really 'bout to go off with that baby-of-a-man?" Issa asks as Molly prepares to leave Kelly's birthday celebration with a young man she meets in the club. "I want to," she responds, sarcastically parroting Issa's earlier call for Molly to consider the impact that her indecisiveness and capriciousness have on her relationship status: "You know it's not like I'm trying to keep a niggah." The club scene cuts quickly to a bedroom where we see Molly and the young man disrobing and Molly aggressively mounting him. An eyeline match then works to cast Molly's one-night stand as an act of defiance in light of the smirk she directs toward Issa, as Issa watches her walk the young man to the door the next morning. The scene cuts to Molly doing yoga on the beach and, later, wine-tasting. The pace and range of transitions in Molly's actions correspond with what Molly verbally admits to Issa at the close of season 1:

> MOLLY: You were right about me. I'm a fucking mess. I don't want to be who y'all think I am.
> ISSA: So don't be.
> MOLLY: How?
> ISSA: You asking me? (Laughter.) But Ima be here while you figure it out.

This concession directs Molly to enter therapy in season 2 and catalyzes the continued formulation of narrative arcs in *Insecure* that directly draw from discourses of mental health and wellness to round Molly's character as a representative black woman.

Seeing Black Women

The coordinates this chapter draws between *Being Mary Jane* and *Insecure* contribute to ongoing conversations about the demands Mara Brock Akil and Issa Rae have long been making for creative spaces to give relief to the range and richness of black women's lived experiences. The financial success both artists are currently experiencing through the platforms of on-demand and streaming media has not made those demands any less urgent. Their collective vision is born out of a consciousness and drive that Brock Akil and Rae share with black women artists of the past, many of whom never saw the fruits of their creative labor but also never stopped creating. This reality, perhaps, best explains why the lens of mental health and wellness functions so pivotally in *Being Mary Jane* and *Insecure*. Through it, audiences see characters whose layered dimensions derive from their confrontation with struggle, embrace of vulnerability, pursuit of balance, and resolve to be complex. black. women.

Notes

1 Cori Murray, "Five of Our Most Influential Storytellers," *Essence*, May 2015, https://www.essence.com/celebrity/shonda-rhimes-ava-duvernay-debbie-allen-mara-brock-akil-issa-rae-essence-cover/.
2 Brittany Spanos, "Can't Stop, Won't Stop," *Rolling Stone*, May 2021, 30–34; Ariane Cruz, "(Mis)Playing Blackness: Rendering Black Female Sexuality in *The Misadventures of Awkward Black Girl*," in *Black Female Sexualities*, ed. Trimiko Melancon and Joanne Braxton (New Brunswick, N.J.: Rutgers University Press, 2015), 73–88.

3   Interview with Eric Deggans, "Issa Rae Is First Black Woman to Create and Star in Premium Cable Show," NPR Morning Edition, radio broadcast, October 7, 2016; Janine Rubenstein, "From 'Awkward' to A-List," *People*, August 7, 2017, 75–76.

4   *Girlfriends* premiered and ran on UPN from 2000 until 2006, the year the CW acquired UPN. It ran for two more seasons on the CW. Over its eight-season run, from September 11, 2000, to February 11, 2008, *Girlfriends* averaged 3.4 million viewers. *The Game* ran for three seasons on the CW, from October 1, 2006, until May 15, 2009. BET picked up the series in 2011, where it ran for six more seasons, from January 11, 2011, until August 5, 2015. The BET premiere episode of *The Game* garnered 7.7 million viewers. Over the series' nine season run, *The Game* averaged 3.6 million viewers. In May 2021, Paramount+, announced that it would air a ten-episode sequel series of *The Game* starring several of the series' original cast members. The rebooted series has run for two seasons. The ninety-minute pilot of *Being Mary Jane* aired July 2, 2013, and garnered 4 million viewers. Over the series' five-season run from January 7, 2014, to April 23, 2019, viewers averaged 1.5 million per season. See trade articles in *Entertainment Weekly* and *Deadline Hollywood* and mainstream and Black press coverage in *Ebony*, *Essence*, and *USA Today*.

5   Breakfast Club Power, "Mara Brock Akil on Bringing *Girlfriends* to Netflix," *The Breakfast Club*, September 11, 2020, YouTube video, 51:58, https://www.youtube.com/watch?v=vBejxZLJgio.

6   Angelique Jackson, "Issa Rae's Next Chapter: How 'Insecure' Creator Is Becoming a Media Mogul with Production Banner Hoorae," *Variety*, March 24, 2021, https://variety.com/2021/tv/news/issa-rae-insecure-hbo-hoorae-1234936020/.

7   The Daily Show, "Issa Rae Is Creating a Pipeline for Underrepresented Artists," April 15, 2021, YouTube video, 8:37, https://www.youtube.com/watch?v=DVTQtvj5HmE.

8   Alice Walker, "In Search of Our Mothers' Gardens," in *In Search of Our Mothers Gardens* (San Diego: Harcourt Brace, 1983), 233.

9   Trudier Harris, "This Disease Called Strength: Some Observations on the Compensating Construction of Black Female Character," *Literature and Medicine* 14, no. 1 (1995):109.

10 Melissa V. Harris-Perry, *Sister Citizen: Shame, Stereotypes, and Black Women in America* (New Haven: Yale University Press, 2011), 200–207.

11 Harris-Perry, 205.

12 See, for example, Aymar Jean Christian, "Beyond Branding: The Value of Intersectionality on Streaming TV Channels," *Television & New Media* 21, no. 5 (2020): 457–474; and Timeka Tounsel, "Productive Vulnerability: Black Women Writers and Narratives of Humanity in Contemporary Cable Television," *Souls* 20, no. 3 (2018): 304–327.

13 *Being Mary Jane*, season 1, episode 8, "Blindsided," directed by Salim Akil, written by Mara Brock Akil, Jessica Mecklenburg, and Erika L. Johnson, aired February 25, 2014, on BET. The intersectional politics and impact of colorism and popular cultural representations of black women have been the source of numerous studies.

14 I use this term as articulated by Angeletta K. M. Gourdine, "Colored Reading: Or, Interpretation and the Raciogendered Body," in *Reading Sites: Social Difference and Reader Response*, ed. Patricinio P. Schweickart and Elizabeth A. Flynn (New York: Modern Language Association of America, 2004), 60–82.

15 *Black Girls Rock!* 2013 aired November 3, 2013, on BET. Video of the acceptance speech is no longer publicly available. A print copy of the speech can be viewed at Rochelle Valsaint, "Some Days You Just Need Reminding," Ms. Inc., January 10, 2017, accessed May 4, 2023, https://msinc.medium.com/some-days-you-just-need-reminding-86adf6f6dd28.

16   Jenna Wortham, "'We Need to Be in Charge,'" *New York Times Magazine*, August 9, 2015, 30.

17   Corey L. M. Keyes, "Mental Illness and/or Mental Health? Investigating Axioms of the Complete State Model of Health," *Journal of Consulting and Clinical Psychology*, 73, no. 3 (2005): 539–548.

18   Keyes, 539. The Centers for Disease Control and Prevention's available data show comparatively low prevalence rates of suicide ideation, major depression, and schizophrenia among black women in relation to their white and Hispanic counterparts. However, the reliability of this data is complicated by well-established findings of high rates of misdiagnoses and cultural barriers to reporting mental health illnesses among black people.

19   Byllye Y. Avery, "Breathing Life into Ourselves: The Evolution of the National Black Women's Health Project," in *Feminism and Community*, ed. Penny A. Weiss and Marilyn Friedman (Philadelphia: Temple University Press, 1995), 147–153.

20   Linda Goler Bount, foreword to *Black Women's Mental Health: Balancing Strength and Vulnerability*, ed. Stephanie Y. Evans, Kanika Bell, and Nsenga K. Burton (Albany: SUNY Press, 2017), xi–xiv.

21   Ruth Chu-Lien Chao, "Well-Being and Resilience: Another Look at African American Psychology," in *Handbook of African American Health*, ed. Robert Hampton, Thomas Gullotta, and Raymond Crowel (New York: Guilford, 2010), 106–120.

22   Barbara Christian, "The Race for Theory," *Cultural Critique*, no. 6 (Spring 1987): 51–63.

23   Beverly Smith, "Black Women's Health: Notes for a Course," in *All the Women Are White, All the Blacks Are Men, but Some of Us Are Brave: Black Women's Studies*, ed. Gloria T. Hull, Patricia Bell Scott, and Barbara Smith (New York: Feminist Press, 1982), 103–114.

24   Here, I point to shortsightedness in Felicia L. Harris and Loren Saxton Coleman's argument that storyline shifts between seasons 1 and 2 facilitate Mary Jane's "betterment" by "foregoing her troubled love life to focus on her career and family." See "Trending Topics: A Cultural Analysis of *Being Mary Jane* and Black Women's Engagement on Twitter," *The Black Scholar* 48, no. 1 (2018): 43–55. The described opening sequence establishes Mary Jane as an already accomplished professional. In addition, her pursuit of a mutually fulfilling romantic relationship is a recurring theme over the series' run.

25   Appreciating the role that these specific songs play in articulating mental health and wellness to the particularities of Mary Jane's and, by extension, black women's experiences requires broad literacy in black culture, especially as expressed through hip-hop. Building this literacy extends beyond the scope of this chapter, but for a brief orientation, see Nghana Lewis, "Prioritized: The Hip Hop (Re)Construction of Black Womanhood in *Girlfriends* and *The Game*," in *Watching While Black: Centering the Television of Black Audiences*, ed. Beretta E. Smith-Shomade (New Brunswick, N.J.: Rutgers University Press, 2012), 157–171.

26   Nsenga K. Burton, "Representations of Black Women's Mental Illness in *HTGAWM* and *Being Mary Jane*," in *Black Women's Mental Health: Balancing Strength and Vulnerability* (Albany: SUNY Press, 2017), 57–73.

27   "TruTru," audio, track 9 on OhNo, *Chips & Hennessy*, 2014.

28   Issa's exact words to Molly are "I think it's sad; it's had enough. If it could talk, I think it would make that sad Marge Simpson groan." Issa's personification of Molly's vagina has been the subject of considerable critical praise of *Insecure*'s first season both for its humor and its invitation to engage "real" conversations about black female sexuality. See, for example, Hahn Nguyen "*Insecure*: Issa Rae Gives a Voice

to Authentic, Flawed Black Women and Even a 'Broken Pussy,'" interview with Issa Rae, *IndieWire*, October 10, 2016, https://www.indiewire.com/2016/10/insecure-issa-rae-hbo-broken-pussy-1201734646/; and Carmel Ohman, "Undisciplining the Black Pussy: Pleasure, Black Feminism, and Sexuality in Issa Rae's *insecure*," *The Black Scholar* 50, no. 2 (2020): 5–15.

29 Ohman, "Undisciplining the Black Pussy," 5–15.

30 In an otherwise solidly substantiated discussion of how *Insecure* functions as a "justice-demanding way of making television" for black women, Caetlin Benson-Allott makes the mistake of characterizing Issa's infidelity as a "self-defeating impulse." Caetlin Benson-Allott, "No Such Thing Not Yet: Questioning Television's Female Gaze," *Film Quarterly* 71, no. 2 (Winter 2017): 65–71.

7

On Air Black

• •

The Breakfast Club, Visual Radio, and Spreadable Media

ADRIEN SEBRO

From the Jazz Age to Jim Crow, from wartime to rock 'n' roll, and from Black Power to hip-hop, locating the pulse of Black America has been a hard-fought battle through the history of radio. With its ability to empower and entertain, radio has proven to be a pedagogical space for Black popular culture, politics, and education. For twenty-five years, before the show ended in 2019, *The Tom Joyner Morning Show* (1994–2019) existed as that sonic space capturing the Black perspective, for us by us. Charting as the nation's number one syndicated urban morning show, Tom Joyner spoke directly to the Black public sphere by super serving the Black population through his progressive political talk, soul music, humor, advice, and celebrity gossip. In this present digital moment, often overlooked in academic discussions, radio has also continued to evolve. With contemporary radio programming such as *The Rickey Smiley Show*, *The Steve Harvey Morning Show*, and *The Breakfast Club*, Black audiences are able to experience these discussions of Black life and culture through sound *and* sight. With a particular focus on Black radio, its history, and shifts to the visual in New York's Power 105.1 FM *The Breakfast Club*, this chapter addresses how *The Breakfast Club* works for and speaks to a contemporary Black audience. Through this case study, I discuss how the turn to visual radio allows *The*

Breakfast Club to super serve the Black community by spreading Black popular culture, livelihood, music, comedy, politics, and current events in radical ways within a growing participatory culture.

Visual Radio

Throughout this chapter, I employ the term *visual radio* to speak for the visual and aural work done by *The Breakfast Club*. Streaming mediums like Revolt TV and YouTube allow audiences to literally see this radio studio, the hosts, and guests, creating a completely new reception experience. The visual brings audiences closer to the subject matter, hosts, and guests on *The Breakfast Club* and allows a new connection that this medium traditionally did not offer. The transition to visual also creates the ability of audience members to participate in interpreting these images in alternative ways, making *The Breakfast Club* into a space of critical pedagogy and debate. I use the term *visual radio* not to be confused with Michele Hilmes's "screen-based radio."

Hilmes posits that "screen interfaces are radio, as much as the audio stream itself," and this is a rapidly evolving combination of digital production, web-based distribution, and mobile digital reception—think audio distribution applications and platforms such as Stitcher, SoundCloud, Apple Podcasts, and so on.[1] Simply put, the shift of hardware from a traditional radio set to the "on the go" access of simply pressing a button on a screen stood for revolutionizing the accessibility of radio programming. With visual radio, I am taking Hilmes's work a step further from sound's convergence with the digital and screen interface to its convergence with the visual.

The convergence of sound, digital, and visual directs attention to the media's function in the real world: as an interlinked hybrid economy of activities, representations, and uses that spread across technological platforms, media professions, textual forms, and audience experiences.[2] Sound industries like radio have remained largely invisible to media industry scholars because of their unique ephemerality and lack of material presence.[3] YouTube has changed this through *The Breakfast Club* channel and its visual casting—transforming an invisible, ephemeral sonic experience to a more tangible, fixed materialization on digital screens, a database for a seriality-produced program speaking directly to Black audiences and culture.

The Breakfast Club is a four-and-a-half-hour morning show featuring DJ Envy, Angela Yee,[4] and Charlamagne Tha God's unrivaled interviews with celebrities, educators, politicians, hip-hop artists, and so on, all from a Black perspective. From megastars like Justin Bieber, Nicki Minaj, and Arnold Schwarzenegger to rap icons such as Rick Ross, Waka Flocka, and Gucci Mane, every guest visiting *The Breakfast Club* is grilled with their signature blend of honesty and humor. The results are often the most circulated radio interviews to be found throughout social media. Their National Radio Hall of Fame biography reads, "Charlamagne Tha God is one of the most potent, influential, and authoritative voices in media. He is a *New York Times* bestselling author as well as creator of the Black Effect Podcast Network. Angela Yee is an entrepreneur and advocate, Gracie Awards winner and an ambassador for the New York Public Library. Also, she is the creator of 'Angela Yee's Lip Service' podcast. DJ Envy is an entertainment industry leader, recording artist, family and businessman. Envy is the creator of 'The Casey Crew' podcast addressing topics on love, family and culture."[5]

Black Radio to the Visual

Black radio, like *The Breakfast Club*, has consistently changed the soundscape of American popular music and culture. Black radio outlets have historically played a crucial role as what William Barlow calls "'the talking drums' of their respective communities"—sources not only of music but also of otherwise inaccessible information about politics, fashion, sports, arts, and culture.[6] It is also a space that Emily J. Lordi deems as crucial for community debate and mobilization, especially during the long civil rights movement. Black radio has been a "major force in constructing and sustaining an African American public sphere."[7]

The Breakfast Club's success is built off the successes of radio programs prior, but it has been perfected in a present spreadable and participatory media culture—talking to a younger, more tech-savvy Black audience of connected viewers. In defining "spreadable media," Joshua Green and Henry Jenkins explain that "powerful new production tools and distribution channels are enabling the mute to speak and the invisible to be seen, [they] are realizing long-deferred hopes for a more participatory culture, embodying the 'technology of freedom.'"[8] The emergence of social networks transforms each of these everyday acts of *The Breakfast Club* and its consumption, giving it greater public visibility, increasing its social dimensions, and ultimately expanding its economic and cultural impact through spreading materials, ideas, and opinions. The convergence and accessibility of media platforms now allows information to be spread and shared in an instant. Information can then be reworked and redistributed as media consumers decide how to participate in the framing of a rapidly expanding culture. In this larger discussion of Black visual radio and spreading Black popular culture, I would be remiss if I did not address the legacy of *The Tom Joyner Morning Show* that set the standard of aural Black communication and its transitions to the digital landscape.

The Tom Joyner Morning Show

Created by veteran Black broadcaster Tom Joyner, *The Tom Joyner Morning Show* aired on urban contemporary and adult contemporary formatted stations across the United States from January 3, 1994, until December 13, 2019. Joyner, perhaps best known for commuting daily by plane between Dallas and Chicago (literally having to physically travel to spread Black popular culture as the Fly Jock), simultaneously hosted local radio programs in both cities. He was the first host of the syndicated television series *Ebony/Jet Showcase* and was signed in 1993 by ABC Radio Networks for a new national show (*The Tom Joyner Morning Show*) to be distributed to urban contemporary stations.[9] Through his illustrious career and impact on the genre, Joyner was the first African American to be inducted into the National Radio Hall of Fame.

The Tom Joyner Morning Show aired live Monday through Friday for four hours, beginning at 6:00 a.m. (EST) and was based in Dallas, Texas. Joyner attributed the national show's success to his complete refusal to serve non-Black audiences. In multiple interviews, Joyner has stated, "We do a show for African Americans. That's what we do."[10] Upon his retirement in 2019, Joyner made even more clear the aims and purpose of his work when he speaks about the responsibility of Black broadcasters, stating, "Don't worry about cross-over. Just super serve, super serve, super serve. Anything that affects African Americans, that's what you do."[11]

Joyner stated on his last program that he made his decision to retire because of repeated salary cuts (claiming that successive cuts had reduced his salary nearly 90 percent) and acknowledged that cultural changes and radicalization among Black audiences ("I think we were more woke then than now") had reduced his influence and thus his listenership and affiliate count. He further stated that his own financial greed drove much of his radio career.[12] The radio industry was rapidly evolving, as were the ideologies of his Black audience base. Joyner knew that it was time to make way for a shifting medium, one where the spread of Black culture takes different approaches in tandem with a younger and more technologically savvy listenership. However, Joyner did expand his platform from traditional radio to follow the digital trends before he departed.

As *The Tom Joyner Morning Show* ascended in popularity, digital advances were beginning to shift the production and reception of radio as it was known: "Internet streaming began in 1994, accelerated with the development of audio software in the late 1990s, and then exploded in the early 2000s as broadcasters of the Recording Industry Association of America worked out rights and royalty issues through SoundExchange."[13] Understood primarily as an ephemeral medium, digital streaming brought radio stations to the web and radio transitioned into a screened medium. Audiences grew their ability to listen to radio programs like *The Tom Joyner Morning Show* through computer screens and other handheld applications in their own time with a simple mouse click of a play button and a still image of *The Tom Joyner Morning Show* logo in the background.[14] Radio became a digital form—a shifting display of textual and visual information—even as it remained a sound experience, replacing a set of prior practices that were scattered and evanescent. Yet as technological advances are constantly in motion, the convergence of aural, digital, *and* visual (what I call visual radio) soon proved to be the more popularized and participatory form of radio consumption.

The Breakfast Club can be what it is now because of what came before. It owes a great deal of its impact to *The Tom Joyner Morning Show* (primarily its engagement with Black audiences and popular culture). Yet it has remixed the format set by both *The Tom Joyner Morning Show* and *The Howard Stern Show* to make its program not only participatory for the modern digital age but also Black.[15] *The Breakfast Club* has harnessed an audience of new technologically savvy individuals who actively participate in spreading the show's messages through various media. Part talk show and part reality, *The Breakfast Club* has been adapted for a postmodern age and allows on-demand access to Black popular culture.

"Wake That Ass Up! . . . Early in the Morning . . . *The Breakfast Club*":[16] The World's Most Dangerous Morning Show

Other than their star-studded interviews, *The Breakfast Club* includes segments such as "Angela Yee's Rumor Report," where Angela shares the latest pop-culture news while Envy and Charlamagne share their unique opinions on each topic; "Donkey of the Day," where Charlamagne chooses a public figure or celebrity to poke fun at after public missteps; and DJ Envy's "People's Choice Mix" featuring twenty-five uninterrupted minutes of DJ Envy's award-winning music mixes.[17] As a hub of Black popular culture, *The Breakfast Club* exists as a space where you can dually receive discussions from Dr. Peniel Joseph on radical Black dignity and radical Black citizenship in one viewing (or listening) and an interview with hip-hop trio Migos about "turning the pandemic to a Band-demic" the next day.[18] *The Breakfast Club* taps into all spaces of Black cultural understanding from hip-hop to celebrity gossip and from Black history to progressive politics. *The Breakfast Club* fluidly reaches its Black audience fan base.

The Breakfast Club was established on New York's Power 105.1 (WWPR-FM) as a morning show serving the local market in December 2010.[19] Soon after, in April 2013, Premiere Networks (a subsidiary of then Clear Channel Communications, now iHeartMedia) launched a weekend version of the show. Four months later, *The Breakfast Club* was rolled out into syndication.[20] As part of iHeartRadio, the national umbrella of iHeartMedia's radio network, *The Breakfast Club* was syndicated through the largest radio broadcaster in the United States—which happens to be white-owned and operated. This nationwide broadcasting helped to spread the message of the radio program to new listeners. However, it wasn't until Revolt TV's simulcasting of *The Breakfast Club* in 2014, that this aural medium not only transitioned into the digital and visual but also garnered an even greater Black audience.

Revolt is a United States–based, music-oriented digital cable television network founded by renowned hip-hop artist and producer Sean "Diddy / Puff

FIG. 7.1 *The Breakfast Club* hosts

Daddy" Combs. With its slogan, "Unapologetically Hop Hip," Revolt is primar-ily dedicated to urban contemporary music, and social justice programming, with music video blocks comprising the majority of the network's afternoon schedule. The hip-hop branding and legacy of Sean Combs helped to establish Black value, credibility, and an established Black audience in this new visual radio space that *The Breakfast Club* began to occupy.

Since its visual casting, the impact of *The Breakfast Club* has continued to rise. In January 2020, *The Breakfast Club* was nominated for an NAACP Image Award in the category of Outstanding News/Information (Series or Special). Concurrently, talk radio industry magazine *Talkers* included it in its 2020 "Heavy Hundred" list of the top one hundred influential talk radio shows, call-ing the show "appointment listening every day for people of color."[21] During the aftermath of the George Floyd protests, the *Los Angeles Times* called it "a radio forum for the nation's racial reckoning,"[22] and as of July 2020, according to Nielsen, the show reached over 8 million listeners monthly.[23] In August 2020, *The Breakfast Club* was inducted into the Radio Hall of Fame, the first program to ever do so with a targeted Black audience.[24]

The Breakfast Club can be digitally streamed through various audio distribu-tion platforms (such as Apple Podcasts, Stitcher, and SoundCloud). However, it is the transition to visual streaming sites that increases the program's audience engagement, access, and spreadability between media. *The Breakfast Club* cur-rently airs in over one hundred radio markets around the country and is also simulcast by the Revolt TV network and streamed on the online video sharing and social media platform YouTube every weekday morning. Common topics of discussion on the show are celebrity gossip (especially in the hip-hop industry), progressive politics, and Black livelihood. Although simulcasted on Revolt TV for subscription holders, with its 5.26 million subscribers and simplicity in archiving episodes and accessibility, *The Breakfast Club*'s YouTube channel is the site most reachable to nationwide fanfare. Having the ability to comment, like, subscribe, and even take part in the community polls, makes YouTube the most lucrative site to discuss the participatory culture of *The Breakfast Club* and its visual radio audience.

As a radio program, the visual casting of *The Breakfast Club* is low tech in production, yet extremely effective. In a similar way to current widespread engagement with podcasts, new media scholar Briana Barner explains that there's a relatively low barrier to entry into the field; access to a microphone, audio software, and a place to host content makes it possible for almost anyone to start a podcast.[25] Of course, *The Breakfast Club* has an established audience base and nationwide reach, but the addition of a handheld camera to Barner's equation is the essential difference in the making of this low-tech visual radio. This easy access to media making has proven to be useful for groups that have historically been excluded from mainstream and traditional forms of media.[26] With its turn to add the visual with YouTube as its host, *The Breakfast Club* captures something that was otherwise ephemeral so that it can spread across other platforms. As stakeholders in the YouTube space, audience members have active agency in shaping what messages spread, the routes they take, and the communities they reach. With the emergence of new media and convergence, we as viewers and consumers, are all appraisers and distributors of media. With its shift toward the visual rather than just aural, *The Breakfast Club* creates a participatory culture where its audience can critique, evaluate, and recirculate *The Breakfast Club*'s content.

Of its many spreadable episodes, *The Breakfast Club*'s "Birdman Goes Off on the Breakfast Club Power 105.1" recorded on April 22, 2016, sits unparalleled to any other episode. With twenty-two million views and counting, this two-minute and twenty-six-second video sits as the most viewed program on *The Breakfast Club*'s YouTube web page. In the program, the rapper and producer Birdman (followed by his entourage) enters the recording booth immediately on the defensive, cursing, and chastising the hosts without answering any interview questions. They abruptly storm out with DJ Envy even calling it "our shortest interview ever."[27] Clearly, a previous confrontation occurred between the hosts and Birdman that isn't addressed here, but Birdman's frustration can simply be deduced through his comment that became an instant social media colloquialism, "Put some respek on my name."

Due to the mass circulation and spreading of *The Breakfast Club* through social media, Birdman's short and emotion-filled interview became a source of capital and publicity. The spread of memes across social media sites (like Instagram, Twitter, and Facebook) such as the one in figure 7.2 not only drove more eyes to *The Breakfast Club* viewership, but Birdman himself soon capitalized off the media frenzy, releasing a series of merchandise revolving around

FIG. 7.2 Birdman on *The Breakfast Club*

his interview quotables. From T-shirts, to hoodies, to even the release of his song, "Respek," Birdman, and in effect *The Breakfast Club*, circulated among the eyes, ears, and even buying power of those invested in Black popular culture.[28] As this short video makes clear, the visual aspects of *The Breakfast Club* as a visual radio forum contribute to its spreadability in ways that simply listening to the interview would not be possible. Moreover, *The Breakfast Club*'s presence throughout these various media proves that this program is a site of mass "textual poaching."

Through the participatory nature its visual casting inspires, it's clear through this short example that *The Breakfast Club* remains a mainstay in Black popular culture. Watching the radio program allows viewers, even casual ones, to participate in how this show is advertised, understood, and even misunderstood. Dedicated audience members of the program may know the conflict between Birdman and the hosts was due to past interviewees speaking negatively about Birdman while on the show. Yet the casual viewer may be engaged simply from only Birdman's reaction. Each viewer has a particular way in which they can spread this interview as popular text. This usage of *The Breakfast Club* as text is an example of "textual poaching." Henry Jenkins uses this term to describe how some fans go through texts like favorite television shows and engage with the parts that they are interested in, unlike audiences who watch the show more passively and move on to the next thing. Specifically, fans use what they've "poached" to become producers themselves, creating new cultural materials in a variety of analytical and creative formats from "meta" essays to fan fiction, fan art, and in this case, memes.[29] In this way, Jenkins argues, fans "become active participants in the construction and circulation of textual meanings."[30] How fans respond to and interact with the program drives the popularity of *The Breakfast Club* with its technologically savvy audience.

Acknowledging the popularity of their platform, the three hosts consistently make it clear who their intended audience is not just the technologically savvy but also Black people. Knowing that the white-executive dollars from their syndicate iHeartMedia services a different base than their Black-owned simulcaster Revolt TV, *The Breakfast Club* welcomes all viewers or listeners but consistently reminds the audience of their narrative perspective. This is seen clearly in not just the majority of their interviewee choices but also the content of the interviews. For example, in an interview with comedian Dave Chappelle, Charlamagne Tha God directly addresses Chappelle's white fans and the risks of cultural appropriation:

CHARLAMAGNE: Where do you draw the line when it comes to cultural appropriation?

CHAPPELLE: I'm not sure how to answer that. No one's going to feel that way more than African Americans. Because we create so much culture and oftentimes it's just siphoned from us and it's almost all that we've ever had. But it is American culture too . . . I don't know.

CHARLAMAGNE: Why do you think white people gravitated towards your comedy?

CHAPPELLE: I think all of us at some point ventured into a cultural crossroads. We're Black people but we're corporate people. We all smoke weed; we traverse the American landscape. I don't think there's anyone in America that I'm incapable of communicating to on some level.[31]

As seen here in this short excerpt from the larger interview, Charlamagne continues to bring a Black perspective forward as he addresses his questions toward Chappelle and the power of his comedy. Just like Chappelle and his comedy, *The Breakfast Club* can speak to mass audiences engaged with popular culture; however, the Black audience is always thought of first.

Other episodes of *The Breakfast Club* are much more direct about the "for us by us" approach that the program often helps push forth. From an interview with clinical psychologist turned social media and memeable mainstay Dr. Umar Johnson, one quote can sum up the critical perspective of Johnson: "White supremacy is disguised everywhere."[32] Clearly making a name for himself with his fifth visit to *The Breakfast Club*, the self-proclaimed "Prince of Pan-Africanism," Johnson has recently become a buzz word in Black popular culture. Umar Johnson is a doctor of clinical psychology and a certified school psychologist who specializes in working with parents of African American children who receive special education and/or are diagnosed with disruptive behavior disorders.[33]

Everything about Johnson is unapologetically Black, and in each of his interviews, he makes that clear. As part of his professional work, he hosts lecture series, created the "Unapologetically Afrikan" Black College and Consciousness Tours, and runs a Black parent boot camp that focuses on special education, ADHD, and generally how Black parents can advocate for their Black children. This latter work comes primarily through a charter school he is working to develop in Wilmington, Delaware, the Frederick Douglass Marcus Garvey Academy. However, his popular culture presence largely comes from social media spread via Instagram and Twitter.

Currently, Johnson's memes are huge among Black Twitter users, as some have taken bite-sized moments from old speaking engagements and Johnson's Instagram live streams and transformed them into bits of comedy. But underneath the flamboyant oration is what skeptics of Johnson find concerning: his conflation of opinions and facts or presenting half-truths as full-truths; his well-documented homophobia and misogyny; and the money he has been given to fund a school that still doesn't exist.[34] So although he speaks truth to power regarding the status of Black people in America, much of his rhetoric can be read as divisive. Unfortunately, with such spread through social media sites, it's difficult to grasp who is laughing *with/in* support of Johnson or who is simply laughing *at* him.

As he appears on visual radio and engages with the products that appear in other media, he is converging all the spaces where his message of Black liberation exists. Whether trivialized or not, Johnson's message is spreading, and a great deal of that is due to his numerous appearances on *The Breakfast Club*. The YouTube platform of this visual radio (coupled with Johnson's rousing personality) allows his message to be spread across various media, liked, commented on, and undoubtedly memed. The importance of this discussion, alongside how the hosts call out present political officials and question what they are doing for Black American constituents, makes clear that *The Breakfast Club* is not simply a forum for "messy" low culture, laughs, and play. It is also a valuable political forum that elected officials are increasingly seeing as important to engage.

Politics and *The Breakfast Club*

The Breakfast Club is not only a program but a platform, a spotlight, a think tank for all things hip-hop / pop culture, community, and politics. Known for their unrivaled interviews and their ability to connect with and engage audiences, *The Breakfast Club* is a must-stop on political campaign trails, especially for reaching Black constituents who may or may not be politically active or knowledgeable. Easier to digest than the often divisive political rhetoric on cable television networks, the political discussions on *The Breakfast Club* aim to reach a voting base that is often ignored. Due to the format of the show, its content, and its consistent reminder of being a space for urban Black perspectives, the vast majority of elected (or potentially elected) officials who visit *The Breakfast Club* on their campaign trails are people of color, more left-leaning, politically progressive, and aligned with the Democratic Party structure. Above all, the political hopefuls who visit the program essentially use *The Breakfast Club* as a space to exercise their "downness" (through body language, word play, and cultural references) in efforts to relate to a younger, urban, and Black constituency that they may otherwise feel unable to communicate.

As its home station Power 105.1 is based in New York City, *The Breakfast Club* invests in and communicates the issues of its local Black community in a myriad of ways. On the brink of the 2021 New York City primary elections, for example, *The Breakfast Club* studio acted as a space for political education, campaigning, and important conversations pertaining to the rights and livelihood of Black voters, particularly in New York City. With interviews from eight different candidates on their political runs (including mayoral, district attorney, and New York City council candidates), *The Breakfast Club* served as a forum for political, economic, and social discussions on issues like poverty, stop and frisk, affordable housing, and investing in education.

It is no secret that these potential elected officials visit the set of *The Breakfast Club* in order to speak directly to their Black audience base. Every question brought into the conversations is consistently in line with "How does this impact Black lives?" The importance of these interviews is even more pronounced as these specific eight interviews are categorized in their own playlist on *The Breakfast Club*'s YouTube channel under the title "NYC Primary Elections 2021."[35] The accessibility in visually archiving these particular interviews offers a digital advantage to how visual radio can now prioritize and highlight more temporal discussions. Of course, radio has always stood as a space for political debate and campaigning, but through the visual radio of *The Breakfast Club*, Black voters (especially the technologically savvy ones) are able to see these candidates while hearing their critical political perspectives. The visual adds so much more to the identity of these candidates that voters often wish to know. Body language, behavior, attire, movement, as well as their political mission statement all play important roles in why someone may vote for a candidate. The advances in visual radio allow audiences this important access and information before heading to the polls.

With a nationwide reach and spread of *The Breakfast Club*'s Black audience, the visual radio program has developed into a respected campaign stop to tap into the Black constituents in not just local elections but also the races of elected officials on the national level. With the increasing number of cases of COVID-19, the world as we knew it shut down amid one of the most critical presidential campaigns in recent times—the contest between the Democratic frontrunner and former vice president Joe Biden and the sitting president Donald Trump. Although locked down in their own homes, teleconferencing software allowed the visual streaming of *The Breakfast Club* to persist and continue its casting of hard-hitting interviews. In a one-on-one interview between Charlamagne and Biden, just months before the election, Biden attempts to use *The*

Breakfast Club as his forum to reach Black voters. Casually sitting in his home wearing a suit with no tie, Biden is projecting an approachability that only visual streaming viewers of the interview are able to experience. As Charlamagne suggests, this discussion centers what Biden will be doing for Black people. Biden, in long-winded responses, consistently highlights his political history, successes, and résumé of Black supporters to prove that he is "that guy":

> CHARLAMAGNE: I've been critical of you, so I want to get to know you today. I want to talk to you about mostly Black stuff.
>
> BIDEN: I'm the guy that said we oughta take hard records and find out exactly how many people in the Black community are getting COVID and are dying from it. . . . Remember when they said "Biden can't win the primaries," I kicked everyone's ass (stumbles), oh excuse me.
>
> CHARLAMAGNE: No, talk like that, I need you to say that![36]

Throughout the interview, Biden continues to play up his downness with the Black community and the support he receives from Black leadership young and old, even declaring that "they are the reason I get elected." As the interview draws to a close, Biden uses *The Breakfast Club*'s platform to double down on the support he needs from Black constituents that engage with the program. From his brief discussion on weed crime reform to even guaranteeing that multiple Black women were being considered as his running mate, Biden taps directly into the issues young Black urban voters deem important.[37]

Without warning, an off-camera member of Biden's team attempts to rush the interview to a close. Charlamagne jumps closer to his computer screen proclaiming, "You can't do that to Black media!" Clearly aligned with the history of Black media being restricted and ignored, Charlamagne takes an important and visual stand against the cutting off of a media source that caters to historically disadvantaged people who, more often than not, do not have a voice. This declarative statement forces Biden to continue the conversation. However, his reactionary proclamation at the end became the only soundbite people know of this interview. Biden states, "If you have a problem figuring out whether you're for me or Trump, *then you ain't Black.*"

Although he would ultimately go on to win the presidential election, seeing Biden claim that one's Blackness inherently means that they are in support of his politics took Black constituents and their fluidity of political identities for granted. "You Ain't Black," as a phrase and hashtag, along with the link to the visual radio interview, spread across numerous platforms of news reporting, op-eds, and social media. In response to his comments, Biden stated, "I was making the point that I never take the vote for granted and in fact, I know in order to win the presidency, I need the African American vote. . . . I shouldn't have been so cavalier."[38] Although Biden attempted to adjust the meaning of his declaration, "You Ain't Black" spread in various ways. Other than the #YouAintBlack

Twitter hashtag that featured Twitter users participating in the dialogue via jokes and serious political commentary on the statement, Biden's declaration also made its spread to network television.

Let's Be Real (2020–2021), on the FOX Network, was a satirical puppet series covering politics and pop culture. The series followed current events and added a comedic flair to them with the use of puppets that represent popular American figures. After the mass circulation of Biden's interview on *The Breakfast Club* and its residual spread throughout various media, *Let's Be Real* created a satirical game-show where Biden's puppet rates the Blackness of its contestants. Albeit meant for laughs, the spread of the phrase "You Ain't Black" and *Let's Be Real's* participatory act of reworking the meaning of Biden's declaration are all due to the visual radio circulation of Black popular culture through *The Breakfast Club*.

Conclusion

As a platform and public space for Black life and culture, *The Breakfast Club* has redefined the possibilities of Black radio with its inclusion of the visual in the digital landscape. Whether through engagement on YouTube, Revolt TV, or social media, with its particular focus on progressive Black politics, celebrities, hip-hop, and livelihood, *The Breakfast Club* speaks to a contemporary and tech-savvy Black audience that merges and spreads information through various mediums of communication. Visual radio as a practice allows *The Breakfast Club* to super serve the Black community by spreading Black popular culture in radical ways, allowing audiences to reinterpret their meanings, participating in the spread of information, and turning *The Breakfast Club* into a site of critical Black pedagogy.

Notes

1 Michele Hilmes, "On a Screen Near You: The New Soundwork Industry," *Cinema Journal* 52, no. 3 (Spring 2013): 180.
2 Hilmes, 177.
3 Hilmes, 178.
4 Angela Yee announced her departure from *The Breakfast Club* to host her own iHeart radio show in August 2022. Her last day was December 2, 2022.
5 Radio Hall of Fame, accessed December 13, 2022, https://www.radiohalloffame.com/the-breakfast-club.
6 Emily J. Lordi, "Black Radio: Robert Glasper, Esperanza Spalding, and Janelle Monáe," in *Are You Entertained? Black Popular Culture in the Twenty-First Century*, ed. Simone C. Drake and Dwan K. Henderson (Durham, N.C.: Duke University Press, 2020), 45.
7 Lordi, 45.
8 J. Green and H. Jenkins, "Spreadable Media: How Audiences Create Value and Meaning in a Networked Economy," in *The Handbook of Media Audiences*, ed. Virginia Nightingale (Wiley-Blackwell, 2013), 109–111.

9 Jericka Duncan, "Retiring Radio Icon Tom Joyner Says He Would Have Stayed for More Money: 'My Goal Was to Die on the Radio,'" *CBS Mornings*, December 13, 2019, https://www.cbsnews.com/news/tom-joyner-radio-icon-retiring-says-he-would-have-stayed-for-more-money/.

10 Duncan.

11 Duncan.

12 Duncan.

13 Hilmes, "On a Screen," 179. SoundExchange is a nonprofit collective rights management organization. It is the sole organization designated by the U.S. Congress to collect and distribute digital performance royalties for sound recordings.

14 "The Tom Joyner Morning Show," accessed June 7, 2023, https://player.listenlive.co/47051.

15 Its success is also built from remixing the foundation of visual radio set forth by *The Howard Stern Show*. *The Howard Stern Show* was the first visual radio show at the intersection of convergence media, taking full advantage of the internet, satellite radio, and visual casting. As an American talk, radio, and comedy show hosted by Howard Stern, this program gained wide recognition when it was nationally syndicated on terrestrial radio WXRK in New York City between 1986 and 2005. *The Howard Stern Show* was the highest-rated morning radio program from 1994 to 2001. Part of this show's highest-rated status came from its move from primarily aural radio to visual radio. In June 1994, robotic cameras were installed in the WXRK studio to film the radio show for a condensed half-hour program on television via the E! Network. See "Howard Stern to Star, Condensed, on TV," *New York Times*, June 1, 1994.

16 Sound bite of *The Breakfast Club*'s daily introduction.

17 "Power 105.1," accessed June 7, 2023, https://power1051.iheart.com/featured/breakfast-club/about/.

18 Breakfast Club Power 105.1 FM, "Peniel E. Joseph on Black Dignity, Radical Revolution + The Lives of MLK & Malcolm X," *The Breakfast Club*, June 15, 2021, YouTube video, 58:52, https://www.youtube.com/watch?v=CTtx8tMYPx8&t=33s; Breakfast Club Power 105.1 FM, "Migos Talk Respect, Relationships, Atlanta's Mount Rushmore and New Album," *The Breakfast Club*, June 16, 2021, YouTube video, 38:21, https://www.youtube.com/watch?v=V6dcrEPmAxk&t=2042s.

19 Ibrahim, Shamira, "'The Breakfast Club' Calls Itself 'The World's Most Dangerous Morning Show'—Maybe It's Time We Listen," *Okayplayer*, accessed May 7, 2023, https://www.okayplayer.com/originals/the-breakfast-club-charlamagne-tha-god-criticism.html.

20 "Clear Channel Begins Breakfast Club Syndication Rollout," *Radio Insight*, August 22, 2013, https://radioinsight.com/headlines/84758/clear-channel-begins-breakfast-club-syndication-rollout/.

21 Stephen Battaglio, "'The Breakfast Club' Is a Radio Forum for the Nation's Racial Reckoning," *Los Angeles Times*, July 15, 2020.

22 Battaglio.

23 Battaglio.

24 Sweenie Saint-Vil, "'The Breakfast Club' Inducted into the Radio Hall of Fame," August 17, 2020, https://www.revolt.tv/2020/8/17/21372571/the-breakfast-club-inducted-radio-hall-of-fame. Tom Joyner and Robin Quivers were the first Black inductees, yet they were inducted as individuals, not for their programs.

25 Briana Barner, "Safe and Sound: How Podcasts Became Audio Enclaves for Black Women," *Bitch Media*, February 26, 2020.

26 Barner.

27 Breakfast Club Power 105.1 FM, "Birdman Goes Off on the Breakfast Club Power 105.1," *The Breakfast Club*, April 22, 2016, YouTube video, 2:26, https://www.youtube .com/watch?v=4jLT7GQYNhI.

28 Ben Dandridge-Lemco, "Birdman Is Now Selling 'Put Some Respek on My Name' Shirts," *The Fader*, April 26, 2016, https://www.thefader.com/2016/04/26/birdman -respek-shirts-release-dates. Also, while on their tour bus, the R&B and Soul group The Hamiltones created a remix song "Put Some Respek on It" based on Birdman's quotables from his interview with *The Breakfast Club*. Breakfast Club Power 105.1 FM, "Birdman Goes Off."

29 C. Tosenberger, "Textual Poachers," in *Encyclopedia of Consumer Culture*, vol. 1, ed. D. Southerton (London: SAGE Publications, 2011), 1446–1447.

30 Henry Jenkins, *Textual Poachers* (New York: Routledge, 1992), 24.

31 Breakfast Club Power 105.1 FM, "Dave Chappelle on Bill Cosby, Charlie Murphy, Being Non-Apologetic, & Much More," *The Breakfast Club*, June 30, 2017, YouTube video, 38:26, https://www.youtube.com/watch?v=YjPoOd8oAbo.

32 Breakfast Club Power 105.1 FM, "Dr. Umar Johnson Speaks on American Racism, Joe Biden's Agenda, Interracial Relationships and More," *The Breakfast Club*, April 26, 2021, YouTube video, 1:16:24, https://www.youtube.com/watch?v=2_lGRkSpugw.

33 Breakfast Club Power 105.1 FM, "Dr. Umar Johnson Speaks."

34 Breakfast Club Power 105.1 FM, "Dr. Umar Johnson Speaks."

35 Breakfast Club Power 105.1 FM, "NYC Primary Elections 2021," YouTube, video playlist, June 22, 2021, https://www.youtube.com/playlist?list=PL -JcXudKgJPZZs8yZpMqQ6u3CBELlWiNU.

36 Breakfast Club Power 105.1 FM, "Joe Biden on Black Woman Running Mate, Democrats Taking Black Voters for Granted and Wiping Weed Crime," *The Breakfast Club*, May 22, 2020, YouTube video, 18:19, https://www.youtube.com/watch?v= KOIFs_SryHI.

37 This is before Vice President Kamala Harris was announced as President Biden's running mate.

38 Eric Bradner, Sarah Mucha, and Arlette Saenz, "Biden: 'If You Have a Problem Figuring Out Whether You're for Me or Trump, Then You Ain't Black,'" CNN, May 22, 2020, https://www.cnn.com/2020/05/22/politics/biden-charlamagne-tha-god-you -aint-black/index.html.

Part III

Monetizing Black

• •

8

Black Women, Audiences, and the Queer Possibilities of the Black-Cast Melodrama

● ●

ALFRED L. MARTIN JR.

To set its narrative wheels in motion, the "quality" series *Pose* (FX, 2018–2021) opens with Damon Richards (portrayed by Ryan Jamaal Swain) being forcibly ejected from his home for being a dancing, Black queer kid. While the series uses Damon's abjection as a narrative catalyst to tell *Pose's* story of alternative kinship networks, it simultaneously casts Black parents as unsupportive of their queer children. As a trope with currency in political and social arenas, Black people as antigay is understood as almost intrinsically linked to the state of Blackness itself. For example, in California during the 2008 voting season that elected Barack Obama president, Black Californians were blamed for the passage of Proposition 8, which was designed to deny same-sex couples the right to marry in California. As Ta-Nehisi Coates writes, "The 70 percent figure for Black support of Prop 8 is wildly overblown, and in conflict with all the other polling done. The [National LGBTQ Taskforce] study concludes that 58 percent is a more likely number. To put that in context, the study also concludes that 59 percent of Latinos supported Prop 8. That isn't one-up-manship—it just means we were about the same."[1] This fallacy about the monolithic nature of Blackness and the interconnectivity of Blackness and antigayness shapes discourse and particularly media discourse.

These discourses about Blackness and imagined Black audiences as monolithic results in what I have elsewhere called a generic closet.[2] As a concept,
generic closet refers to the Black-cast sitcom's episodic engagement with Black
gayness as well as the industrial imagining of Black audiences as bigoted, uned-
ucated, religious, and poor compared to white audiences (particularly white
"quality" audiences). However, the popularity of series across the television
landscape like *The Real Housewives of Atlanta* (Bravo, 2008–), the *Love & Hip
Hop* franchise (VH1, 2011–), *The Game* (UPN, 2006–2009; BET, 2011–2015),
and *Scandal* (ABC, 2012–2018) was cause for the industry to reconsider this
imagination. Targeting Black women, many of these programs regularly
achieved ratings success, and films like *Baggage Claim* (2013, dir. David E. Tal-
bert) included gay supporting characters while achieving box office success. Of
course, in their personal lives, many Black women have engaged with Black gay
men often through the beauty industries, churches, and other organizations.
The ad industry not only took note of Black women's rising spending power but
also paid attention to their tastes when considering content and which stories
to tell. As a commercial medium concerned with selling eyeballs to advertisers, the industry needed to understand the Black women who were tuning in to
Black-led and Black-cast series that ran the gamut from the "respectable" to the
"ratchet."

This chapter explores Black-cast television production's simultaneous turn to
the Black-cast melodrama *and* its long-term narrative engagement with Black
gayness. Unlike the Black-cast sitcom, which only engaged with Black gayness
episodically, Black-cast melodramas like *The Haves and the Have Nots* (*Haves*;
OWN, 2013–2021) and *Being Mary Jane* (*BMJ*; BET, 2013–2019) included
Black gay characters as part of the televised biological Black family and work-
place. On May 28, 2013, OWN debuted *Haves*, a show described as the network's answer to the British series *Downton Abbey* (PBS, 2010–2015).[3] Among
the family of "haves" in the series' title are the Harringtons, a wealthy Black
Savannah family who have a gay son, Jeffrey (Gavin Houston). Jeffrey has a
contentious relationship with his mother, Veronica (Angela Robinson), around
his sexuality. The series' first season averaged 3.7 million viewers.[4] Premiering
July 2, 2013, as a movie event, *Being Mary Jane* follows Mary Jane Paul, played
by Gabrielle Union, as she navigates life and love as a television news anchor.
BMJ's first three seasons included Mark Bradley (Aaron D. Spears), an initially
closeted Black gay man who is also Mary Jane's coanchor and friend. The series
debut was the highest-rated original series on cable with 4 million viewers overall and 2 million in the coveted eighteen to thirty-four demographic.

I center these two series as originary texts that begin a larger trend in the
Black-cast melodrama's engagement with Black gayness. This chapter explores
these two series and their imaginations of Black female audiences and, thus,
how each series engages with Black gayness. I attempt to understand how the
melodrama shapes and is shaped by audience imaginations and the narrative

moves a text makes with respect to Black gayness specifically. Examining genre as not only textual but also industrial, this chapter engages the queer possibilities the Black-cast melodrama provides for Black gay visibility via Black women.

Black-Cast Melodrama and the Making of Black Women Audiences

I do not employ melodrama pejoratively. Like Jason Mittell, this work does not take genre "at face value, using the categorical labels that are culturally commonplace without much consideration of the meanings or usefulness of those self-same labels."[5] Genre generally, and the melodrama specifically, are what Mittell calls cultural categories in which a genre is not simply about what occurs within a given text but is also located in how audiences understand generic formations *and* how media industries activate genre as a means to hail particular audience segments.

At its core, Tom Schatz suggests that melodrama is called such because it "refers to those narrative forms which combine music (*melos*) with drama. . . . Generally speaking, 'melodrama' was applied to popular romances that depicted a virtuous individual (usually a woman) or couple (usually lovers) victimized by repressive and inequitable social circumstances, particularly those involving marriage, occupation, and the nuclear family."[6] Similarly, Peter Brooks argues that melodramatic narratives indulge "strong emotionalism; moral polarization and schematization; extreme states of being, situations, action; overt villainy, persecution of the good, and final reward of virtue; inflated and extravagant expression; dark plottings, suspense, breathtaking peripety."[7] While Schatz and Brooks argue that melodrama can be found within narrative, Jane Feuer partly suggests the genre is affective as well as narrative. She argues that melodramas create "an *excess*, whether that excess be defined as a split between the level of narrative and that of *mise-en-scene* or as a form of 'hysteria,' the visually articulated return of the ideologically repressed."[8] This discussion of the affective register of the melodrama gestures toward the ways the genre hails women as ideal viewers. I want to point out that the melodrama is not necessarily generically different from daytime soap operas or so-called quality dramas like *The Sopranos* (HBO, 1999–2007), *Breaking Bad* (AMC, 2008–2013), and *Fargo* (FX, 2014–). Rather, these generic demarcations—the melodrama, the drama, and the daytime soap—are more concerned with hailing audience segments than necessarily differentiating among one another based on textual properties. The melodrama, and specifically the Black-cast/Black-led melodrama because of its appeals to emotional/affective responses, imagines Black women as ideal viewers.

In contrast, the Black-cast sitcom frequently imagines a monolithic mass Black audience. In the "common knowledge" of Black folks, this mass Black audience is imagined as antigay. As veteran television producer Ed Weinberger told me in 2013, "I don't think [Black-focused networks] have encouraged gay Black characters because they are fearful of alienating their audience. I think they're afraid that there is still a prejudice."[9] Thus, some television channels' move toward the Black-cast/Black-led melodrama demonstrated an attempt to segment Black audiences in new ways within media discourse.

This new audience imagination and segmentation is rooted in at least three industrial turns. First, the 1980s were a time when the expansion of cable resulted in the launch of networks that targeted smaller audience segments. In 1980, BET, or Black Entertainment Television, launched as a mix of Black entertainment and public affairs programming. And in 1984, Lifetime launched and by 1985 was branding itself as "talk television" in a bid to draw a mass female audience. Additionally, the FOX network began broadcasting in 1986 and immediately targeted a neglected mass Black audience (and auxiliary young, white, male hip-hop consumers) through a commodification of hip-hop sensibilities. While FOX ultimately abandoned Black viewers for more lucrative white ones, BET retained its focus on Black viewers—even as critics of its programming charged the network with mediating disreputable Black images.[10] The need to bifurcate Black audiences became apparent when BET purchased syndication rights to *The Game* after the CW canceled the series in 2009. In reruns on BET, *The Game* garnered "higher numbers than they did when they originally aired on The CW," leading BET's senior vice president of original programming to state that *The Game* was "the beginning of what scripted programming means to BET."[11] Two years later, BET had greenlit new episodes of the series to capture Black female audiences.

On Martin Luther King Jr. Day in 2004, TVOne launched in a bid to break BET's monopoly on Black audiences. With an initial schedule filled with syndicated Black-cast sitcoms, TVOne began producing original programming in 2010 with *The Ultimate Merger* (TVOne, 2010–2011), a spinoff of *The Apprentice* (ABC, 2004–2017) starring Omarosa Manigault as an eligible bachelorette looking for love. In 2009 BET launched Centric, a channel that set its focus on upscale African American viewers. While the network initially sought to segment Blackness by socioeconomic status (and expendable income levels), the network soon shifted that focus to upscale Black women audiences. The network's first original program, *Keeping Up with the Joneses* (Centric, 2009–2010), was described in its press release as a "docu-soap" that captured "the non-stop drama of the high society world of the beautiful and sassy Editor-in-Chief of *Jones* magazine."[12] Alongside *Keeping Up with the Joneses*, Centric also premiered *Model City* (Centric, 2009–2010), a program that followed the lives of four male models—including one Black gay male model. SueAnn Tannis, a public relations executive who runs the personal blog *Sooo Fabulous!*, not only predicted that "a good few women will be tuning in when [*Model City*] premieres" but also understood the series as melodramatic by suggesting it is "chock-full of drama, getting up close and personal as the guys try to master handling rejection, exhausting schedules, jealous girlfriends, and the personal insecurities that can come along with the job."[13] Ultimately, Centric rebranded itself to more precisely target Black female audiences to increase the effectiveness of its advertising.

The second industrial turn at capturing Black women finds TV showrunner Shonda Rhimes vaunting ratings successfully with her blindcast melodramatic series *Grey's Anatomy* (ABC, 2005–present) and *Scandal* (ABC, 2012–2018). Kristen Warner describes blindcasting as an industrially "useful tool" that allows "showrunners and television writers to avoid explicitly writing race into the script with the confidence such actions could create equal opportunity for actors of diverse backgrounds. . . . Blindcasting ultimately helped [*Grey's Anatomy*] become a runaway success because it appeared to reinforce a multicultural society that could attract a number of audience demographics."[14] Blindcasting relies on a racelessness that seeks to make white viewers forget characters are Black through the evacuation of any (or much) cultural specificity (similar to Sut Jhally and Justin Lewis' study of *The Cosby Show* [NBC, 1984–1992]).[15] Simultaneously, blindcasting relies on Black viewers', and specifically Black women's, Pavlovian response to "being seen" in media.[16] However, as Rhimes's programs started to come under fire for Black female characters' lack of cultural specificity, BET and OWN (reluctantly) began producing programming like *Being Mary Jane* (BET, 2013–2018) and *The Haves and the Have Nots* (OWN, 2013–2021) that spoke more directly to the specificities of Black womanhood.

The third industrial shift, related to the increase in Black representation within melodramatic series, involves advertising industry behemoth Nielsen compiling reports about the buying power of African American consumers in 2011. Its first report, "The State of the African American Consumer," revealed that Black households typically spend "an average of seven hours 12 minutes each day—or 213 hours per month—watching [television]. This amounts to about 40% more viewing time than the rest of the population."[17] The most-watched program among Black viewers older than two years old excluding sports, variety, awards, and special programming was the long-running soap opera *The Young and the Restless* (CBS, 1973–present). When discussing Black adults aged eighteen to forty-nine, coincidentally the ad industry's most-coveted demographic, the top program (excluding sports) was BET's reboot of *The Game*.

While the series retained the thirty-minute format from its iteration on the CW, it employed a hybrid production style that blended multi- and single-cam shooting. Additionally, similar to Kristal Brent Zook's work on Black-cast sitcoms of the 1990s, *The Game* blended comedic and dramatic moments to create a sitcom that hewed more closely to the melodramatic. Rounding out the top three programs were the mostly Black-cast docusoap *The Real Housewives of Atlanta* (*RHOA*; Bravo, 2008–present) and the Black-cast sitcom *Let's Stay Together* (BET, 2011–2014). Aside from their popularity among African American women, each of these series also included some engagement with Black

FIG. 8.1 State of the African-American consumer

gayness. In its iteration on the CW, *The Game* featured two episodes about a football player coming out as gay. *Let's Stay Together* featured Darkanian (Tony Bravado), a Black football player who goes from womanizer to declaring his gayness in a press conference over seven episodes and two seasons. And *RHOA* regularly featured Black gay celebrity hairstylists Derek J and Miss Lawrence. While I have elsewhere called *The Game* and *Let's Stay Together* Black-cast sitcoms, largely because of their thirty-minute format and use of the laugh track, they depart from the sitcom form in their use of serial rather than episodic storylines. In utilizing more melodramatic storylines and centering Black women within the main series narratives, *The Game*, *Let's Stay Together*, and *RHOA* imagined themselves as series that would appeal most to women generally, and Black women specifically.

Additionally, the 2011 Nielsen report began to single out Black women as a growth market for potential advertisers. Nielsen reported that African American consumer buying power was nearly one trillion dollars annually, buoyed by "trends in education and a rising number of professional African-American women in the work force."[18] The report argued that this trend presented an opportunity for advertisers with Black women specifically because they "tend to be the primary decision makers for most household buying decisions."[19] Some networks paid attention to these trends. VH1 and other networks began producing programming that appealed to Black women, and upstart networks like BounceTV (2011) and Aspire (2012) launched to further challenge BET's hegemonic hold on Black audiences in the industrial imagination.

The 2012 Nielsen report "African American Consumers: Still Vital, Still Growing" stated Black households are "127% more likely to include a single parent, most often a woman."[20] With this insight, some networks began to double down on producing melodramas appealing to Black women. After all, the top ten prime-time series in African American households were *The Game*, *Love & Hip Hop* (VH1, 2011–present), *Basketball Wives* (VH1, 2010–2013; 2017–present), *Single Ladies* (VH1, 2011–2014; Centric, 2014–2015), *T.I. and Tiny* (VH1, 2011–2017), *Whitney Houston: Her Life* (CNN, 2012), *La La's Full Court Life* (VH1, 2011–2014), *Scandal*, and *Braxton Family Values* (WE tv, 2011–present). These series run the gamut with respect to their major narrative thrusts; however, I argue that apart from CNN's *Whitney Houston: Her Life*, each of the top ten series appealed to Black women and could be considered melodramatic.

Amid the industry's turn to Black women as a viable audience segment, Oprah Winfrey launched OWN, the Oprah Winfrey Network, in 2011. Although series like *Love & Hip Hop*, *Basketball Wives*, and *Scandal* were scoring in the ratings in Black households and with advertisers, some segments of Black communities were less than thrilled with how these series trafficked in disreputable images of Blackness generally and Black womanhood particularly. In fact, at OWN's launch, Winfrey said her network would be "fun and entertaining, without tearing people down and calling them bitches."[21] For her starting lineup, Winfrey largely relied on people whose careers she had helped earlier through *The Oprah Winfrey Show* (syndicated, 1986–2011) like Dr. Phil, Suzie Orman, Dr. Oz, and her best friend and journalist, Gayle King. However, the network struggled to find an audience, which ultimately resulted in laying off thirty employees and a seemingly ever-changing roster of executives.[22]

Less than a year after its launch, Winfrey, the previous queen of daytime, was at the helm of a fledgling network. Rather than targeting a mass audience as the network had at its launch, Winfrey turned to her friend Tyler Perry for content, greenlighting *The Haves and the Have Nots*, an hour-long melodrama, and *Love Thy Neighbor* (OWN, 2013–2017), a half-hour comedy. The network's turn to Perry is significant in that it signaled Winfrey's engagement not only with women but with *Black* women through the network's programming. And it was not just OWN that turned to Black women. By 2014, ABC was branding its Thursday night prime-time lineup under the hashtag TGIT (thank God it's Thursday) and, as Eleanor Patterson details, using Black women's viewership of Shondaland series *Grey's Anatomy*, *Scandal*, and *How to Get Away with Murder* and their adoption of social media to harness the power of this recently discovered market segment.[23] In fact, Black women's Thursday night social media activity around Shondaland series was so well-known that Beyoncé released her "surprise" 2013 self-titled record at 11 p.m. (EST), at the conclusion of *Scandal*'s midseason finale (which attracted 9.23 million viewers). Interestingly, as networks began producing Black-cast/led melodramas, this programming also began to include Black gay characters. In *Being Mary Jane* and *Haves*, Black gayness finally bursts out of the generic closet via Black women, achieving mainstream visibility within the fabric of series rather than being trotted out for short narrative arcs.

Being Mary Jane and *The Haves and the Have Nots* Come Out of the Generic Closet

The generic closet, as I have argued elsewhere, shapes the imagination of the Black-cast sitcom's audience as well as its narrative engagement with Black gayness. Like their Black-cast sitcom counterparts, the Black gay characters within *BMJ* and *Haves* begin their respective show lives under the presumption of heterosexuality. However, both series are important because they not only assert Black gay men's rightful claim to Blackness, but they also engage storylines beyond these characters coming out as gay.

BMJ introduces Mark Bradley in the pilot episode, where he initially appears to simply be a fellow anchor at Atlanta-based Satellite News Channel (SNC). He hosts *The Mark Bradley Hour*, the show that, in terms of flow, precedes Mary Jane's *Talkback with Mary Jane Paul*. While he and Mary Jane exchange pleasantries and share fandom for ABC's prime-time melodrama *Revenge* (ABC, 2011–2015), it is not until the third act of the pilot episode that scribe Mara Brock Akil reveals that they are close friends: Mary Jane goes to Mark's home when she is having a crisis about not having married and borne children yet. As Mark consoles Mary Jane on his sofa, the sound of a door opening is heard. Shortly thereafter, a white man enters the scene, asks if Mary Jane is OK, and then leans in to kiss Mark. And with that, Mark is gay, not through a speech act but a physical one.

Mark's gayness is, on the one hand, a surprise because he did not offer the kinds of context clues sitcom television writers often provide when trying to help viewers detect a character's gayness. On the other hand, the matter-of-fact way Brock Akil reveals Mark's gay identity dovetails with what she told me about the place of gayness in her storytelling: "Because I've always had gay men in my life—my children have gay uncles—it never occurred to me to not include gay characters in the stories I'm telling."[24] In other words, for her, the revelation of gay identity is not necessarily a big narrative event (although it was in *The Game*'s two episodes with a Black gay character). At the same time, *BMJ* casting director Tracy "Twinkie" Byrd revealed that because the character's gayness is not revealed until late in the pilot, and gayness was not part of the character breakdown, "I had a number of actors who came in and didn't realize it was [a gay role] . . . as it was written, it was just written as a great character. And [they] didn't realize until one of the last lines or two words or something. . . . And they're like, 'Wait a minute. . . .' They had that moment in the [casting] room. Because we didn't want to make it a big deal."[25] On the one hand, Byrd's suggestion that Mark's gayness was not central to the breakdown actors were provided points to a kind of postgayness that suggests gayness is but a small part of one's identity. On the other hand, it signals the ways in which the series would attempt to center his Blackness more than his gayness.

However, after the first episode, it is revealed that Mark has only told Mary Jane that he is gay. Thus, in some ways, although he appears across twenty episodes of *BMJ*, the major thrust of his narrative arc revolves around his gay identity. In many of the episodes in which Mark appears, he deals with work issues (the fledgling ratings of his show and its attendant rebranding) and his relationship to Mary Jane. However, in the season two episode "Freedom," Mark comes out to his parents after his mother, who is visiting from out of town, directly asks if he is gay. In the "Freedom" episode as well as the next episode in which he appears ("Sleepless in Atlanta"), not only does Mark begin to lean into his gay identity, but he also centers his Black identity. He reveals the issues he is having with his white boyfriend, Eric (Daniel Thomas May), partly stem from racial differences. This narrative accomplishes two things. First, it centers Mark as a Black gay man, not a gay Black man. As Darieck Scott argues, gay Black men have "political, social and cultural allegiances . . . to 'white' gay politics, to 'white' gay men and to 'white' cultural forms."[26] Conversely, Black gay men center their Blackness and, thus, Black love.

Second, Mark's centering of his Blackness demonstrates the producers' intent to make the series "Black on purpose." As Kristen Warner describes, "Black on purpose" represents "a strategic way of writing [*Being Mary Jane*'s] African American characters . . . that allows them to be seen as 'unapologetically Black.' That is, through the writing, it is evident that these characters are Black, and equally as important, are written by Black folks."[27] In the dissolution of his relationship with Eric in the episode "Sleepless in Atlanta," Mark suggests Eric was jealous of Mary Jane because she "always got where [Mark] was coming from. [Eric] kinda felt like an outsider." While Mark partly grieves the end of his relationship with Eric ("One Is the Loneliest Number"), he mostly shifts into being a friend and confidante to Mary Jane, sharing relationship and love woes. This gestures toward the series' treatment of the character as more than his gayness, a

FIG. 8.2 Mark and Mary Jane

treatment I argue is rooted in his character's existence within a "women's genre" and in a series whose appeal and target are almost singularly Black women.

Mark ultimately leaves *BMJ* (or more aptly is written out of *BMJ*) when he becomes embroiled in a scandal in which he has been photographed having sex in public. Although he had only been out to his parents and Mary Jane, the scandal results in SNC not only embracing the scandal but proposing that Mark use it to revamp his show to focus on the intersections of foreign policy and LGBT rights. Rather than use his sexuality to lift his ratings and get himself out of the scandal, Mark decides to leave SNC ("If the Shoe Fits"), again asserting that his Black identity is important to his intersectional identity. On the one hand, Mark being written off the show for its remaining twenty-three episodes and its made-for-TV movie finale perhaps gestured toward the enduring nature of the generic closet for Black-cast series. On the other hand, Mark being out from the beginning of the series with no "detective work" needed to figure out his sexuality suggests he is a different kind of Black gay character: one whose Blackness was centered until he was written off the series.

While *BMJ* expands the generic closet in centering the intersection of Blackness and gayness, *Haves* develops Black gay televisibility by not only further integrating Black gayness into the series but also disrupting tropes associated with Black gayness and Black traditional family formations. Jeffrey, the Harringtons' Black gay son, is part of a Black family of "haves" in the series title and appears in 135 of the series' 215 episodes. A substance abuse counselor when the series begins, Jeffrey is charged with assisting Wyatt Cryer (Aaron O'Connell), a recovering drug and alcohol abuser. As in *BMJ*, Jeffrey begins the series as presumably heterosexual. However, in the second episode of the first season ("Playing in the Deep End"), Candace (Tika Sumpter), one of the series' villains, meets Jeffrey and tells her friend, Amanda (Jaclyn Betham), who is trying to set the two up on a date, that Jeffrey is gay.

> AMANDA: So... what do you think about Jeffrey?
>
> CANDACE: OK... that man is gay.
>
> AMANDA: What? No, he's not.
>
> CANDACE: Yes, he is.
>
> AMANDA: Are you sure?
>
> CANDACE: Trust me. I know a gay man when I see one.
>
> AMANDA: I've known him most of my life. There's no way.
>
> CANDACE: OK... Fine.
>
> AMANDA: Gay? Really?
>
> CANDACE: Mmhmmm. Now. Will you drop it? He's obviously in the closet and uncomfortable about it.

Similar to the ways the generic closet sets the detection phase in motion, *Haves* uses Candace to raise questions about Jeffrey's sexuality. As I have argued elsewhere, detection "raises those questions not directly but by presenting something as slightly 'off' with a character within the gay episode. This 'offness' can range from a character being too polite or perfect . . . or wearing colors out of step with approved scripts of Black masculine sartorial choices."[28] For Candace, she used her gaydar to "know a gay man when [she sees] one." Once Amanda tells her brother Wyatt that Jeffrey might be gay, he devises a scheme to try to figure it out for himself. Because Wyatt knows Jeffrey will come to his room to check on him, Wyatt pretends to be asleep in nothing but his underwear and records his bedroom door on his laptop, ultimately catching Jeffrey staring longingly at his nearly naked body.

In "The Truth Will Set You Free," the fifteenth episode of the first season, Wyatt convinces Jeffrey to admit that he is gay (and in love with Wyatt). In the next episode, "No More Hiding," he comes out as gay to his parents. In the scene, unlike the ways Black masculinity has historically been mediated, Jeffrey's father, David (Peter Parros), supports his son's homosexuality while his mother, Veronica (Angela Robinson), says she will never be OK with his gayness. In fact, the scene ends with David hugging Jeffrey as Jeffrey cries and the screen fades to black. The scene also reveals how melodrama takes the second act (declaration/discovery of the generic closet) and uses it to begin another narrative cycle, never advancing toward discarding the Black gay character. Because the Black-cast sitcom discards Black gay characters post–coming out, the reception to the newly out person must be a warm welcome. In Jeffrey's case, his mother is unwilling to accept his homosexuality and expresses her belief that God has continued to punish her by allowing Jeffrey to live (when other pregnancies had not gone full term) and making him gay. Third, Perry disrupts the trope of unsupportive Black fathers and Black gay sons. Although it is David's political career that could be in jeopardy (given his antigay political stances), he ultimately embraces his son for who he is.

Within this melodrama, Jeffrey's story continues with him being gay and engaging in a few relationships, but he is also entangled in other narratives that are inconsequential to his sexuality. Despite Perry's work in Black-cast sitcoms, he had never before included a Black gay character. It is Perry's turn to the melodrama and his full lean into a televisual form hailing women as viewers that frees him to include a recurring Black gay character.[29]

Black Gayness in the Black-Cast Melodrama

The Black-cast/led melodrama has been a relative boon for Black gay representation that extends beyond the act of coming out. While neither *BMJ* nor *Haves* abandons the narrative drama that can be mined through the act of coming out, they demonstrate that Black gay men can center their alliances with Blackness and Black politics. They also demonstrate a myriad of stories in which Black gay characters can be involved that do not center gayness.

After *BMJ* and *Haves* demonstrated that Black women would consume content with recurring Black gay characters, other Black-cast melodramatic series, including *Empire* (FOX, 2015–2020) and *Greenleaf* (OWN, 2016–2020), have also included recurring Black gay characters. However, visibility is not enough—if it ever were. Three things are important about the ways *Empire* moves the bar past mere representational politics. First, the series was executive produced by Black gay showrunner Lee Daniels, who also directed the Oscar-nominated film *Precious* (2009). Second, Jussie Smollett was hired to play Jamal, the series' Black gay character. While Smollett was not necessarily publicly out as gay, he told Ellen DeGeneres that the people who needed to know were aware of his sexuality (before being forced to come out in a "special" backstage interview with DeGeneres).[30] Third, unlike *BMJ* and *Haves*, *Empire* not only centered Jamal's political allegiances to Blackness but seemed to follow Joseph Beam's pronouncement that "Black men loving Black men is the revolutionary act" by coupling Jamal with mostly Black men throughout the series.[31]

Additionally, *Greenleaf* created three stories involving Black gay characters across the series' five-season run on OWN and attempted to break the myth that tightly connects Black religiosity and homophobia.[32] The series includes Carlton Cruise (Parnell Damone Marcano) as the series' fictional church's out gay music director, who appears on sixteen of *Greenleaf*'s sixty episodes, and Kevin Satterlee (Tye White), who begins his forty-two-episode run questioning his sexuality and married to Charity Greenleaf-Satterlee (Deborah Joy Winans). Lastly, *Greenleaf* includes Aaron Jeffries (William H. Bryant Jr.), who is an attorney and a Greenleaf family friend who becomes romantically involved with Kevin during his twenty-three-episode story arc. Like *Empire*'s Smollett,

Marcano is an openly Black gay man playing a Black gay character, although the other two roles are played by Black heterosexual men performing gayness.

While representation is always simulacra and can never be real, it *can* resonate with Black viewers. The fact is that OWN and BET targeted Black women through the use of Black-cast/led melodramas and likely also expected that these series would appeal to Black gay viewers through their melodramatic affect and via the act of mediating Black gayness. Perhaps the Black gay stories of *BMJ, Haves, Empire, Greenleaf, Love & Hip Hop: Atlanta's* sixth season (VH1, 2012–present), *Love & Hip Hop: Hollywood's* second season (VH1, 2014–2019), and others yet to come might shift the hegemonic understanding of Blackness as congruous with heterosexuality and gayness as always-already white. While networks have frequently turned to (and away from) Blackness—including FOX, UPN, the WB, the CW, and TBS—and the media and ad industries create new audience segments, the Black-cast melodrama unlocked Black queer possibilities for television. Regardless of what the future of televisual Black gayness in the melodrama holds, the discovery of Black women as a viable and valuable audience was an important moment for Black gay representation. However, as of this writing, Black gayness has again mostly disappeared from the Black-cast television landscape with *Haves* concluding in July 2021.[33]

Notes

1 Ta-Nehisi Coates, "Prop 8 and Blaming the Blacks," *Atlantic*, January 7, 2009, https://www.theatlantic.com/entertainment/archive/2009/01/prop-8-and-blaming -the-blacks/6548/.

2 Alfred L. Martin Jr., *The Generic Closet: Black Gayness and the Black-Cast Sitcom* (Bloomington: Indiana University Press, 2021), 105.

3 Tim Molloy, "OWN Announces Tyler Perry's Answer to 'Downton Abbey,'" *The Wrap*, January 5, 2013. https://www.thewrap.com/own-announces-tyler-perrys -answer-downton-abbey-71536/.

4 Rick Kissell, "Ratings: OWN's 'The Haves and the Have Nots' Hits Series Highs," *Variety*, September 23, 2015, https://variety.com/2015/tv/ratings/the-haves-and-the -have-nots-series-highs-ratings-1201600918/.

5 Jason Mittell, *Genre and Television: From Cop Shows to Cartoons in American Culture* (New York: Routledge, 2004), 2.

6 Thomas Schatz, *Hollywood Genres: Formulas, Filmmaking, and the Studio System* (New York: Random House, 1981), 221–222.

7 Peter Brooks, *The Melodramatic Imagination* (New Haven: Yale University Press, 1976), 11–12.

8 Jane Feuer, "Melodrama, Serial Form and Television Today," *Screen*, 25, no. 1 (1984): 8.

9 Ed Weinberger, interview with author, March 19, 2013.

10 For a fuller discussion, see Beretta E. Smith-Shomade, *Pimpin' Ain't Easy: Selling Black Entertainment Television* (New York: Routledge, 2007).

11 Trevor Kimball, "*The Game*: Season Four Starts on BET in January 2011," TV Series Finale, October 12, 2010, https://tvseriesfinale.com/tv-show/the-game-season-four -bet-18759/.

12 BET Networks, "'Keeping Up with the Joneses' Never Looked So Beautiful Nor
    So Deliciously Wicked as Centric Premieres Docu-Soap Following the Life of
    Media Queen in Houston High Society," press release, March 16, 2010, http://www
    .thefutoncritic.com/news/2010/03/16/keeping-up-with-the-joneses-never-looked-so
    -beautiful-nor-so-deliciously-wicked-as-centric-premieres-docu-soap-following-the
    -life-of-media-queen-in-houston-high-society-34959/20100316bet01/.

13 SueAnn Tannis, "All-New Reality Show 'Model City' Premieres Thursday," Sooo
    Fabulous!, February 15, 2010, https://sooofabulous.com/2010/02/15/all-new-reality
    -show-model-city-premieres-thursday/.

14 Kristen Warner, *The Cultural Politics of Colorblind TV Casting* (New York: Rout-
    ledge, 2015), 13.

15 Sut Jhally and Justin Lewis, *Enlightened Racism: The Cosby Show, Audiences, and the
    Myth of the American Dream* (New York: Routledge, 1992).

16 Kristen J. Warner, "ABC's *Scandal* and Black Women's Fandom," in *Cupcakes, Pinter-
    est, and Ladyporn: Feminized Popular Culture in the Twenty-First Century*, ed. Elana
    Levine (Urbana: University of Illinois Press, 2015), 37; and Alfred L. Martin Jr., "Fan-
    dom While Black: Misty Copeland, *Black Panther*, Tyler Perry and the Contours of
    US Black Fandoms," *International Journal of Cultural Studies* 22, no. 6 (2019): 742.

17 Nielsen Company, "The State of the African American Consumer," September 2011, 10,
    https://www.nielsen.com/insights/2011/state-of-the-african-american-consumer/.

18 Nielsen Company, 6.

19 Nielsen Company, 9.

20 Nielsen Company, "African American Consumers: Still Vital, Still Growing,"
    September 2012, 4, https://www.nielsen.com/insights/2012/african-american
    -consumers-still-vital-still-growing-2012-repo/.

21 "On Her OWN," *Emmy* 32, no. 7 (January 2010): 72.

22 "OWN Scripts Growth Strategy with Help from Tyler Perry; *The Haves and the Have
    Nots, Love Thy Neighbor* to Build Up Midweek Schedule," *Broadcasting & Cable*,
    May 27, 2013, 21.

23 Eleanor Patterson, "Must Tweet TV: ABC's #TGIT and the Cultural Work of Pro-
    gramming Social Television," *Transformative Works and Cultures* 26 (2018).

24 Mara Brock-Akil, "A Conversation with Mara Brock-Akil and Salim Akil," interview
    at the ATX Television Festival, season 6, Austin, Tex., June 11, 2017.

25 Jennifer Euston, Tracey Lillienfield, Tracy "Twinkie" Byrd, "Reflective Casting:
    Trends or Content? Presented by Casting Society of America," panel discussion
    conducted at the ATX Television Festival, Austin, Tex., June 5, 2015.

26 Darieck Scott, "Jungle Fever? Black Gay Identity Politics, White Dick, and the Uto-
    pian Bedroom," *GLQ: A Journal of Lesbian and Gay Studies* 1, no. 3 (1994): 300.

27 Kristen J. Warner, "*Being Mary Jane*: Cultural Specificity," In *How to Watch Televi-
    sion, Second Edition* (New York: New York University Press, 2020), 108–109.

28 Martin, *Generic Closet*, 16.

29 Although through his Madea films, Perry mostly hails this same audience.

30 Luchna Fisher, "Jussie Smollett of 'Empire' Comes Out to Ellen DeGeneres," ABC
    News, March 9, 2015. https://abcnews.go.com/Entertainment/jussie-smollett-empire
    -ellen-degeneres/story?id=29510347.

31 Joseph Beam, *In the Life: A Black Gay Anthology* (Los Angeles: Alyson Books, 1986).

32 Elijah G. Ward, "Homophobia, Hypermasculinity and the US Black Church," *Cul-
    ture, Health & Sexuality* 7, no. 5 (2005): 493–504.

33 Editor's Note: Hope lives in the televisual tunnel. Katori Hall's critically acclaimed
    series *P-Valley* (Starz 2020–) centers Black male gay (and Black lesbian) stories, iden-
    tity, and desire to the delight of its voluminous, multiplatform audience.

9

In a '90s Kind of World, I'm Glad I Got My Shows!

••••••••••••••••••••••

Digital Streaming and Black Nostalgia

BRIANA BARNER

In April 2018, on a spring day in Oakland, California, two men were enjoying the weather and grilling at Lake Merritt, a local park. A white woman named Jennifer Schulte decided that these men made her uncomfortable and deemed them to be a threat. She called the police and reported that instead of using a charcoal grill, they were using a non-charcoal grill—in a designated grilling area, nonetheless—and wanted the situation handled "immediately." Videos and pictures surfaced of Schulte on the phone with the police, looking hysterical and frightened, claiming that she was being harassed. This incident was part of a larger string of events in which white people called the police on Black people doing seemingly harmless activities—like grilling at the park with their families.

The pictures and videos of "BBQ Becky," as Schulte was later labeled, went viral, and memes were instantly created. These memes reimagined BBQ Becky calling the police for a number of "offenses" related to Black popular culture. One of the memes that emerged from this unfortunate event placed Schulte in the middle of the image with a caption reading, "Hello? Yes. There are homegirls standing to my left and my right." The homegirls flanking each side of her are the four main cast members of the 1990s television series *Living Single* (1993–1998).

FIG. 9.1 BBQ Becky and *Living Single* cast. Author's own screengrab. Creator of the meme unknown.

The humor of this meme is layered: the series featured a group of Black friends enjoying life and each other. BBQ Becky, seemingly sensing Black people gathered joyfully, calls the police to report another noncrime while a line from the popular theme song is inserted into the narrative. Because *Living Single* is an important part of the 1990s television series trajectory and therefore an important part of the American and Black popular culture landscape, this added to the humor and, ultimately, ridiculousness of BBQ Becky's antics.

The theme song of *Living Single*—performed by one of its stars, rapper Queen Latifah—is just as popular as the show. For context, BBQ Becky went viral in 2018. Thus, placing the line from the song into the meme, over two decades *after* the show went off the air, further cements the series' relevance in the Black cultural imaginary. Anyone familiar with at least the theme song of the show would instantly recognize the cast and understand the reference. The meme also harkens to the current trend of nostalgia for the 1990s. This is apparent in the popularity of fashions from yesteryear, such as "mom" jeans, and the many television series that have been rebooted—whether these series have been successful or not is a different story. But it remains: America longs for the "good ole days" of the 1990s.

Explosion of Black Representation

The representation of Blackness in the 1990s was a big deal, but it was also not something that "just happened." The increase in Black content was intentional and dated back to the 1980s when the fourth broadcast network (FOX) was created and broke up the domination of the three broadcast television networks that ruled the airwaves up until that point—ABC, CBS, and NBC. While cable television was growing more popular, many Black viewers were still watching the broadcast networks and had yet to navigate over to cable. FOX needed to cultivate an audience that would help build the network and turned to young Black audiences as their targeted demographic to do that work. This resulted in FOX offering multiple series with primarily Black casts.[1] After the success of FOX, smaller networks UPN and WB followed this same formula and targeted underserved Black audiences with a slew of primarily Black-cast shows.[2] Remembering this glorious time vividly, there seemed to be no shortage of Black shows.

Yet as each of these new networks developed and set their sights on becoming more mainstream, the target audience switched. Most of the series were canceled in favor of television shows with casts appealing to white audiences. Black-cast shows, the thinking went, only appealed to Black audiences, and Black audiences were no longer the intended audience. The networks did not want (or need) Blackness to be part of their identity as they rebranded and shifted.

Courting Black audiences like start-up networks did in the 1990s as nostalgia for the '90s continues, streaming platforms have become more interested in series that were not seen as popular or strong contenders previously and therefore had not been added to their growing content libraries. Black audiences' nostalgia for '90s shows is unique in that this was a particular period in which an explosion of Black representation arrived where little existed. Black audiences are not necessarily underserved in the current moment, but it is difficult to stream many of the shows that were loved from this era. So what does it mean to be a fan who wants to participate in nostalgia but can't due to a lack of availability?

The delay in putting Black shows from the 1990s and early 2000s onto streaming platforms demonstrates a continued lack of investment in Black series and audiences, replicating previous industrial waves of Black representation. I am largely interested in exploring what this sudden interest in Black nostalgia means for Black audiences. Using the video announcement from Netflix's "Strong Black Lead" Facebook page, this chapter analyzes the industrial response to the acquisition of these series and how the actors framed the series as part of what Alfred L. Martin calls "must-see blackness."[3] As described by Martin, must-see Blackness refers to the imperative that Black audiences and fans feel to support Black media in all its forms. Black fans, Martin continues, are also aware of the precariousness of Black media, which heightens the urgency in supporting it. I discuss the labor of these shows' fans—whom the "Strong Black Lead" spotlighted in its news release about the acquisition, as these fans recognize the importance of remembering these shows—and the danger of them being forgotten or not seen as valuable enough to be added to streaming platforms.

Nostalgia

The nostalgia for the 1990s is complicated. On the one hand, this nostalgia and longing are the results of anxiety and angst over the events happening since 9/11, which also include the 2008 recession.[4] The current pandemic can also be added to the list. In the cultural imagination, the 1990s were a simpler time, a more prosperous time. Media produced in the 1990s, then, are also a reflection of this imagined simpler time. But it is also important to put into context why the 1990s were a significant period in Black popular culture.

Those who consumed Black media from this era, presumably, have different reasonings for longing for what some call the "golden era of Black representation." During this time, over seventeen top series appeared with primarily Black casts. Films with Black leads were also popular, thanks to heavy-hitter directors such as Spike Lee, John Singleton, and Julie Dash. The 1990s were a time when immense Black pride was displayed in the media. Many top television series such as *Martin* (1992–1997), *Living Single*, *The Cosby Show* (1984–1992), and *A Different World* (1987–1993) featured cast members sporting African-themed clothing or paraphernalia from historically Black colleges and universities (HBCUs).

The 1990s were the place to be—at least according to the growing interest in this particular decade. Neil Ewen describes the decade's appeal:

> The decade of the 1990s is often constructed in the contemporary imagination as a peaceful fin de siècle, or an interregnum: in this case the period between the fall of the Berlin Wall in 1989 and 9/11. Frequently lauded by liberal critics as a time of hope, during which the hard edges of Reaganism and Thatcherism were softened by the rise of the Third Wave, the 1990s in this narrative is a decade that started in recession, but which grew hopefully toward the new century. As such, it signifies the point in history immediately before anxiety became the defining issue of the present era, arising from the so-called "War on Terror," the 2008 financial crisis, debt and precarity.[5]

Kristal Brent Zook further contextualized the 1990s through the lens of Blackness. Media producers of Blackness in the 1990s grappled with the very essence of Blackness. Zook states that while the 1960s and 1970s brought new economic stability for many Black people, the 1980s brought anxiety around Black identities. These questions continued into the 1990s: "Black productions of the 1990s were individual autobiographies as well as communal outpourings of group desire—collective rememberings not unlike slave narratives. During this period, black producers and consumers engaged in awkward modes of resistance and representation. It seemed that we wanted both capitalism and communalism; feminism as well as a singular, authentic self; patriarchy plus liberation; Africa the motherland *and* the American dream. These yearnings were explored, celebrated, and contested in black-produced shows of the '90s."[6] Explorations of race, Blackness, and identity were themes represented within 1990s Black television. This was also a period with an increased presence of Black actors and actresses on predominantly Black-cast series.

It is important to note that this so-called heyday or renaissance of Black television is part of a larger pattern in television. The pattern consists of industrial waves of interest in Black television series and films. The 1990s were a particularly crucial period for a couple of reasons: (1) the addition of the FOX, WB, and UPN networks broke up the domination of the original television networks, and (2) these networks took a calculated risk[7] in investing in young Black audiences that had previously been ignored.[8]

The series acquired by Netflix are just a slice of the shows available during the 1990s and early 2000s.[9] Predominantly Black casts were a normal sight throughout the week on the three start-up networks—FOX, UPN, and the WB. This period contributed to a rethinking of what Blackness meant and how it was defined and expressed. This could also explain the visceral attachment to this period for many Black folks and particularly why fans of Black culture would embrace and long for this period during a pandemic and time of racial reckoning.

Nostalgia for the "renaissance" of Black television also signals a desire for a time when explicit Black representation was plentiful. This is not to say that nostalgia for these shows and this cultural moment isn't without its problems. Although outside of the scope of this chapter, viewing the content of these series through the lens of 2022 reveals lots of cracks in the representational foundation. A simpler time for Black audiences and fans of Black-cast shows is not simple. Nonetheless, I focus on the desire to see shows from this era via streaming platforms and their "always on" content libraries.

Responsibility of Remembering

In the wake of the murders of Breonna Taylor, George Floyd, and Ahmaud Arbery in 2020, and in the middle of the pandemic, many companies began participating in what was being touted as a "racial reckoning." Streaming platforms were no exception. Companies released statements, emails, anything to make their antiracist stance known. Black Lives Matter became the refrain of the summer, despite the movement being very present for almost a decade at that point.

For their part, Netflix pulled a very surprising move. In July 2020, at the height of the racial reckoning, it announced via its "Strong Black Lead" brand that over the span of the next few months, it was bringing back multiple shows from UPN and WB. Most of these series had never been available on other streaming platforms, and some of them were not even available to purchase as boxed DVD sets like other television series. So for many of us, particularly those of us without access to cable where many of the shows' episodes were in syndication, this was the first time we were able to see these series since they stopped airing.

In the announcement of the deal, the stars of the series acknowledged that fans had been requesting Netflix to acquire the rights to these shows for years. I know because I am one of those fans. When *Living Single* came to Hulu in 2018, I was ecstatic. Finally! But there were no other big acquisitions like it. I still couldn't find many of the shows I wanted to watch. But Netflix changed this in the middle of a pandemic when everyone was forced to sit inside, growing tired of the ever-increasing new content on all the streaming platforms. Audiences would finally have the chance to rewatch (or discover) series like *One on One*, *Girlfriends*, and *Half and Half*. But why now? Although this question is diffi-cult to answer, as Netflix has not released the details of its acquisition deals, one can't help but see similarities to this courting of Black audiences with the same series that other new networks used to entice them decades prior.

Before focusing on Netflix's acquisition of several classic Black shows, I turn back to the marketing of these acquisitions. Writing for the *Washington Post*, Helena Andrews-Dyer points to the addition of *The Fresh Prince of Bel-Air* to HBO Max's (now Max) lineup. In an ad for the debut of the series on the platform, HBO Max states, "The celebrated sitcom has never been available to stream—until now."[10] One possible reason for its appearance could be the race to have exclusive rights to stream previously unavailable series. In the case of HBO Max, *The Fresh Prince of Bel-Air* could recruit old and new audiences to the platform and be lauded for "finally" bringing the series to a streaming plat-form. As the debut of *The Fresh Prince of Bel-Air*'s reunion crept closer, it helped bolster interest in both the reunion, which was new and original content for the new platform, and the old episodes of the series, which were not available on other platforms. With the continued interest in 1990s nostalgia, HBO Max debuted as a platform anchored by the promise of reunions of fan favorites such as *The Fresh Prince* but also *Friends*. Nostalgia was proving to be a profitable risk.

Fans of Blackness and Black popular culture are aware of the industrial nar-rative of Black media scarcity. And regarding nostalgia, Black fans have had the responsibility to do the remembering, to keep alive the memories of the Black beloved shows of yesteryear. Martin's concept of must-see Blackness is use-ful here. He writes, "Economic consumption drives must-see blackness in the sense that black fans are cognizant of the precariousness of blackness' existence in spaces that are either historically white and/or have been hostile to the pres-ence of blackness."[11] Fans of television shows from the Black TV renaissance are aware of the urgency of their support for these series coming to streaming plat-forms. Due to licensing and syndication rights, there could be fewer opportuni-ties to get these series onto platforms, particularly as home networks get more and more serious about holding tight to their own libraries, essentially holding some of these series hostage. Netflix's acquisition deal could lead to more series seeing the light of day. After showing little interest in syndicated Black series for years, could it be that networks are finally paying attention to the pleas of fans to make these shows available or, more likely, (re)recognizing another potentially lucrative revenue stream?

Streaming the Absent

Content is king for streaming platforms. Platforms like Netflix, which largely rely on subscriptions, need viewers to have a reason to come back day after day, week after week. In order to build and sustain audiences, a steady stream of appealing content is needed to not only bring them to the platform on a consistent basis but also keep them from canceling their subscription when a desired series ends.[12] In order for that to happen, something must attract them and be worthy enough for their subscription dollars.

Streaming platforms and legacy television are often viewed as competition, for good reason. Platforms like Netflix, Hulu, and Amazon compete not only with each other but also with other start-up platforms and legacy television networks that are trying to join the streaming competition (looking at you, Disney+). There is an ever-revolving door of original content on networks like Netflix. This original content forms a big part of the identity of these platforms and helps add to the prestige of streaming. But original content cannot solely sustain networks—not yet, at least, as these platforms are still very much in their infancy. Similar to legacy television, streaming platforms must also rely on reruns and "old" network programming to attract viewers. Anne Gilbert writes about how this important model replicates legacy television: "Subscription services build a brand on the combination of their original content, convenience and reliability of the streaming service itself, and the notion that they have a vast, 'always on' library of content to appeal to their viewers. Such [content] libraries [are comprised] largely of licensed programming that originated on legacy television; this programming has a newfound economic value and cultural role, worthwhile more for its quantity and the volume of entertainment hours offered than for specific program titles."[13] Having a steady stream of older television programs that audiences are familiar with is a crucial component of the popularity of streaming platforms. The "always on" aspect of their libraries not only aligns with the bingeing viewing practices that Netflix popularized but also puts the power in the hands of the viewers. Always on means the viewer can ideally watch whatever they want, whenever they want. Gilbert writes, "As the ultimate 'pushed' content, television reruns have persisted as a comfortable form of television that viewers watch because it is convenient and familiar and, most importantly, because it is on."[14]

This "always on" aspect of television reruns looks slightly different within online television. Legacy television has a schedule to adhere to, and reruns help serve as fillers for when original content is not airing. Although online television does not have to adhere to the same scheduling demands as legacy TV, having a rotating list of available content is key to prioritizing a variety of audiences. This also means that streaming platforms have different risks they can take when choosing which "old" television shows to add to their libraries and therefore "creat[ing] a new market for old television."[15]

Although reruns of 1990s shows can be seen on various broadcast networks, many series are also widely available on streaming platforms. For instance, up until January 2020, *Friends* (1994–2004) was available on Netflix in the United States (as of the writing of this chapter, American-based fans can now stream the show via Max).[16] This means that young audiences can discover the show even though for many, they were not born when the show was on air. Having access to older series on streaming platforms is important to help understand how young people navigated the world during a very specific time.

Friends vs. Living Single

Friends debuted in the same era and shared similarities in particular with *Living Single*. In 2020, one of the stars of *Friends*, David Schwimmer, caused controversy when discussing the possibility of a reboot. Schwimmer stated that instead of a reboot of the show, there should be an "all-Black *Friends* or an all-Asian *Friends*."[17] The comment downplayed the success of *Living Single* while also ignoring the many comparisons between the series. Cast member Queen Latifah said the following about the similarities in responding to Schwimmer's comments: "It was one of those things where there was a guy called Warren Littlefield, who used to run NBC, and they asked him, 'When all the new shows came out, if there was any show you could have, which one would it be?' And he said *Living Single*. . . . And then he created *Friends*."[18] Although there were so many similarities, *Living Single* never received the attention nor level of success of *Friends*. *Friends* went on to be available in multiple countries and streaming platforms and, subsequently, introduced to new and younger audiences long after the show went off the air. Along with a few others, *Living Single* became available on the major streaming platform Hulu in January 2018.

Series like *Friends* have remained popular mainstays on streaming platforms and become fan favorites as younger and newer audiences get introduced to the series. As mentioned prior, *Friends* also aired during the Black TV renaissance, and the main premise of the show has often been compared to *Living Single*. Yet *Friends* has also been heavily criticized for its lack of representation, specifically of Black characters, while being set in a culturally diverse New York City. Like the nostalgia for the '90s, *Friends*'s popularity seems to be the result of "a nostalgia that glosses over the racial tensions of that decade."[19] The series is said to be representative of the experiences of young people living in an urban setting, which presumably also echoes the continued popularity of modern young people experiencing similar challenges and dilemmas—mostly to the exclusion of Black and brown people.

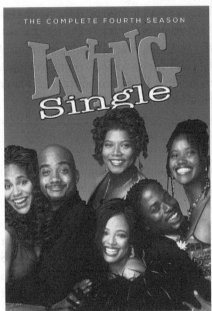

FIG. 9.2 *Living Single* and *Friends*

"For Whatever Reason . . ."

In 1996, *Living Single* creator Yvette Lee Bowser, along with some of the stars of the series, discussed her frustration with the lack of attention given to the show in comparison to its counterpart, *Friends*. Bowser noted that while *Living Single* had no merchandising opportunities, *Friends* had a plethora of them. David Janollari, executive vice president of creative affairs for Warner Bros., said the following about the disparities between the series: "'Friends,' for whatever reason, has become a national phenomenon, the likes of which we haven't seen in the last decade. Naturally, in a case like that, the merchandising soars. That comes out of the show becoming a mega-hit. It doesn't work in reverse. 'Living Single' was a very special and important show when we launched it. I wish it had become as much of a mega-hit as 'Friends.' If we felt there were merchandising opportunities, we would sure exploit them."[20]

For Bowser, however, the "whatever reason" that *Friends* became as successful as it did was not by happenstance. She stated, "It's disappointing that we have never gotten that kind of push that 'Friends' has had. I have issues with the studio and the network over the promotion of this show."[21] The lack of promotion continued past the series no longer being aired. The value was not seen in *Living Single*, and the same can be said for so many other Black television series that have finally been given the light of day on streaming platforms.

The Ringer's Victor Luckerson explored why so few Black shows from that golden era were available to stream.[22] At the time of the article (October 2016), only three of the seventeen 1990s Black-cast shows were available to stream: *A Different World* (Netflix), *In Living Color*, and *The Cosby Show* (both on Hulu). Since the publication of that article, more series have been added, but a large number of them are still not available on streaming platforms.

Netflix to the Rescue?

On July 29, 2020, Netflix announced its acquisition of the rights to seven "classic" Black series. The news was released via Netflix's "Strong Black Lead" brand, which focuses on Black content through various mediums such as podcasts, original content, and social media. The news was accompanied by a video featuring some of the stars of these series, thanking the fans and sharing their excitement of having their shows on Netflix. "Strong Black Lead" is credited with strengthening the perception of the Netflix brand as one that believes in highlighting Black content. According to a letter to its stakeholders, Netflix intended to spend $17 billion on content in 2021. (In 2020, it spent $11.8 billion, as the pandemic halted production on many shows, but went on to spend another $17 billion in 2022.) Although the acquisition deals were not made public, it is presumed that this more expansive budget helped with acquiring these important shows (and in turn, reaching new audiences and maintaining current subscribers with this "new" but old content). Netflix can thus be celebrated for an increase in Black representation and continued courting of Black audiences along with the ever-present "Strong Black Lead" brand and its "Representation Matters" collection, which also debuted in 2020.[23]

In the video announcement, actors like Tia Mowry, Wendy Racquel Robinson, and Tim Reid discuss their series, recounting memorable moments and catchphrases from their respective shows while also emphasizing the role fans played in helping to bring these shows back. Different stars are shown saying the following statement: "A little birdie over at Strong Black Lead told me that you guys have literally been asking for these shows for like years, and years, and years."[24] According to the announcement, fans' labor, which aligns with Martin's must-see Blackness, was an essential part of this deal. Yet again, Black audiences had to prove that they were worth being courted. Due to the limited availability, being a fan of these shows meant putting in the work to remind networks of their relevance.

The video announcement also positioned Netflix as a platform interested in taking a chance on these series. Of course, the actors do not say this acquisition could have happened years prior. They fail to mention the racial reckoning happening during this particular cultural moment. Mara Brock Akil, a Black TV powerhouse and creator of *Girlfriends* and *The Game*, hints at it when she says that she could "use a laugh right about now." In this instance, she harkens instead back to the nostalgic desire of "simpler times" or of using the reruns and "return" back to these shows as a distraction from the raging global pandemics.

In a combined statement from the announcement, the various actors of the series say, "It's going to give an opportunity for a whole new generation of folks that's gonna be watching on Netflix."[25] Audiences who hadn't seen these shows now have the chance to experience a portion of the Black '90s TV renaissance, which of course takes on a different representational meaning as we exist in an industrial wave of interest in diversity and representation. While a plethora of content with diverse representations exists, the actors caution that there is still work to be done: "These shows changed the face of television as we know it. And it helps for Black creators, both in front and behind the camera."[26] However, the actors don't explicitly state how this will help Black creatives. The relevance of these shows when they originally aired and the urgency of supporting them as they come to streaming platforms, specifically Netflix, are understood as Black creatives speak to Black audiences and those interested in Black popular culture. At the end of the video, a tearful Wendy Raquel Robinson (who, in addition to starring on *The Game*, also starred on *The Steve Harvey Show*, which at the time of this writing, is available to stream on Tubi and Pluto TV) says, "And thank you 'Strong Black Lead' for giving new life and new reimagination to shows like this."

Conclusion

As an avid fan of Black TV, I am beyond thrilled to have the opportunity to watch so many of my favorite shows again. At the beginning of the pandemic, before I fully understood the magnitude of what was to come, I looked forward to finally having time to watch all the shows that had been on my list to watch eventually. But as the months dragged on, I became less and less interested in the overwhelming amount of content available on the many streaming services. I was overwhelmed, stressed out with life, and not interested in beginning new series.

A comfort level exists in watching familiar content but particularly during a pandemic. A return to a "simpler time" also meant pre-COVID and a great escape where I could pretend like I wasn't existing in multiple pandemics. Like Mara Brock Akil, I could also use a laugh, and the classics made available on Netflix provided the perfect vehicle and nostalgia. Netflix's growing content budget could indeed be a sign that acquisitions like this are on the horizon. It could also spur heightened interest in other series from the '90s TV renaissance. Beyond Netflix, Amazon, Hulu, and Max all seem to be interested in this nostalgic turn as well.[27] For example, in March 2021, Amazon premiered the much-anticipated follow-up to Eddie Murphy's film *Coming to America*—its sequel, *Coming 2 America*.

Popular, mainstream television series are viable options for streaming platforms but will presumably become more and more difficult to obtain as legacy networks seek to build their own streaming platforms and hold tighter to their own libraries. We can see this in the removal of the smash-hit *The Office* from Netflix in 2020, when it was placed on parent company NBC's streaming service Peacock. Nonetheless, more series being made available on streaming platforms opens up the cultural archive and imaginary to include those who were there all along. Fans of Black TV will not let these shows be forgotten. In the Netflix video announcement, the stars vehemently acknowledge the labor of their fans: "So thanks to everyone who has ever made a social media post or left a message asking about these shows. It didn't go unnoticed. You did it!"[28] Even as fans celebrated these series, social media users commented asking about other shows from that '90s heyday, such as the ever-popular *Martin*, which is available on Amazon Prime via subscription to BET's streaming service, BET+. Only time will tell which series get added to other platforms and how long these shows remain on those platforms. In the meantime, I enjoy expanding my young son's cultural imagination and understanding of Black popular culture through these newly available series. In a '90s kind of world, I'm glad I got my shows!

Notes

1 Kristal Brent Zook, *Color by FOX: The FOX Network and the Revolution in Black Television* (New York: Oxford University Press, 1999).
2 Brent Zook, 3.
3 Alfred L. Martin Jr., "Fandom While Black: Misty Copeland, *Black Panther*, Tyler Perry and the Contours of US Black Fandoms," *International Journal of Cultural Studies* 22, no. 6 (2019): 737–753.
4 Neil Ewen, "'Talk to Each Other like It's 1995': Mapping Nostalgia for the 1990s in Contemporary Media Culture," *Television & New Media* 21, no. 6 (2020): 574–589.
5 Ewen, 576.
6 Brent Zook, *Color by FOX*, 3.
7 Jennifer Fuller, "Branding Blackness On US Cable Television," *Media, Culture & Society* 32, no. 2 (2010): 285–305.
8 Herman Gray, *Cultural Moves African Americans and the Politics of Representation* (Berkeley: University of California Press, 2005).
9 Netflix acquired the series *Moesha* (1996–2001); *The Game* (2006–2009), the first three seasons (which aired on The CW, the network that was created after the merger of The WB and UPN); *Sister, Sister* (1994–1999); *Girlfriends* (2000–2008); *The Parkers* (1999–2004); *Half and Half* (2002–2006); and *One on One* (2001–2006).
10 Helena Andrews-Dyer, "Classic Black Sitcoms like 'Fresh Prince of Bel-Air' and 'Living Single' Are Finally Streaming. Why Did It Take So Long?" *Washington Post*, 2020, https://www.washingtonpost.com/arts-entertainment/2020/07/09/black-sitcoms-streaming/.
11 Martin, "Fandom While Black," 737–753.
12 Anne Gilbert, "Push, Pull, Rerun: Television Reruns and Streaming Media," *Television & New Media* 20, no. 7 (2019): 687–701.
13 Gilbert, 687.
14 Gilbert, 689.
15 Gilbert, 691.

16 Shelley Cobb, Neil Ewen, and Hannah Hamad, "*Friends* Reconsidered: Cultural Politics, Intergenerationality, and Afterlives," *Television & New Media* 19, no. 8 (2018): 683–691.

17 Christopher Rosen, "David Schwimmer Meant 'No Disrespect' to *Living Single* over *Friends* Diversity Comment," *Vanity Fair*, 2020, https://www.vanityfair.com/hollywood/2020/02/david-schwimmer-living-single-friends-erika-alexander.

18 The series creators for *Friends* deny the theft, the similarities, and even knowledge of *Living Single* before creating *Friends*. See *History of the Sitcom*, episode 5, "Facing Race," directed by Marshall Jay Kaplan, written by Robert Eaton, aired August 1, 2021, on CNN.

19 Cobb, Ewen, and Hamad, "*Friends* Reconsidered," 688.

20 Greg Braxton, "'Single' Looks for a Little Help against 'Friends,'" *Los Angeles Times*, February 1, 1996, https://www.latimes.com/archives/la-xpm-1996-02-01-ca-30941-story.html.

21 Braxton.

22 Victor Luckerson, "Why Isn't 'The Fresh Prince of Bel Air' on Netflix?," *Ringer*, October 19, 2016, https://www.theringer.com/2016/10/19/16038496/classic-black-shows-not-on-netflix-fresh-prince-of-bel-air-a081092b31b5#.7iws5xpjx. In the article, Luckerson focused on *The Fresh Prince of Bel-Air*, which was not available to stream on any platform in America (although it was available internationally). In 2020, new platform HBO Max (now Max) added the show to its library in addition to producing a reunion of the cast.

23 These numbers do not transfer to Netflix's workforce, however, as only 7 percent of its employees are Black.

24 Strong Black Lead, "Your UPN faves are coming to Netflix!," Facebook, July 29, 2020, https://www.facebook.com/NetflixStrongBlackLead/videos/1225252637825715.

25 Strong Black Lead.

26 Strong Black Lead.

27 As of the writing of this chapter, these networks have added several of these '90s shows to their platform such as *The Jamie Foxx Show* and *Family Matters*.

28 Strong Black Lead.

10

Tyler Perry's Too Close to Home

• •

Black Audiences in the Post-Network Era

SHELLEEN GREENE

In this chapter, I examine Tyler Perry's partnership with TLC (The Learning Channel), which produced the short-lived *Tyler Perry's Too Close to Home* (2016–2017, henceforth *Too Close to Home*), the first scripted program for the network. Canceled after two seasons, *Too Close to Home* may be considered a failed Perry venture, but the series' production and media coverage allows for an examination of the circulation of the Perry brand in the post-network environment. Unlike the majority of his productions, *Too Close to Home* was the first Perry series to have a white-led cast. This decision on Perry's part may have been motivated by a desire to expand the scope of his productions, which have traditionally focused on Black-centered narratives. However, *Too Close to Home* can also be read as an attempt to capture new niche audiences in the post-network era, one characterized by the convergence of traditional and social media.

In "To Brand and Rebrand: Questioning the Futurity of Tyler Perry," Leah Aldridge asks, "What are some of the future potentialities and possibilities of Perry's media and branding machine? In this neoliberal moment, what is the market logic of Perry's celebrity and how does race as commodity complicate that logic?"[1] I contend that *Too Close to Home* is an extension of Perry's role as a "central, albeit controversial, figure in the visibility, circulation, and exhibition of Black media in American public and popular culture."[2] It can be read as Perry's attempts to both develop new television production models and diversify his own brand with multiracial-cast programming that appeals to multiple niche audiences. While recent edited volumes have examined Perry's history from theatrical productions to his multimedia empire, his representation of African American communities, and in particular, his representation of African American women, Perry's television oeuvre remains understudied in terms of its aesthetics and innovative production model.[3] As Beretta Smith-Shomade states, "While many may disagree with and/or dislike the stories he tells, he's one of the very few Black producers/writers who is getting to tell [Black stories] at this televisual moment," and further, Perry's work allows us to "paint a fuller picture of what Blackness can mean (will mean) in our future mediated landscape."[4]

Since producing his first television series, Perry has negotiated several lucrative network agreements, including his breakthrough deal with TBS (Turner Broadcasting System / Time Warner, Inc.), his 2012 exclusive partnership with OWN (Oprah Winfrey Network), and his 2017 agreement to produce original programming for Viacom networks, including BET. Perry's expansion into television was made possible through the strength of his brand name, garnered from his theatrical and film productions, with his films alone generating over one billion dollars in profits both domestically and abroad. Beginning with his work as a playwright, director, and producer on the urban theatrical circuit, Perry's productions have centered African American communities and cultivated Black audiences who have followed him to film, television, and other media platforms. As Samantha Sheppard argues, "Perry's strategic media convergence relies on the migratory behavior of his loyal audience who seek out his work in a variety of spaces, across mediums, and on different platforms, including on stage, screen, television, and in the bookstore."[5] The success of Perry's agreements has depended on his audiences "traveling" to new networks with the expectation of seeing the Perry brand.

While arguably, like other Perry productions, *Too Close to Home* may be criticized for its "weak plots, reductive characters, and questionable politics,"[6] this chapter seeks to examine the dialogues that emerged between Perry and his Black audiences during the run of the program. I suggest Perry navigates this complex terrain by making universalist claims for the appeal of *Too Close to Home* while working within a convergence model to draw varied audiences from traditional and social media. *Too Close to Home* also features African American characters who acknowledge and speak to the various socioeconomic class dynamics of Black audiences, allowing for moments of identification within the program's diegesis. The series also cultivates dynamic and prolific Black audiences that motivated a debate around the program. Through their presence at cast Q&As and on social media platforms such as YouTube, Black audiences elaborated a dialogue regarding Perry's casting for the program, demonstrating how they navigate the post-network era via modes of active reception (both material and virtual). Ultimately, *Too Close to Home* demonstrates Black audiences' use of social media to elaborate their position vis-à-vis Perry's brand and representational politics.

Tyler Perry and the Post-Network Era

Since 2006, Tyler Perry has produced, written, and directed over fifteen television programs for OWN, BET, TBS, and TLC. While some of his scripted television programs, such as *Tyler Perry's House of Payne* (TBS, 2007–2012; BET, 2020–), *Meet the Browns* (TBS, 2009–2012), and *The Paynes* (OWN, 2018), expand on Perry's existing stage and film franchises, his other programs vary from prime-time soap operas—such as *The Haves and the Have Nots* (OWN, 2013–2021), *If Loving You Is Wrong* (Oprah Winfrey Network/OWN, 2014–2020), and *The Oval* (BET, 2019–)—to sitcoms like *Tyler Perry's Assisted Living* (BET, 2020–). Perry's television programs expand his existing media empire, now centered around the Tyler Perry Studios in Atlanta, Georgia. These programs carry with them the controversies and criticisms leveled against Perry's cultural productions, which build upon racial stereotypes, circulate conservative Christian beliefs, and "thematically pair representations of Black identity with tales of betrayal, morality, incest, domestic violence, and trauma."[7] While Perry has come under considerable criticism for his theater, film, and television productions, he has become a formidable global media producer, ranking among the highest-paid professionals in the Hollywood industry.

Perry achieved his initial success through theatrical productions beginning with *I Know I've Been Changed* (1998), a play based on his childhood experiences of abuse and economic precarity. In 2000, Perry's *I Can Do Bad All by Myself* debuted his signature Mabel "Madea" Simmons character, his rebellious, transgressive matriarch. Due to Madea's overwhelming popularity, Perry wrote the character into his next play, *Diary of a Mad Black Woman* (2001). As Artel Great argues, Madea's success can be attributed to Perry's connection to historic African American theater: "Perry's urban-themed Christian tinged plays are situated within a Black theatrical tradition that traces its roots back to the works of the 'Chitlin Circuit' and the Theater Owners Booking Association (TOBA) in the early twentieth century."[8] With the profits from his theatrical productions and their DVD sales, Perry produced his first film, the adaptation of *Diary of a Mad Black Woman* (Lionsgate, 2005). It grossed over $50 million domestically.[9]

After subsequent Hollywood successes, Perry began his foray into television with the sitcom *Tyler Perry's House of Payne* (TBS, 2007–2012; BET, 2020–). Now standing as the longest running Black-led sitcom, *Tyler Perry's House of Payne* was the product of Perry's deal with TBS in which the network purchased one hundred episodes for $200 million, making it "the first of its kind and the

FIG. 10.1 *Tyler Perry's House of Payne* cast

largest such agreement in cable television history."[10] In 2012, Perry established an arrangement with OWN in which his studios would provide original scripted programs such as *The Haves and the Have Nots*, *If Loving You Is Wrong*, and *Love Thy Neighbor* (2013–2017). In 2017, Perry entered another major agreement with Viacom to create original scripted programs for its networks that will run through 2024.[11] In the case of his deal with OWN, Perry joined with another Black media mogul, Oprah Winfrey, to enhance his production profile and "brand." At the time, OWN was known primarily for reality television and "women-centered" programming, including *Iyanla, Fix My Life* (2012–2021) and *Welcome to Sweetie Pie's* (2011–2018). As Sheppard has argued, by leveraging his success in theater and film, Perry, with the addition of his television ventures, "operates not only across multiple media platforms (e.g., theatre, film and television) but also functions as a media platform (i.e., operates as cultural and industrial leverage for others via partnerships and co-productions)."[12]

Perry's function as a "media platform" can be seen in his partnership with OWN, which experienced significant ratings increases after the introduction of Perry's scripted programs. Perry's agreement with TLC replicates the OWN deal in its introduction of scripted programming to a reality-TV-centered network. However, while the OWN scripted programs created ratings success, primarily by drawing Black audiences to the network, *Too Close to Home* failed to produce a similar impact. The cancellation was attributed to, among other reasons, the program being "out of place between episodes of [TLC's] reality-based lineup" and the overall weakness of the program.[13] However, as stated previously, *Too Close to Home* provides insights into Perry's brand as it circulates within the post-network era.

Perry's move into television takes place during the transition to the post-network era. Beginning in the 1980s, the multichannel period was characterized by greater programming options beyond the three formerly dominant networks (ABC, NBC, CBS). Due to the development of new networks, cable outlets, niche programming, and new screen and storage technologies, the "nonlinear" post-network era becomes characterized by television networks' new approaches to their audiences. Amanda Lotz writes, "The increased fractionalization of the audience among shows, channels, and distribution devices has diminished the ability of an individual television network or television show to reinforce a certain set of beliefs to a broad audience in the manner we long believed to occur. Although television can still function as a mass medium, in most cases it does so by aggregating a collection of niche audiences."[14] Even in the era of post-network narrowcasting, Black audiences operate within an environment with greater viewing options and opportunities for media creation and active reception as bloggers and YouTubers, on Twitter and various other social media.

The 2018 Nielsen Company's Diverse Intelligence Series report, "From Consumers to Creators: The Digital Lives of Black Consumers," suggests Black audiences have been active producers within the post-network era through "their adoption of social media and technology platforms."[15] Scholars Jacqueline Stewart, Anna Everett, and Robin Means Coleman argue that Black audiences have always used media to respond to and critique their representations in U.S. film and television, and these reception practices extend into the digital era.[16] Herman Gray furthers, "The activities and meanings produced by Black audiences are also structured by the social location of audiences within a historical field and by the organizational structures and industrial imperatives of global technologies that are changing the signifying practices of media. . . . The way in which these synergistic innovations structure and signify cultural meanings bear increasingly on what we can say about how meanings are made and where."[17] In the case of *Too Close to Home*, produced by a prominent media mogul who has traditionally produced work targeted to Black audiences, Black YouTubers and anonymous participants in live Q&As demonstrate Black audiences' use of traditional and social media to comment on this particular expansion of the Perry brand. In reading the YouTube reviews and Q&As in relation to the program, varied responses indicate that while Perry's Black audiences "follow" his brand in terms of narrative, they also question his casting decisions.

Tyler Perry's *Too Close to Home*

Too Close to Home was one of the first scripted programs to be filmed in Perry's three-hundred-acre studios in Atlanta. Like many of his programs, *Too Close to Home* was shot on a compressed schedule. Whereas most television program seasons are filmed over a two- to three-month period, Perry shot one season of *Too Close to Home* in approximately ten days.[18] This accelerated production schedule places different pressures on actors and crew, for instance, with actors learning lines within very short time frames. Courtney Burrell, an actor who portrays the character Nelson in the second season, notes that Perry hires "actors and actresses who pick up on the craft really fast and who are ready and prepared" to learn lines quickly for the episodes.[19]

Too Close to Home was described as "new programming fare" for the TLC network.[20] In the press and promotional events, Perry speaks of his production model as a corrective to the inefficient system of television and film production. In an August 16, 2016, premiere Q&A, one actor commented, "There's no wasted time on a Tyler Perry set. . . . I just kept saying 'Jesus take the wheel!'" while another stated, "You watch how fast he shot it and you see the production value . . . you know, it's kind of a wake-up call, and I think a lot of the networks are going to have a wake-up call." In the same Q&A, Perry states,

> I didn't learn here. I didn't come in through this door. I didn't come up in this system. So, when I came, everything seemed wrong. I was on this one movie and we shot twelve hours while they were shooting these fight scenes, and I was just completely shocked at the amount of wasted time and I found it so egregious. So, what I've learned to do, because I was broke, and I had to do everything myself, I had to learn how to do everything myself. As I'm shooting, I'm editing all the time. I know when the cuts are coming.[21]

Perry also promotes a "family" oriented work environment on set. As Burrell states, "[Perry] goes in there and starts the day off praying. We all hold hands, the production team, the actors and actresses. And Tyler leads the prayer in a big circle around the set. It becomes like a family vibe. He makes me feel like I'm not alone."[22] While the cast members speak of the family environment cultivated on Perry's sets, the accelerated schedule (including the writing of scripts) may have compromised the quality, if not the production value, of the program's narrative, leading to some expressions of confusion and boredom from reviewers. However, Perry's production model merges a Christian belief system with capitalism alongside democratic ideals of rugged individualism, efficiency, productivity, innovation, and frugality.

This invocation of capitalist democracy, what Jodi Melamed has called neoliberal multiculturalism, also entails a mode of racial equivalency in which economic inequality is separated from institutional and systemic racism.[23] This false

FIG. 10.2 *Tyler Perry's Too Close to Home* cast

equivalency becomes apparent in one interview with lead actor Danielle Savre. An African American woman audience member asks Savre, "Were you familiar with Tyler Perry's work before you started *Too Close to Home*?" to which Savre responds, "No, I'm sorry." The audience member continues, "And if you were, did your imagination of what it would mean to be part of a Tyler Perry production . . . is it what you thought it would be?"[24] Savre's response, rather than discussing the question of race to which the question alludes, speaks of the program's production model, costume, and makeup and of her admiration for what Perry "had done in the industry." Race is both invoked and denied through an emphasis on industrial success by way of Perry's innovation, a gesture that is prevalent in the promotional materials for *Too Close to Home*.

Producing *Too Close to Home*

The series concerns Annie Belle (Anna) Hayes (Danielle Savre), a young white woman from a working-class background who, after achieving economic and social upward mobility through a position in the White House, is forced to move back to her hometown of Happy, Alabama, after a scandal caused by her affair with the president. Despite relatively stable ratings, TLC canceled the series, comprised of sixteen episodes, after its second season.[25] While the program's racy affair between a White House aide and the U.S. president drew comparisons to the Clinton-Lewinsky affair, Perry states that the political scandal was not the immediate inspiration for the series. However, the presidential primary and the eventual Trump–Hillary Clinton presidential race, as well as other political scandals, were in mind when the series was in development.[26]

As the first scripted series for TLC, *Too Close to Home* builds on the existing programming of the network, one dominated by reality television, including popular programs such as *Here Comes Honey Boo Boo* (2012–2014), *Hoarding: Buried Alive* (2010–2014), and *My 600-Pound Life* (2012–). Indeed, in its narrative, *Too Close to Home* draws on these series, appealing to the network's existing audience base. Perry states that in the development phase of the series, he suggested to TLC and its owner, the Discovery network, that *Too Close to Home* should be comprised of TLC's "[many] reality shows" and continued, "[I said let's] pull the bits and pieces out of all the shows you have on TLC and see what happens. . . . So it was designed for this particular audience of TLC."[27] Since its rebranding in 2006, TLC's largest audience has been women in the twenty-five to fifty-four age bracket.[28] In the case of the TLC agreement and the resulting series, the Perry and TLC "brands" merged to create a program that would appeal to its primary audiences but also draw Perry's base. TLC includes a slate of programs that offers diverse casting, including *90-Day Fiancé* (2014–), *Doubling Down with the Derricos* (2020–), and *Sister Wives* (2010–). Distributed through Discovery Networks International, TLC also broadcasts throughout African, Latin American, Asian, and European markets.[29] *Too Close to Home* offered Perry an opportunity to distribute his brand across TLC's domestic and global markets.

However, *Too Close to Home* features a white-led cast, a departure from Perry's productions. As would be expected given his other ventures with OWN and Viacom, TLC may have wanted Perry's brand to bring a larger Black audience to their network. However, *Too Close to Home* was almost immediately received with criticism for its white casting, to which Perry responded that it was a form of "reverse racism."[30] In terms of his decision, Perry mentioned his own experience of living in a trailer park with relatives and also stated, "We all got the same dramas, so I'm not seeing color as much as I did anymore in the sense of our stories. Our stories are so similar."[31] The responses to *Too Close to Home* can be seen in the paratexts of the program where the racial politics unfold.

Black Audience Responses to *Too Close to Home*

In an Essence Live feature entitled "Is Tyler Perry's All White Cast 'Slayed' or 'Shade,'" commenters were asked to respond to Perry's interview on *The Tom Joyner Morning Show* where he defended his casting for *Too Close to Home*. Perry invoked Norman Lear's production of Black-cast sitcoms such as *Good Times* (CBS, 1974–1979) and *The Jeffersons* (CBS, 1975–1985) and reiterated his statement that "people are people."[32] The first reviewer, Charles McBee, "slayed" Perry because of what he believed was Perry's circulation of negative stereotypes in his work but ultimately ended with "Let him set white people back a couple of years. We need a break from the Madeas and the Browns. . . . Go ahead Tyler Perry, do your thing." Christina Coleman, who offered an ambivalent response stated, "As a Black creator you should be giving these opportunities to Black people, but also, let the man do what he got to do, he got to make his money. I mean white people write stories about Black people. . . . Like he said, people are people. I also agree. But I was also like but you have a responsibility, you also got to give your brother a job." Sevyn Streeter summarized the responses by saying,

> I feel like as a creative being, he wants to spread his wings a little bit. He's done a lot of movies that have predominately Black casts whether people feel like they . . . you know, they represent us in the right way, if we are just talking about in terms of whether his casts are predominately white or predominately Black, I gave him slayed because he's done a lot of them, the majority of them, truth be told, that have predominately Black casts and he just wants to show his diversity. Do I think he could do more movies with Black casts that show . . . represent us in a better light? You know, I think he could do that a little better. . . . I think we'll see that from him in the future. But I think that it's ok for this one movie [sic] of all the movies he's done, he has a cast that is predominately white. He's been around for a minute, let's see what he does next.[33]

The segment next goes to producer Kayla Rodriguez, who reads the live feed responses. Rodriguez reports that user "Jasmine Johnson" wrote, "People are people, but he was checking for those Black audiences when he was making his 'come up,' so please." User "Armilla Jackson" wrote, "Tyler Perry has been a lot for people, and a lot for the Black community. Let him make his money!" The responses on #ESSENCELive suggest an ambivalent reception to *Too Close to Home*, one that acknowledges Perry as a "creative being" who should be able to produce a white-led cast program, but also one attentive to the need for more diversified Black representations beyond "the Madeas and the Browns" as well as the economic dynamics of the media industry. Ultimately, they support Perry "making that money." In the feed, Black representation on film and television is negotiated by participation within a market economy and an awareness of representational politics.

The question of casting also arises in a *Too Close to Home* premiere Q&A with Perry and the cast members. Perry appears on stage flanked by the program's white cast members. An African American audience member begins his question by stating that the program is a "departure from what we normally see from Tyler Perry, especially when it comes to the cast."[34] Perry at first responds humorously: "Working with white people is hard!"[35] However, Perry both answers and does not answer the question. He continues,

> Seriously, there is no difference. . . . People are people [and] what was going on for me is that I had these ideas in my head and usually when I sit down and start to write, I don't necessarily see color, size, race [or] anything like that when I'm starting to write a story . . . unless it's Madea. . . . I know that she's Black. But when

I started this show, I just started writing and as I was writing and seeing these characters and hearing from them, when I started to cast it, I started to see the people that you see up here, and they are doing a phenomenal job on the show, and I'm pretty excited about it.[36]

An African American woman audience member pushes at the equivalency that Perry suggests in his statement: "[Can we say] 'poor white trash' is kind of like saying 'Black trash'? . . . You know what I'm trying to say, like ghetto is ghetto."[37] Perry responds with a broad statement: "There is no difference in all of us, we all share the same ability to have the same amount of pain, the same amount of love, the same amount of forgiveness, so it's just another side of a story that I wanted to tell."[38] The audience member adds, "It's about the money . . . the economics."[39] Once again, the audience member's hesitant questioning of the racial dynamics of the casting resulted in a color-blind response that emphasized class rather than race dynamics, as though they were exclusive. For Perry, *Too Close to Home* is about "family, faith, and forgiveness," themes that can also be found in his Black-led films and television series. Perry's responses in a *Good Morning America* (*GMA*) interview and Q&A indicate a tension between Perry's universalist claims and his traditional association with Black American communities. What the Q&As and online commentaries reveal is that Black audiences navigate pleasure and enjoyment of the Perry brand through an intersectional approach that negotiates *Too Close to Home*'s representation of race, class, gender, and sexuality.

Perry's Self-Positioning in the Post-Network Era

This ambivalent Black audience response extends to the promotional media for *Too Close to Home*. In the previously-referenced *Good Morning America* interview held in his home, Perry speaks about the series with movie posters of iconic African American performers, including Bessie Smith and Cab Calloway, surrounding him.[40] As Sheppard argues, "An innovator in Black cultural production, Perry works in the vernacular tradition of other Black pioneers, including actor and director Spencer Williams," and further, "By aligning himself with such figures, he places himself as an integral next step in the teleological history of black production and representation in American cinema, declaring that he belongs in the cultural conversation with the aforementioned figures."[41]

However, after a brief montage featuring his Madea character and his various television programs, Perry appears seated with the two program stars, Kelly Sullivan and Brock O'Hurn. As the two romantic leads, the *GMA* segment builds on their previous celebrity status, Sullivan's work in soap operas, including *General Hospital* and *The Young and the Restless*, and O'Hurn's social media presence as the "man bun" guy.[42] The interview provides a preview of Perry's next Madea release, *Boo! A Madea Halloween*, then turns to Perry's recent fatherhood.

While the program's predominately white cast is not discussed, Perry is contextualized by his primarily African American productions and featured as a multimedia mogul and parent. The narrative provided by the interview is one of hard work, upward mobility, and of the auteur who can create various stories, even ones without majority Black casts. In some ways, the interview suggests a rebranding not only of TLC but also of Perry, now branching out from his primarily Black-cast-driven narratives. In seeking new markets, as Aldridge argues, Perry's productions must necessarily move away from his "niche" demographic to "broader market saturation."[43] The *GMA* interview puts forth both a representation of Perry as African American auteur and a multimedia mogul seeking audiences from daytime soap operas, reality television, and social media. Simultaneously, Perry once again points to Norman Lear—the Jewish television writer responsible for *All in the Family*, the legendary program about a bigoted white man who is confronted with the liberal politics of the early 1970s—as well as predominately Black-cast programs such as *Good Times*, *Sanford and Son* (NBC, 1972–1977), and *The Jeffersons*. In this way, Perry both places himself within a television lineage, one in which television programming becomes a means of debating current racial politics, and defends his decision to lead a predominately white cast production.

Suturing Black Audience

Perry's intersectional negotiation can be found in the program's placement of key secondary African American characters within the predominately white working-class community at the center of the drama. While several Tyler Perry television programs feature multiracial casting, including *The Oval* and *The Haves and the Have Nots*, African American actors serve as leads in these series, while white actors are often supporting characters. In *Too Close to Home*, the Black characters may be read as placed within the narrative world to serve as points of identification for Black audiences. Certainly, this may have been the case in the second season, in which, as a response to the widespread criticism the program received for its casting, the number of African American characters with storylines increased significantly. However, as indicated by YouTube reviewer responses, this identification was negotiated along the lines of race, gender, and socioeconomic class. In an examination of two African American characters from the program, Valerie and Frankie, I suggest that *Too Close to Home* attempted a multivalent approach to drawing niche Black audiences, appealing not only to Perry's African American viewers but also to Black viewers familiar with the self-improvement narratives circulated on TLC's reality programs. The merging of the TLC and Perry brands allows for a particular reading of the secondary African American characters that demonstrates the complexity of Black audiences' identification and responses.

In the first season, Valerie (Ashley Love-Mills), one of Anna's close group of D.C. friends, is the only African American featured character. Out of the group of friends, Valerie is also the one who is most critical of Anna's conduct, fearing its impact on her and their cohort's careers. In an early episode, Valerie and another friend, Dax (Nick Ballard), visit the trailer home of Anna's obese mother, Jolene (Trisha Rae Stahl). They are looking for Victor (Charles Justo), Dax's boyfriend, who after driving Anna back to Alabama becomes the victim of a hate crime. Upon their arrival in Happy, we view Dax and Valerie walking across the grounds of the trailer park. While Dax remains somewhat neutral to the surroundings, it is Valerie who becomes the focus of affective response to Jolene's living conditions. She comments, "What in the hell? Who lives like this?" After a tense encounter in which Jolene announces to Dax that she doesn't "speak to his type," Dax and Valerie leave the trailer with Valerie heaving due to the stench. The scene plays out a stereotypical "poor white trash" attitude toward race and sexuality and stages an encounter between progressive politics and the regressive attitudes of the town locals. However, drawing upon TLC's reality programming, which spectacularizes chronic health issues such as obesity, the program's representation of Jolene resonates with TLC's programs such as *My 600-Pound Life* and *Obesity Med*. Valerie's affective response can be positioned in relation to that of a reality program viewer, who as an outsider, observes Jolene's condition.

As the only African American character, Valerie stands "outside" in terms of race, gender, and class, and her positioning within the narrative allows her to articulate observations and judgments that may resonate with both Perry's and TLC's Black audiences. However, Valerie is not written as a sympathetic character. She is ambitious, at one point vying to become the president's mistress, and is particularly judgmental. In some ways, Valerie conforms to the stereotypical representation of Black female antagonists in Perry's productions. For instance, YouTube reviewers Ashley Miller and Random TV Reviewers (Stanley and Lynette) found Valerie's initial lack of support and disregard for Anna's feelings unbecoming. Valerie received similar criticism in the later episode depicting the visit to the trailer park. Random TV Reviewers stated of the scene: "Now Val is pissing me off. . . . Now I understand if you're all upset your friend put you in the middle of some bullskit [*sic*], which she did, but why are you at this level of disrespect?" While critical of the behavior of the white residents of the town, the reviewers perceived Valerie as an elitist outsider who did not respect the rules of the culture she entered.

In the second season, several African American characters are introduced into the narrative. Octavia Robertson (Angela Marie Rigsby) is a resident of the trailer park community who lives with her sister-in-law, Regina (Azur-De Johnson), who's having an affair with another African American resident, Elm (Nelson Estevez). Additional African American characters include Tina (K. D. Aubert), Elm's wife, and Nelson (Courtney Burrell), Octavia's brother, who returns to Happy after his military service. We also meet Frankie (Crystle Stewart), a therapist who is working with obese hoarder Jolene and who is central to helping Jolene emerge from her trailer. Unlike Valerie, the second-season African American characters are decidedly working-class and are placed as members of the trailer park community, living and working alongside their white counterparts. These characters partially stem from Perry's personal history of having lived in a trailer park and as a response to criticism of the program's casting.

Frankie is introduced as a therapist who resides in the trailer park. After the town sheriff notices the extent of Jolene's hoarding and brings together park residents to help clean her home, he asks Frankie to work with Jolene to help her emerge from her trailer. Incorporating the spectacle of self-improvement reality television, Frankie's role is to introduce the therapeutic solution—working through the feelings of anger, resentment, and shame that are fueling Jolene's obesity and hoarding. As introduced within the series, Jolene is an unsympathetic character who we learn prostituted her children to acquire money for drugs. However, the program's conclusion is consistent with the intervention narratives found on TLC's reality programs, and Frankie's character is integral to this process. The reworking of domestic trauma and the therapeutic solution are also familiar tropes in Perry's oeuvre and are familiar to his Black audiences who encounter such stories in Perry's theater, film, and televisual works. In this sense, Perry brings together "the fictional, the autobiographical, and media appropriation in order to convey difficult, traumatic emotions and affects."[44] Frankie's character brings together the shared characteristics of both the TLC and Perry brands in order to appeal to niche Black audiences. Ultimately, the characters of Valerie and Frankie reveal a complex, multivalent identification on the part of Black audiences, not only one that speaks to the tensions between the new South of the twenty-first century but also one in which progressive politics intersect with the legacies of the Jim Crow South and the challenges of appealing to niche Black audiences in the post-network era.

Conclusion

The narratives and controversies surrounding *Tyler Perry's Too Close to Home* demonstrate the complex and nuanced ways in which Black audiences interact with the Tyler Perry brand in the post-network era. *Too Close to Home* stands as a particular experiment that demonstrates how Black audiences deploy social media as a form of active response and participation within a globalized media industry that produces and circulates representations of African American communities. In the case of Tyler Perry, Black audiences' expectations of his brand and its focus on Black-centered narratives motivated a debate concerning racial representation in the media industry and a questioning of Perry's turn to colorblind discourse as a means of reaching multiple niche audiences, a discourse embedded within his production model.

I suggest that the varied responses to *Too Close to Home* stem from the new models of production, distribution, and exhibition heralded by the post-network era. In his expansion into new niche markets, Perry created a program that attempted to speak to multiple demographics. Black audiences of *Too Close to Home* attempt to navigate Perry's universalist claims and the intersectionalities of race, gender, sexuality, and class presented in this text. Yet since the cancellation of *Too Close to Home*, TLC has not produced another scripted drama series for the network, focusing on its hybrid reality/scripted programs. And since *Too Close to Home*, Perry has produced predominately Black-led cast programs, including *Sistas* (BET, 2019–), *The Oval* (BET, 2019–), *Bruh* (BET+, 2020–), and *All the Queen's Men* (BET+, 2021–). Given Perry's breadth as an actor, producer, director, and writer, the experiment of *Too Close to Home* suggests that the Perry brand will continue to expand its offerings to attract various audiences, at times, through recourse to a color-blind, universalist rhetoric. However, Black audiences, too, will continue to adapt to the complexities of the post-network era, shaping and refining their interpretation of his representations on-screen through active reception practices.

Notes

1   Leah Aldridge, "To Brand and Rebrand: Questioning the Futurity of Tyler Perry," in *From Madea to Media Mogul: Theorizing Tyler Perry*, ed. TreaAndrea M. Russworm, Samantha N. Sheppard, and Karen M. Bowdre (Jackson: University of Mississippi Press, 2016), 229.

2   Samantha N. Sheppard, "'Tyler Perry Presents . . .': The Cultural Projects, Partnerships, and Politics of Perry's Media Platforms," in Russworm, Sheppard, and Bowdre, *From Madea to Media Mogul*, 3.

3   Beretta E. Smith-Shomade, "Introduction: I See Black People," in *Watching While Black: Centering the Television of Black Audiences*, ed. Beretta E. Smith-Shomade (New Brunswick, N.J.: Rutgers University Press, 2012).

4   Smith-Shomade, 9.

5   Sheppard, "Tyler Perry Presents," 9.

6   Aymar Jean Christian and Khadijah Costley White, "One Man Hollywood: The Decline of Black Creative Production in Post-Network Television," in Russworm, Sheppard, and Bowdre, *From Madea to Media Mogul*, 138.

7   TreaAndrea M. Russworm, "Introduction: Media Studies Has Ninety-Nine Problems . . . But Tyler Perry Ain't One of Them?," in Russworm, Sheppard, and Bowdre, *From Madea to Media Mogul*, xv.

8   Artel Great, "Bring the Payne: the Erasure of the Black Sitcom and the Emergence of *Tyler Perry's House of Payne*," in Russworm, Sheppard, and Bowdre, *From Madea to Media Mogul*, 161.

9   Great, 162.

10 Great, 159.

11 Sophie Haigney, "Viacom Signs Tyler Perry, a Blow to Oprah Winfrey's Network," *New York Times*, July 14, 2017, https://www.nytimes.com/2017/07/14/arts/television/viacom-poaches-tyler-perry-from-oprah-winfreys-network.html.

12 Sheppard, "Tyler Perry Presents," 4.

13 Rodney Ho, "Confirmed: TLC's 'Tyler Perry's Too Close to Home' Cancelled after Two Seasons," *Atlanta Journal-Constitution*, November 2, 2017, https://www.ajc .com/blog/radiotvtalk/confirmed-tlc-tyler-perry-too-close-home-cancelled-after -two-seasons/P1HcSzugbCLjyJ3QWC9otL/.

14 Amanda Lotz, "Understanding Television at the Beginning of the Post-Network Era," in *The Television Will Be Revolutionized*, 2nd ed. (New York: New York University Press, 2014), 33–34.

15 Cheryl Grace, Andrew McCaskill, and Mia K. Scott-Aime, "From Consumers to Creators: The Digital Lives of Black Consumers," Diverse Intelligence Series, The Nielsen Company, 2018, accessed October 20, 2021, https://www.nielsen.com/wp -content/uploads/sites/2/2019/04/from-consumers-to-creators.pdf.

16 See Jacqueline Stewart, *Migrating to the Movies: Cinema and Black Modernity* (Berkeley: University of California Press, 2005); Anna Everett, *Returning the Gaze: A Genealogy of Black Film Criticism, 1909–1949* (Durham, N.C.: Duke University Press, 2001); and Robin R. Means Coleman, *Say It Loud! African American Audiences, Media, and Identity* (New York: Routledge, 2002).

17 Herman Gray, foreword to Means Coleman, *Say It Loud!*, iv.

18 Andre Lamar, "Dover Man Stars in Final 'Madea' Film," accessed May 15, 2023, https://www.delawareonline.com/story/news/2019/02/28/dover-man-stars-in-final/ 5792299007/.

19 Lamar.

20 Elizabeth Wagmeister, "Tyler Perry Drama Marks TLC's First-Ever Scripted Series," *Variety*, accessed June 2021, https://variety.com/2016/tv/news/too-close-to-home -tyler-perry-tlc-drama-1201742668/.

21 TheMovieReport.com, "Too Close to Home Premiere Q&A with Tyler Perry, Heather Locklear & Cast," August 16, 2016, YouTube video, 20:40, https://www .youtube.com/watch?v=AoJo1vaEs1Y.

22 TheMovieReport.com.

23 Jodi Melamed, "The Spirit of Neoliberalism: From Racial Liberalism to Neoliberal Multiculturalism," *Social Text* 24, no. 4 (Winter 2006): 1–24.

24 BUILD Series, "Danielle Savre Discusses Her Show, 'Too Close to Home,'" March 22, 2017, 30:15, https://www.youtube.com/watch?v=mFDkpyyUol4.

25 "Tyler Perry's *Too Close to Home* Is TLC's First Scripted Series," Tyler Perry, accessed June 15, 2021, https://tylerperry.com/tyler-perrys-too-close-to-home-is-tlcs-first -scripted-series/.

26 TheMovieReport.com, "Too Close to Home."

27 TheMovieReport.com.

28 Armete Mobin, "Niche Representation: A Case Study of TLC," *Medium*, June 25, 2020, https://medium.com/@armete/niche-representation-a-case-study-of-tlc -2656281ae734.

29 George Szalai, "TLC's Reach to Cross 100 Million Homes Internationally Next Week," *Hollywood Reporter*, October 25, 2011, https://www.hollywoodreporter.com/ news/general-news/tlcs-reach-cross-100-million-252811/.

30 Liz Calvario, "Tyler Perry Says Backlash against His TLC Show's White Cast Members Is 'Reverse Racism,'" *IndieWire*, December 30, 2016, accessed June 8, 2021, https://www.indiewire.com/2016/12/tyler-perry-says-backlash-against-tlc-shows -white-cast-reverse-racism-1201763892/.

31 Jonathan Landrum Jr., "'Too Close to Home:' Tyler Perry on White Cast," *Detroit News*, January 3, 2017, accessed June 8, 2021, https://www.detroitnews.com/story/ entertainment/television/2017/01/03/tyler-perry-white-starring-cast-close-home -tlc/96021832/.

32 "Slayed or Shade: Tyler Perry's *Too Close to Home*," *Essence*, August 30, 2016, updated December 6, 2020, accessed October 15, 2021, https://www.essence.com/videos/tyler-perrys-decision-cast-all-white-people-slayed-or-shade/.

33 "Slayed or Shade."

34 TheMovieReport.com, "Too Close to Home."

35 TheMovieReport.com.

36 TheMovieReport.com.

37 TheMovieReport.com.

38 TheMovieReport.com.

39 TheMovieReport.com.

40 "Tyler Perry Talks Fatherhood, 'Too Close to Home,'" *ABC News*, 2:44, https://abcnews.go.com/GMA/video/tyler-perry-talks-fatherhood-close-home-41563084.

41 Sheppard, "Tyler Perry Presents," 9.

42 Sheppard, 9.

43 Aldridge, "To Brand and Rebrand," 230.

44 Ben Raphael Sher, "'All My Life I Had to Fight': Domestic Trauma and Cinephilia in Tyler Perry's Archive of Feelings," in Russworm, Sheppard, and Bowdre, *From Madea to Media Mogul*, 96.

Part IV

Feeling Black

• •

11

"I'm Trying to Make People Feel Black"

●●●●●●●●●●●●●●●●●●●●●●●

Affective Authenticity in *Atlanta*

BRANDY MONK-PAYTON

Three black men sit on a tattered couch in the middle of a field across the street from an apartment complex. They are smoking weed. The scene almost seems as if it is a dream were it not for the casual conversation about the material realities of being broke as a young adult. The rap business might be their ticket out of impending poverty, and this becomes the deceptively simple premise of the pilot episode of cable comedy *Atlanta* (FX, 2016–2022). *Atlanta* premiered on September 6, 2016, and follows the adventures of Earnest "Earn" Marks (Donald Glover), Alfred "Paper Boi" Miles (Brian Tyree Henry), and Darius Epps (Lakeith Stanfield) as a trio of misfits living and working—or hustling, as the case often is—in the city that is seen as the African American mecca of the south. The half-hour series created by multihyphenate artist Donald Glover was widely lauded as a fresh entry into representations of blackness on the small screen. As a headline for *Essence* magazine stated, "*Atlanta* Is the Slightly Dark, Introspective Dramedy the Black Community Needs."[1] Indeed, prior to the program's release, the decade of the 2010s in black network and cable television in the United States was largely dominated by the likes of Shonda Rhimes melodramas and Tyler Perry sitcoms. Along with Issa Rae's *Insecure* (HBO,

2016–2021), *Atlanta* ushered in a new era of black programming developed by African American millennial media makers.

Such programming that spans genres strives to emphasize the different contours of black life in the United States across geographies. They are often notable for their highly localized depictions of African American experience at the intersections of race, class, and gender in cities such as Los Angeles, New York City, Chicago, and Atlanta. Ideologically, these television programs are not beholden to a conventional politics of representation that can stifle black creativity. Instead, the choices that are deployed in form and content are more provocative. *Atlanta* in particular attempts to function for viewers on a deeper level of meaning-making via an affective register. Glover states of the series, "I'm trying to make people feel black."[2] This intentional desire to cultivate an emotional and perceptual encounter with blackness pervades every frame and sequence.

In this chapter, I argue that the program generates a structure of feeling for spectators that allows for an authentic engagement with black ways of being and knowing. Though it is a contested term, I see value in employing the language of authenticity because it still circulates and holds purchase within television industry discourse, which includes the assessment of TV texts by audiences and critics. For example, AJ Springer writes for *Ebony* magazine that "*Atlanta* . . . delivers what many Black viewers have been clamoring for: an authentic Black experience that shows real life depictions of Black masculinity, which beats caricatures seven days a week."[3] *Atlanta* invites viewers to "feel black" through its mise-en-scène, dialogue, performances, and soundscape. While Glover and the *Atlanta* production team promote verisimilitude, they also construct a televisual milieu that deftly blends realism and surrealism. The fantastical elements of the series attest to the uncanny moments of black existence that are often difficult to articulate. In these ways, *Atlanta* should not be considered an example of what Kristen Warner deems "plastic representation" or "synthetic elements put together and shaped to look like meaningful imagery, but which can only approximate depth and substance because ultimately it is hollow and cannot survive close scrutiny."[4] *Atlanta* goes beyond a superficial portrayal of black community on-screen through risky storytelling that infuses its characters as well as narrative environments and situations with subtle complexity.

Not only does *Atlanta* provide a uniquely complicated black perspective, but it also experiments with a black gaze. As Tina Campt argues of the new crop of black creative projects in popular media culture, "While blackness is now seen (i.e. made visible to a wider audience), it is not necessarily something to be felt."[5] A black gaze, then, refuses such "traditional ways of seeing blackness" and "requires *labor*—the labor of discomfort, feeling, positioning, and repositioning—and solicits visceral responses to the visualization of Black precarity."[6] *Atlanta* demands active engagement on the part of the viewer who becomes a witness to the experiences of the mostly black millennials on the series who "loiter at the margins of their own output."[7] Thus, the fictional series resonates with this population's social, political, and economic realities in the twenty-first century. This chapter articulates how *Atlanta* attempts to resist reproducing the hegemonic white gaze of seeing blackness by creating a diegetic atmosphere at the limits of legibility. With millennial creative Glover at the helm, the series allures yet challenges its ideal viewing demographic by inciting both spectatorial pleasure and displeasure with its uniquely dark humor.

Locating the Black Millennial Television Audience

Dividing a population into generational categories according to age is an instructive, albeit increasingly contested, classification system for understanding cultural attitudes across history for marketing purposes. Oftentimes, whiteness becomes the default for broad assertions about the disparate life conditions and consumptive habits of different age groups in the United States, from baby boomers to Gen Z. *The New Republic* published an essay in February 2019 entitled "The Missing Black Millennial." In the piece, author Reniqua Allen reflects on the plight of black millennials who are rendered invisible within "a generation profoundly shaped by the events of its time—9/11, the Iraq War, the Great Recession, climate change—and baleful socioeconomic trends: growing income inequality, staggering levels of student debt, stagnant wages."[8] Black millennials, born between the early-to-mid-1980s and the mid-1990s, acutely experienced these crises and more. For example, they also eagerly watched the ascendancy of Barack Obama to president of the United States and the swift backlash against him that burst the bubble of a postracial America. As black faces reached higher places (such as the top political office in the country), ordinary folks continued to deal with disenfranchisement and oppression. Slogans championing "hope" and "change" turned into the rallying cry "I can't breathe." Black millennials found themselves toggling between #blackexcellence and #blacklivesmatter on social media. The generation navigated structural racism and anti-black violence in a way both all too similar yet somehow different from their elders during the civil rights movement. Allen writes, "The black millennial, then, is composed of contradictions and ambiguity. . . . In many ways, the story of the black millennial is as much about consistency as it is about change—which is to say that the story of the black millennial is the story of what it means to be black, period."[9]

At the time of *Atlanta*'s release, African American millennials comprised 14 percent of the entire millennial population.[10] However, they hadn't been hailed as a lucrative audience demographic for legacy television in the same way as their white counterparts with programming fare such as *New Girl* (FOX, 2011–2018), *Girls* (HBO, 2012–2017), *Broad City* (Comedy Central, 2014–2019), and *Mr. Robot* (USA, 2015–2019). With the advent of streaming platforms, black millennials began to be addressed through narrowcasting with the multicultural ensemble dramedy *Orange Is the New Black* (Netflix,

2013–2019), *Master of None* (Netflix, 2015–2021), and *Dear White People* (Netflix, 2017–2021). Yet before the streaming takeover there was the web series, specifically *The Misadventures of Awkward Black Girl* (YouTube, 2011–2013). Issa Rae's indie web series became a "creative and promotional outlet amidst personal and professional precarity."[11] Rae stars as her alter ego "J," who navigates a kind of arrested development in her millennial awkwardness; the program embraces an aesthetic of abjection (across race, gender, and class) as its primary locus of humor.[12] *The Misadventures of Awkward Black Girl* made the transition to linear television in the form of HBO's *Insecure* (2016–2021), a risky business move for the premium network that works because it masterfully straddles storytelling that is both culturally specific and universal.[13] In contrast to *Girls*, it courts an audience of black millennials (especially women) and speaks directly to their desires at the same time that it attempts to grapple with general concerns about success and failure as a young adult.

Many of the television programs created by millennial showrunners of color like Rae, Aziz Ansari, and Donald Glover can be considered what Taylor Nygaard and Jorie Lagerwey call "Diverse Quality Comedies," which they define as "critically acclaimed, award-winning, aesthetically innovative, niche-market comedies with a grim outlook on the political, social, and economic world in which their characters live."[14] These programs primarily seek to address millennial audiences of color who have been underserved for television fare with which they can identify. Alfred L. Martin Jr. names the racialized quality audience of high-production-value black-cast dramas the BLAMP, which stands for "black, liberal, affluent, metropolitan professional viewers."[15] I suggest that the black millennial audience demographic that watches diverse quality comedic programs like *Atlanta* should be seen as interconnected yet distinct from its BLAMP-y counterpart. Black millennial viewers can be highly educated and upwardly mobile, but they embody a particular sensibility toward life predicated on their emergent adulthood during the early 2010s. This means that they might eschew the label of liberal in favor of progressive or even radical to describe their political orientation. Their affluence is circumscribed within the precarious labor conditions of the gig economy. Due to stressors related to racial macro- and microaggressions, black millennials might also experience high degrees of burnout.[16] Thus, the black millennial audience segment doesn't resemble an earnest "buppie" (black yuppie) so much as it offers up an image of the cynical "blipster" (black hipster). Such cynicism reflects their distinct subject position vis-à-vis their disparate economic realities, which contributes to a different sense of success. Ultimately, they are searching for an alternative black aesthetic and politic that speaks to their status as postmodern subjects in an anti-black world.

Arguably no celebrity creative embodies the wry millennial outlook more than Glover. As a black millennial, Glover appeared on the cover of *AdWeek*'s 2016 class of Young Influentials that profiles people under forty who are changing business and culture.[17] Glover is in part influential because he under-stands how his age demographic's media consumption is inextricably inter-twined with the rise of the internet and digital technology more broadly. Indeed, part of the innovative aspect of *Atlanta* is its attentiveness to the importance of social media flows in black millennial experience and especially those related to hip-hop culture. In addition to being a black millennial showrunner, Glover can also be considered within the paradigm of the showrunner-as-auteur who comes to serve as a figure of legitimation.[18] As *Atlanta* showrunner, creator, star, writer, and occasional director, the entertainer authenticates the television text through his own brand of black nerd that appeals to a wide variety of publics.

The Crossover Success of Donald Glover

In October 2013, Donald Glover posted photographs on Instagram of handwrit-ten notes on stationary paper from the Marriott Hotel. The series of notes read like a stream of consciousness from someone anxious about their rising fame. In shaky penmanship, he wrote down thoughts such as "Im afraid of the future, Im afraid people think I hate my race, I feel like Im letting everyone down, Im afraid people hate who I really am, Im afraid I hate who I really am."[19] These musings made clear his struggle with his own identity as an African American man on the precipice of mainstream popularity. Glover occupies a unique status within the entertainment industry. Not only is he a creative who is successful across mediums, but he also appeals to black and white audiences alike. He is a famous black individual who has achieved crossover stardom by crafting distinc-tive personas both on the television screen and on the web.

Glover was born and raised in the suburban sprawl of Stone Mountain, Geor-gia, where his mother was a daycare provider and his father worked for the postal service. He came from modest middle-class means and grew up with his biologi-cal siblings—sister Brianne and brother Stephen—alongside numerous children that his parents fostered over the years. Notably, the entertainer was raised in a Jehovah's Witness household, and such religious upbringing also comes to inform some of his creative pursuits. Glover graduated from New York University's Tisch School of the Arts and did improv comedy before Tina Fey hired him as a writer on *30 Rock* (NBC, 2006–2013) when he was just twenty-three years old. He joined the cast of *Community* (NBC, 2009–2015) playing Troy Barnes, an arrogant jock-turned-sensitive-nerd, which catapulted him to mainstream public recogni-tion. His stint on the single-camera sitcom was not without conflict; for instance, he has divulged being on the receiving end of racist microaggressions committed by colleague Chevy Chase on the set.[20] Nonetheless, working on network sitcoms both behind and in front of the camera after attending NYU introduced Glover to white liberals and made him palatable to such an audience.

Though white liberals became endeared to him through television, the per-former had already been cultivating a diehard fan base with the internet savvy multicultural millennial demographic. Indeed, Glover made a name for himself on social media by posting frequently on Twitter and producing viral content as part of the Derrick Comedy group on YouTube such as the highly popular 2006 parody video *Bro-Rape: A Newsline Investigative Report*. Moving from sketch comedy into stand-up, Glover was featured on an episode of *Comedy Central Presents* (Comedy Central, 1998–2011) in 2010 that led to his first hour-long TV special *Donald Glover: Weirdo*, which premiered on the cable network a year later. In both performances, he makes use of college frat boy gross-out humor resembling his material with Derrick Comedy and tells numerous jokes centering on using the N-word and being a black nerd who likes things that are "strange and specific" in front of a racially diverse crowd.[21]

In a piece for *The Village Voice*, "Donald Glover Is More Talented Than You," writer Bill Jensen outright labels him a black hipster and an "emo with a fro" who "represents a new archetype of entertainer—a black nerd who can like white stuff."[22] Glover's proximity to white popular culture contributes to his recognition in this arena. Notably, he guest stars for two episodes on the second season of *Girls* as Sandy, the black Brooklynite and Republican boyfriend of Hannah Horvath (played by Lena Dunham). The appearance seemed to be a tongue-in-cheek response to criticisms of that program's lack of racial inclusivity. In his last scene, Hannah argues with Sandy about how his conservative politics are contradictory to his African American identity, which leads to their breakup. Thus, Glover-as-Sandy ends up as another fetishized black guy to be discarded when no longer of narrative use in such a white vision of millennial experience.

Despite his tokenization on *Girls*, Glover's roles in two 2015 films instantiate the claim that, per his personal and professional background, he is actually the "two-headed hydra of Black geekdom and Atlanta ratchet."[23] In *The Martian* (2015), he appeared as astrodynamicist Rich Purnell who uses scientific ingenuity to solve the primary predicament of the film. He portrays the "absolutely adorable Andre" in *Magic Mike XXL* (2015) who descends a staircase shirtless wearing a hat to serenade a young black woman with a freestyle song. The latter appearance is crucial here, as it solidifies his status as an object of affection for black female audiences with his sweet and soulful style. Glover continued to cultivate crossover success in his cinematic choices from his foray playing a young Lando Calrissian in *Solo: A Star Wars Story* (2018) and voicing Simba in the live-action remake of Disney's *The Lion King* (2019) opposite superstar Beyoncé Knowles. In addition to a robust television and film career, Glover also began to make music in 2011, rapping under the pseudonym of Childish Gambino. His experience with the hip-hop scene heavily contributes to the feel of *Atlanta*, which will be discussed later in this chapter.

Whether he is Childish Gambino or Donald Glover, his multiple media ventures allow him to retain an enigmatic status as someone who makes meaning differently for a variety of audiences. As a creative chimera, he maneuvers within and across music, film, and television in a way that is difficult to pin down. Glover deftly practices a "strategic ambiguity" with his persona, which Ralina Joseph conceptualizes as "carefully created constructions designed to wink at certain audiences and smile blandly in the face of others."[24] Following this, a project like *Atlanta* can be seen as a media product that not only makes use of strategic ambiguity but also resides in a liminal space of racialized experience situated between familiarity and estrangement.

With the development of the series, Glover remarked that he "wanted to show white people, you don't know everything about black culture."[25] Such a statement simultaneously seems to court a white viewership yet also refuses to cater to this racial demographic's hegemonic epistemologies. In fact, pleasure on the part of *Atlanta*'s creative team seems to be derived from making the show illegible in some respects to the white gaze. John Landgraf, the chairman of FX network, affirms the wholly black perspective of the series: "Donald and his collaborators are making an existential comedy about the African-American experience, and they are not translating it for white audiences."[26] In this way, *Atlanta* might invite non-black viewers in but also refuses to educate or indulge them in favor of generating resonance with its black and millennial audience.

Blackness, Resonance, and *Atlanta*

While promoting *Atlanta* at the Television Critics Association press tour in 2016, Glover claimed that "the thesis with this show was to show people what it's like to be black, and you can't write that down. You have to feel it."[27] *Atlanta* relies on viscerally touching its spectators through its distinct televisual rhythms and reverberations. In his essay "The Feel of Life: Resonance, Race, and Representation," Herman Gray theorizes how racial feeling manifests through quotidian black expressivity that calls attention to "subjection to racism and the resilience and imagination to challenge it."[28] While he observes such circuits of ordinary affect in new media ecologies, they are also present in a television series like *Atlanta* and its distinctive approach to connecting with spectators.

A primary reason why *Atlanta* resonates on an affective level is that the series has an all-black writers' room (including Glover's younger brother, Stephen) with many of those on staff never having written for TV before. Glover recalls that he "wanted people with similar experiences who understood the language and the mindset of the characters and their environment."[29] Here, a lack of expertise is advantageous and gives the program a nonformulaic and fresh quality. Glover's longtime collaborator Hiro Murai—who is known for his work on music videos—has directed most episodes of the series. The Tokyo-born and Los Angeles–raised Murai articulates the organic quality of making each episode in which the production team puts itself "in a situation where [they] can thoughtlessly doodle and then make something that feels honest to that moment."[30] This is exhibited from the very first scene of the pilot, titled "The

FIG. 11.1 FX *Atlanta* cast

Big Bang." The crew (Earn, Al, and Darius) find themselves in an altercation in front of a liquor store that quickly escalates with weapons drawn. A stray dog randomly appears. A gunshot is heard before a cut to the title sequence. While the series is invested in mimetic realism in which representation is a reflection of material realities, there are also frequent inexplicable and fantastical sequences that can be considered surreal. Later in the episode, Earn rides a bus while holding his sleeping daughter, Lottie, and has a philosophical conversation with a stranger. He states defeatedly to the man, who may or may not be a Jehovah's Witness, "I just keep losing." The stranger aggressively demands that Earn bite a Nutella sandwich. When Earn turns to the window as a police car goes by, the man seems to disappear into thin air from the bus only to be briefly seen walking into the woods (with the aforementioned stray dog) in the dead of night. *Atlanta* actively generates ambiguity in order "to create a world where nothing is guaranteed."[31] The series indexes black social life and all its intrigue in oftentimes unconventional and even esoteric ways that exceed semiotic coherence.

Within the coveted eighteen to forty-nine target demographic, the debut episode became the most watched of any basic cable prime-time scripted comedy series since the 2013 premiere of *Inside Amy Schumer* (FX, 2013–2016).[32] FX renewed the program for a second season after only the first two episodes had aired. A Nielsen article celebrated the influence of black content on mainstream culture and highlighted data from the 2016–2017 television season, including the fact that "half of viewership for the newcomer *Atlanta* is non-black."[33] This statistic reveals that, as Nygaard and Lagerwey argue, the series is highly successful at offering "a consistently subtler, more continuous negotiation of the tension between White 'quality' aesthetics and culturally specific critiques of structural racial inequality."[34] In its claims to such aesthetics, *Atlanta* captures the attention of white audiences, who are then made privy to the prestige program's invocation of an unapologetic blackness in every frame.

Atlanta's production models a televisual version of John L. Jackson's concept of "racial sincerity" that "wallows in unfalsifiability, ephemerality, partiality, and social vulnerability."[35] The dialogue and performances are both intuitive and intentional, which contributes to the affective authenticity of the series. Though he is white, cinematographer Christian Sprenger emphasizes details in each shot that connote quotidian black ways of living and being together. Take the mise-en-scène of Van's (Zazie Beetz) bedroom that highlights its intimate quarters where she sometimes sleeps with her baby daddy Earn, or Al's living room and kitchen that are cluttered with stuff. The trio of friends is often depicted sitting (perhaps languishing) on the multiple shabby couches in the apartment, which conveys their personal and professional stasis. However, the program is as much about mobility as it is about stasis. Frequent use of aerial and tracking shots situate the viewer within the urban landscape and showcase different parts of the city and region, including real Atlanta food spots like J. R. Crickets. Characters are seen driving on roads and highways, and overall, the streets of Atlanta are prominently featured as points of encounter.

Indeed, another main character in the series is the city itself. Television representations of the southern metropolis include the glitz and glam of reality docudramas like *The Real Housewives of Atlanta* (Bravo, 2008–), *Married to Medicine* (Bravo, 2013–), and *Love & Hip Hop: Atlanta* (VH1, 2012–). Yet as Maurice J. Hobson notes, Glover's comedy series challenges this view of the city as "Hotlanta" and upends the myth of Atlanta as a black mecca to expose its seedier underbelly. *Atlanta* "targets the experiences of Atlanta's black indigenous citizens, offering a beautifully crafted demonstration of the pageantry of black Atlantan vernacular culture, peculiar to some and spot on to many."[36] The program does not fetishize those who are marginalized by their economic status but rather treats such poor and working-class black folks with care as valuable sources of racialized knowledge. For example, in season 2's "Barbershop," the sacred space of black male talk is depicted through Al's visit to Bibby the barber. Bibby (Robert S. Powell III) is a recognizable denizen of the black community who is somehow always distracted from his job at hand by talking on his phone with Bluetooth technology—which prevents him from actually cutting hair, much to Al's exasperation. When Bibby suddenly has to leave the shop to go see his girl, he tells Al he can come with him to finish, but they have to "go out the back way" because "them people be out there." The scene's hilarity is due to how familiar and resonant it is to anyone who has spent time in a black barbershop. Yet it also still retains a sense of strangeness and mystery as Al is taken on a wild ride where he—and the viewer—never know what obstacle will be put in front of him next.

It is these kinds of scenarios connected to black masculinity along with the trials and tribulations of "homosocial bonds" that are foregrounded in the program's exploration of identity politics.[37] In particular, a major conflict in the series emerges from the consequences of mixing family with finances as Earn continually tries and fails to be an effective business manager for his cousin Al. The young black adults in the series maneuver different forms and degrees of precarity across race, class, and gender. Al's friend Tracy (Khris Davis) appears as a foil to Earn in the second season. Tracy has just been released from prison and dons a white wife-beater, chain, and do-rag. He is clearly a country black dude who knows how to scam. When Tracy and Earn go to the mall to use illegal gift cards on a shopping spree, Tracy remarks that Earn seems like "the preppy type." They are browsing in a shoe store where Tracy excitedly picks up a pair of black dress shoes for a job interview. He casually inquires to his friend's cousin, "You went to Princeton, right? How should I talk to these white folks?" Earn is set in contrast to Tracy here as having the ability to code-switch (resembling Glover himself) in white spaces. When Earn tells him just to be confident, Tracy then promptly steals the shoes because the store has a "no chase" policy, to Earn's disbelief. He goes to his interview clad in a button-down, a tie, khakis, new stolen shoes, and hair waves. The white interviewer tells him he has potential but that there are no positions available, to which Tracy accuses the company of racism, shouting "AmeriKKK" on his way out. Here, the series engages disparities in treatment and life outcomes of those formerly incarcerated black folks who are continually marginalized.

Though *Atlanta* has been less progressive concerning LGBTQIA issues, its depictions of black womanhood and motherhood have become more nuanced through the character of Van. Similar to Earn, Van grapples with her personal and professional decisions in emerging adulthood. In the episode "Helen," Van's black childhood friend Christina introduces her to others as simply "Lottie's mom" at a slightly odd and predominantly white German festival in the mountains. Later, Van is shocked when Christina notes that she "chose" black because she "needed that identity." The episode highlights not only Van's shaky romantic relationship with Earn but also her embrace of an intersectional identity with all its messiness.

The shenanigans of this motley crew can be amusing to watch. Yet Glover comments of the audience, "I don't even want them laughing if they're laughing at the caged animal in the zoo. . . . I want them to really experience racism, to really feel what it's like to be black in America."[38] Here, "them" refers to *Atlanta*'s white viewers. Glover is cognizant of the potential for the program's unabashed blackness to be objectified by white audiences, and perhaps especially young white men who have always been part of the entertainer's fandom. *Atlanta* turns this phenomenon of othering on its head in episode nine of the second season, "North of the Border," where Earn, Al, Darius, and Tracy drive to Statesboro, Georgia, for a concert at a university. A series of unfortunate events results in their arrival at a white fraternity house where they sit trapped under a Confederate flag and become privy to a hazing ritual in which the pledges must dance to the D4L rap song "Laffy Taffy" in two lines blindfolded and naked. The simmering tension that has built up between Earn and Al throughout the episode finally breaks as they burst out laughing at the spectacle. The moment exemplifies how "many contemporary satires force our disavowal of the conventional silence surrounding race by imagining what racial essentialism might look like if whiteness were made observable."[39]

Atlanta has been deemed a "new black Gothic" comedy in which its dark humor is derived from how quotidian black experience can become horrific when it is confronted by white supremacy.[40] The program constructs the city of Atlanta as an urban dystopia in which character anxiety and paranoia are justified due to the racial terror that they meet at every corner. Its mundane quality is made to seem always eerie and haunting. Glover attests again, "I want people to feel scared, because that's what it feels like to be black. . . . Amazing things can happen, but it can be taken away in a moment."[41]

As much as the series places emphasis on that which is concrete about black experience, it just as often veers into abstraction with its disjointed narratives that tap into existential life questions that go largely unanswered. *Atlanta* pushes the bounds of what is permissible on television by creating a black Justin Bieber character or a Michael Jackson–esque reclusive figure named Teddy Perkins. Lest African American audiences become distanced by its alienating address, the program always returns to comforting content, such as the black famous comedian Katt Williams's memorable guest star appearance as the eponymous "Alligator Man" in the first episode of the second season. The series blends introspective character study with satirical commentary on the media and black cultural politics. In the award-winning season 1 episode "B.A.N.," Paper Boi appears as a guest on *The Montague Show*, an interview program on the fictional Black American Network within the diegetic universe of the series. Television operates according to segmentation amid flow in order to sell audiences to advertisers. The episode cleverly includes faux commercials that are meant to target black audiences and signify a cable network like BET and its essentialist marketing.[42]

In season 4, Van becomes a day player on a Tyler Perry–esque comedy series in an episode entitled "Work Ethic!" The Perry-inspired character, Mr. Kirkwood Chocolate, is introduced as an omniscient voice of God who surveys the set and barks orders to the actors through an intercom. As Van searches for her daughter at the vast Kirkwood Chocolate Studios, which has stages named after black actors like John Witherspoon, she gets into a heated conversation with studio staff about the politics of representation and bad black art that sells. "The Goof Who Sat by the Door" is the eighth episode of the fourth season that serves as a mockumentary of the making of *A Goofy Movie* (1995), retrospectively branded as a black nerd classic.[43] Such self-awareness and reflexivity are also integral aspects of the quirky comedy's address to millennial viewers.

With its unique style and narrative, *Atlanta* has received numerous prestigious accolades, including a 2016 Peabody Award, Best Television Series–Musical or

FIG. 11.2 *Atlanta* "B.A.N." episode

Comedy at the 2017 Golden Globes, and Outstanding Directing for a Comedy Series at the 2017 Prime-time Emmy Awards, the latter category of which Glover also became the first African American to win. During his Golden Globes win speech for the series, he thanked the city of Atlanta and its people as well as the Georgia-born rap group Migos for making their song "Bad and Boujee." It was a moment that received laughter from the audience, but on a deeper note, the shoutout recognizes the importance of the YouTube generation and the circulation of hip-hop music through these digital platforms.

Indeed, *Atlanta* understands that viewers are attracted to black online content from Twitter to TikTok. In the pilot, the notorious WorldStarHipHop video aggregating site is mentioned. The comedy series is heavily influenced by both the local rap mixtape game and virtual SoundCloud distribution craze. Paper Boi's burgeoning celebrity from his underground song and low-budget music video provides much fodder at the intersection of art and commerce (for instance, Al gets annoyed when he watches a white girl do an acoustic cover of his hit track online). *Atlanta* comments on the music industry and the role of radio airplay in fostering the success of underground acts. In addition to the plot that centers artist development, from hip-hop to funk, music infuses the overall sonic environment of the program; critics state that "even with its relative obscurity and unobtrusive placement, the soundtrack . . . is crucial to [*Atlanta*'s] next-level specificity, regional intimacy and obsession with atmosphere."[44] The production team thoughtfully curates songs across genres and decades to generate particular kinds of energies for the series and its viewers, from Kodak Black's "Patty Cake" to The Delfonics' "Hey! Love." Glover relays that "good music is all tone. It's like, 'This just feels good' . . . and I felt like in television, it's important to try that, especially if we're going to be tackling a lot of black perspective."[45] The sound of *Atlanta* is a crucial way that the series cultivates its vibe and vibrations by infusing its black gaze with another perceptual register.

For Us by Us

This chapter has traced the emergence of the black millennial audience and the television industry's targeting of such a viewing demographic. Donald Glover's rise as an entertainer is indebted to his appeal to both black and white millennial viewers in his career as a comedian, actor, and musician. With the production of *Atlanta*, Glover was able to "Trojan-horse" FX by pitching a vision of a show that he actually never made.[46] Instead of a joy ride of a conventional rap series, *Atlanta* immerses those who watch it in candid and grim depictions of African American social experience. In his overall analysis of the series, Bijan Stephen definitively states, "There's no pandering to an audience, either. If you don't get the jokes, you don't get them. If that seems strange—a show about day-to-day black life in one of the country's largest metropolises that doesn't exactly have a point or message—then it's probably not for you. But then it wasn't made with you in mind, either. It's the same ethos that powered the brand FUBU: For us, by us. More than anything, *Atlanta* is a love letter to black people and black culture, specifically the people and culture you find in the titular city."[47] Glover echoes this sentiment: "The thing that I'm most proud of with this show is that we got away with being honest."[48] Such racial sincerity on-screen came to be manifest by virtue of the program's writers and performers embracing a fugitive creative tactic that generates radical potential for black television.

Atlanta's affective authenticity emerges from an unapologetic Southern black poor and working-class audiovisual vernacular that has increasingly gone viral in current digital media culture. The program requires much of its audience as it directly disturbs the senses in the play between black belonging and alienation. Thus, watching *Atlanta* isn't easy, and its black mode of storytelling is not diluted to be palatable for white viewers. Beyond such spectatorial address, the series is also a magical odyssey that pushes televisual limits, transforming itself with each episode and season. The penultimate episode of *Atlanta*'s second season, entitled "FUBU," provides audiences with a glimpse into Earn's childhood. The episode's problematic revolves around the young Earn, who pleads with his mother to buy him a FUBU shirt, only to realize that the piece of clothing is fake when he wears it to school. The episode plays on 1990s black nostalgia that resonates with millennial coming-of-age experience and, with its title, also slyly addresses the program's overall status in the TV industry with respect to its unflinching black quality.

Half of *Atlanta*'s third season does not even take place in the titular city but rather follows its characters to Europe. In a teaser trailer for the season, Afrofuturist artist Sun Ra's track "It's after the End of the World" haunts a mysterious montage of images like an empty auditorium, a quiet street at night, a sculpture, and chairs assembled on top of one another in front of television sets before the camera finally zooms in on a bewildered Al sitting at a table wearing a large gold cross and a sweat shirt with the word "Fake" on it. *Atlanta* returned to its roots in the fourth and final season as the main characters continued their odyssey in the black metropolis that they call home. The series finale aired on November 10, 2022, and solidified the program's exploration of the familiar and strange comedy of black life. "It Was All a Dream" opens with *Judge Judy* playing on a television set as Darius, Earn, and Al watch. Darius informs his friends that he has an appointment at a wellness center that offers float therapy in a sensory deprivation tank. Darius slips in and out of a dreamlike state and begins to question the boundaries of his reality to the point at which he—and the viewers—are unclear about whether the entire series has actually been a figment of his imagination. He broaches this perhaps far-fetched idea with the gang and Van, who all eat Popeye's in the last act of the episode, yet the series leaves audiences with no definitive answer.

Atlanta concludes with the ultimate unverifiable claim that stays true to its overall surreal nature amid black material existence. At the end of the program's run, cultural critic Touré writes, "We are in a golden age of Black TV, a time when there are more great, authentic Black shows than ever and there are more empowered Black TV creators than ever, and still, in an era of stiff competition, 'Atlanta' shined above them all as the Blackest."[49] In a twenty-first-century renaissance moment of television by and for African Americans, *Atlanta* provides an innovative take on being black and an irreverent approach to knowing blackness that registers on a deeply affective level for those who venture to watch.

Notes

1 Sonaiya Kelley, "'Atlanta' Is the Slightly Dark, Introspective Dramedy the Black Community Needs," *Essence*, October 26, 2020, https://www.essence.com/entertainment/atlanta-review-black-comedy/.
2 Matt Wilstein, "'Atlanta' Star Donald Glover Wants to 'Make People Feel Black,'" *The Daily Beast*, September 6, 2016, https://www.thedailybeast.com/atlanta-star-donald-glover-wants-to-make-people-feel-black.
3 AJ Springer, "FX's 'Atlanta' Offers Rarely Seen Depictions of Black Masculinity," *Ebony*, September 13, 2016, https://www.ebony.com/entertainment/fx-atlanta-review/.
4 Kristen J. Warner, "Plastic Representation," *Film Quarterly* 71, no. 2 (Winter 2017): 35.

5 Tina M. Campt, *A Black Gaze: Artists Changing How We See* (Cambridge, Mass.: MIT Press, 2021), 7.

6 Campt, 17.

7 Justin Charity, "Donald Glover Blacks Out on 'Atlanta,'" *The Ringer*, September 6, 2016, https://www.theringer.com/2016/9/6/16042054/atlanta-fx-show-donald-glover-737e59619a4a.

8 Reniqua Allen, "The Missing Black Millennial," *The New Republic*, February 20, 2019, https://newrepublic.com/article/153122/missing-black-millennial.

9 Allen.

10 Nielsen, "Young, Connected and Black," *Nielsen*, October 17, 2016, https://www.nielsen.com/us/en/insights/report/2016/young-connected-and-black/.

11 Stefania Marghitu, "*Broad City* and *Insecure*'s Millennial Showrunners: From Indie Web Series to Cable and Streaming Crossovers," *Feminist Media Studies* 19, no. 7 (2019): 2.

12 Rebecca Wanzo, "Precarious-Girl Comedy: Issa Rae, Lena Dunham, and Abjection Aesthetics," *Camera Obscura* 31, no. 2 (2016): 26–59.

13 Kristen Warner, "[Home] Girls: *Insecure* and HBO's Risky Racial Politics," *Los Angeles Review of Books*, October 2016, https://www.lareviewofbooks.org/article/home-girls-insecure-and-hbos-risky-racial-politics/.

14 Taylor Nygaard and Jorie Lagerwey, *Horrible White People: Gender, Genre, and Television's Precarious Whiteness* (New York: New York University Press, 2020), 157.

15 Alfred J. Martin, "Notes from Underground: WGN's Black-Cast Quality TV Experiment," *Los Angeles Review of Books*, May 31, 2018, https://lareviewofbooks.org/article/notes-from-underground-wgns-black-cast-quality-tv-experiment/.

16 Tiana Clark, "This Is What Black Burnout Feels Like," *Buzzfeed*, January 11, 2019, https://www.buzzfeednews.com/article/tianaclarkpoet/millennial-burnout-black-women-self-care-anxiety-depression.

17 Jason Lynch, "Donald Glover," *AdWeek* 57, no. 32 (October 3, 2016): 22.

18 Michael Z. Newman and Elana Levine, *Legitimating Television: Media Convergence and Cultural Status* (New York: Routledge, 2011).

19 Jesse David Fox, "Read Donald Glover's Handwritten Notes about Leaving *Community*," *Vulture*, October 15, 2013, https://www.vulture.com/2013/10/glover-handwrote-notes-about-leaving-community.html.

20 Tad Friend, "Donald Glover Can't Save You," *New Yorker*, February 26, 2018, https://www.newyorker.com/magazine/2018/03/05/donald-glover-cant-save-you.

21 *Comedy Central Presents*, season 14, episode 9, "Donald Glover," created by Paul Miller, aired March 19, 2010, on Comedy Central.

22 Bill Jensen, "Donald Glover Is More Talented Than You," *The Village Voice*, April 13, 2011, https://www.villagevoice.com/2011/04/13/donald-glover-is-more-talented-than-you/.

23 Michele Prettyman, "The Persistence of 'Wild Style': Hip-Hop and Music Video Culture at the Intersection of Performance and Provocation," *Journal of Cinema and Media Studies*, 59, no. 2 (Winter 2020): 154.

24 Ralina Joseph, *Postracial Resistance: Black Women, Media, and the Uses of Strategic Ambiguity* (New York: New York University Press, 2018), 29.

25 Rembert Browne, "Donald Glover's Community," *Vulture*, August 22, 2016, https://www.vulture.com/2016/08/donald-glover-atlanta.html.

26 Friend, "Donald Glover Can't Save You."

27 Liz Shannon Miller, "'Atlanta': Donald Glover Wants You to Feel What It's like to Be Black," *IndieWire*, August 9, 2016, https://www.indiewire.com/2016/08/donald-glover-atlanta-fx-hiro-murai-trump-1201714877/.

28 Herman Gray, "The Feel of Life: Resonance, Race, and Representation," *International Journal of Communication* 9 (2015): 1115.

29 Allison Samuels, "Inside the Weird, Industry-Shaking World of Donald Glover," *Wired*, January 19, 2017, https://www.wired.com/2017/01/childish-gambino-donald-glover/.

30 Amy Wallace, "The Extraordinary Vision of Hiro Murai," *GQ*, November 30, 2018, https://www.gq.com/story/hiro-murai-breakout-profile-2018.

31 Wallace.

32 Josef Adalian, "FX's *Atlanta* Premiere Had the Best Ratings of Any Basic Cable Comedy in Three Years," *Vulture*, September 2016, https://www.vulture.com/2016/09/fx-atlanta-premiere-ratings-strong.html. The premiere drew 1.8 million total viewers and 1.2 million telecast viewers.

33 "For Us by Us? The Mainstream Appeal of Black Content," *Nielsen*, February 8, 2017, https://www.nielsen.com/us/en/insights/article/2017/for-us-by-us-the-mainstream-appeal-of-black-content/.

34 Nygaard and Lagerwey, *Horrible White People*, 178.

35 John L. Jackson, *Real Black: Adventures in Racial Sincerity* (Chicago: University of Chicago Press, 2005), 18.

36 Maurice J. Hobson, "All Black Everythang: Aesthetics, Anecdotes, and FX's Atlanta," *Atlanta Studies*, November 15, 2016, https://doi.org/10.18737/atls20161115.

37 Danielle Fuentes Morgan, *Laughing to Keep from Dying: African American Satire in the Twenty First Century* (Urbana: University of Illinois Press, 2020), 68.

38 Friend, "Donald Glover Can't Save You."

39 Morgan, *Laughing to Keep from Dying*, 70.

40 Sheri-Marie Harrison, "New Black Gothic," *Los Angeles Review of Books*, June 23, 2018, https://lareviewofbooks.org/article/new-black-gothic/.

41 Liz Shannon Miller, "'Atlanta': Donald Glover."

42 Beretta E. Smith-Shomade, *Pimpin' Ain't Easy: Selling Black Entertainment Television* (New York: Routledge, 2007). Such satirical content around Black consumer culture can also be seen in filmmaker Spike Lee's *Bamboozled* (2000).

43 Austin Williams, "The Enduring Legacy of Disney's Black Millennial Classic 'A Goofy Movie,'" *Vice*, February 22, 2017, https://www.vice.com/en/article/8qkxe5/the-enduring-legacy-of-disneys-black-millennial-classic-a-goofy-movie.

44 Joe Coscarelli, "In 'Atlanta,' a Soundtrack That Subtly Whispers Its Locale," *New York Times*, October 13, 2016, https://www.nytimes.com/2016/11/01/arts/music/atlanta-donald-glover-music-supervision.html.

45 Lynch, "Donald Glover," 22.

46 Trace William Cowen, "Donald Glover Reveals How He Convinced FX to Make 'Atlanta,'" *Complex*, February 26, 2018, https://www.complex.com/pop-culture/2018/02/donald-glover-reveals-how-he-convinced-fx-to-make-atlanta.

47 Bijan Stephen, "Atlanta Dreaming," *Dissent* 65, no. 3 (Summer 2018): 7.

48 Wilstein, "'Atlanta' Star Donald Glover."

49 Touré, "Why Atlanta Is the Blackest Show Ever," *New York Times*, November 11, 2022, https://www.nytimes.com/2022/11/11/opinion/atlanta-finale.html.

12

I'm Digging You

• • • • • • • • • • • • • • • • • • • •

Television's Turn to Dirty South Blackness

BERETTA E. SMITH-SHOMADE[1]

Black popular culture began serving up the Black South for larger U.S. and world consumption in the 1990s. For example, Aaliyah's "Are You That Somebody"—made for the *Dr. Doolittle* cinematic soundtrack—is remembered more for its intro rather than the song itself: "Dirty South, (uh-huh) can y'all really feel me?" Turn to the first quarter of the twenty-first century that finds television and digital media narratives contesting the disciplining gaze of whiteness similarly. In this moment, the blackest of Black manifests in our critical and visual consciousness, particularly opening audiences to a certain Blackness and rurality no one has wanted to think or talk about until now. New narratives complicate and toss out altogether the recurrent triumphs and multiple tragedies of living while Black, poor, and rural (or certainly other urban) in the Dirty South.

New Southern-based television series demonstrate not only the difficulties of living while Black but also the resilience and fight Black people employ in their determination to claim, stay, and walk in their birthright. OWN's *Queen Sugar* (Ava DuVernay, 2016–2022) and Starz's *P-Valley* (Katori Hall, 2020–) reckon with a past tinged with the scent of burning Black flesh and spurred by Black Lives Matter. Using frames of queering and informal economies, I discuss how this contemporary rebuke of white-is-right continues to reverberate through Southern Black mediated culture and why it resonates with Black audiences.

Migrating South

Media scholar Victoria E. Johnson writes about the ways in which television traditionally displays dominance, normalcy, and whiteness—locating mattering (white) audiences between coasts in the middle of the United States. Thus, even when new networks emerge such as PAX (1998–2006, now ION), their programming imagines a sensibility where everybody knows my name—my white, Christian name. This is not new. In the 1960s, to distract an audience distressed with a myriad of social unrests, the television industry turned to reimagining the South as a presumed gentler and better place than the actual history (and lived reality) suggested. Lily white and simple (-movement and -minded) narratives like *The Andy Griffith Show* (CBS, 1960–1968), *The Beverly Hillbillies* (CBS, 1962–1971), *Petticoat Junction* (CBS, 1963–1970), *Hee Haw* (CBS, 1969–1971), and later, the good ole boys of the *Dukes of Hazzard* (CBS, 1979–1985) provided contrast to the rise of the northern suburbs and rioting streets and brought CBS out of their last-place position in the broadcast wars. This success was temporary because once the powers-that-be received better demographic data that showed who the class of people watching these series was, they canceled them.[2] This whitewashed South belied its actual population and situation, even with the massive Black migration northward that had taken place since the beginning of the twentieth century. It reflected a gap between the imagined plantation South and the South of the enslaved.

Half a century later, studies conducted by Pew Research found that the U.S. Southern region hosts the highest share of the country's Black population. They showed 56 percent of all Black folks live in the South, deviating from previous Black living patterns. While the early twentieth century watched Black folks migrating from the South in droves, since 1970, the number of Blacks living in the South has grown.[3] This return to the South has not been so much a valuation of it but a recognition that the lives of many Black folks haven't been all that they were cracked up to be up North and out West. When Gladys Knight sang about her man getting on the midnight train to Georgia, she understood it and joined his return. This was 1973. By 2021, *New York Times* writer Charles Blow called for Blacks to go back to the South to take up political power that has already been structured and built by Blacks who remained and supported by those who have returned. He suggests in returning, you can not only face *The Devil You Know* but also mount "the most audacious power play by Black America in the history of the country."[4] These demographic shifts alongside television industry expansion and Black creative voices visioning differently are all part of the reason we see more stories centering Southern Black life in television and digital media.

Screening the South Now

With new corporate mandates to target Black audiences, the Dirty South returns with the voices and visions of those whose ancestors built its foundation. Even when harkening to the past with Southern series like *Underground* (WGN, 2016–2017) and *The Underground Railroad* (Amazon Prime Video, 2021), contemporary iterations hit different. For example, *Underground* creators Misha Green and Joe Pokaski explore slavery in Georgia but to the beat of Kanye West's 2013 "Black Skinhead." The series is introduced with the sounds of dogs barking and snarling, running, breathing, and a banging drumbeat. For audiences of a certain generation, the rap may mean nothing beyond its contemporary and energized sound. However, for millennials and some Generation Z who later catch the series, this soundtrack calls them to attention. It signals defiance, a reshaped understanding of respectability, and a reimagined history.[5] Even in a narrative about a period hundreds of years before their birth, these audiences get connected to the right-nowness of the fictionalized trauma through Kanye—helping to birth a divergent narrative and trajectory altogether.

These are not the routes and *Roots* of a historicized Virginia of the 1970s. This time, audiences view the enslaved's fight—the brutality and their hard work—but also their collective determination to live and live differently within the savage and slaveholding Dirty South. Producer David Wolper positioned *Roots* as an immigrants' tale of Black men with helpful, crying Black women.[6] *Underground* shows audiences something more, a position from the unbowed.[7] When television scholar Brandy Monk-Payton argues for certain televisual reparations, this series might not be it (if "it" is even possible), but it certainly offers a more plausible acknowledgment and remembrance of what happened before and rationale for why everyone needs to fight like hell to not let it happen again.[8]

The Dirty South is beginning to be reimagined across media platforms. The charming Southern 1960s humor of whites as fish out of water or as the nouveau riche has melted away in favor of sweltering heat, crippling corruption, and glistening Black bodies. In defining the Dirty South, hip-hop scholar Regina N. Bradley believes that in addition "to the physical renderings of the word 'dirty,' that is, red clay, dirt, or mud, the term also connotes the dirtiness of the treatment of Southern [B]lack folks, even in the post-civil rights era, which deromanticizes the belief that the movement ended the racial and socioeconomic tensions facing Southern [B]lack communities."[9] African American studies scholar L. H. Stallings enlarges this understanding of the Dirty South by insisting it exists as the simultaneous place and practice of "intersectional politics, critiques of moral authority, and the development of regional aesthetic philosophies whose purpose is dismantling and reinventing Southern public spheres."[10] These updated and energized conceptualizations of the Dirty South help shape a rationale and necessity for contemporary Southern Black stories. They also draw awareness to a tension with the marketing of and works emerging from what is considered the capital of the Dirty South, the wished-for chocolate city, Atlanta.[11]

As a televisual hub of Southern Blackness, Atlanta has become almost spiritual in its mixed connotations of Black mecca, Motherland, and "forty acres and a mule" promises for African-Americans and Blacks of the diaspora. It provides a context and home for the closeness of peoples and beliefs of descendants from the African continent. The larger cultivated narrative of Atlanta, Georgia, as a welcome place specifically for Black folks has resounded strongly since the 1970s—encouraging people from all over the country to pack their things and return (or move) to this promised land. In Atlanta, an abundance of professional energy and possibilities thrives. African diasporic peoples *appear* prosperous. They own grand houses, serve as television news anchors, graduate from the best HBCUs (Atlanta University Center [AUC]), claim their influencer status, drive high-end cars, run politics, and dress in designer clothes. Atlanta is home to Tyler Perry Studios. Aspirational descriptions get trotted out as a city "too busy to hate." While historian Maurice Hobson argues sweepingly about Atlanta's Black mecca narrative against its poor Black masses (its palpable class divide), 2019 found 3.6 million Black people who claimed Georgia as home. I call attention to Atlanta because of the multiplicity of fictional and nonscripted narratives that emanate from there and the standing the city holds in the Black imagination about Black progress. However, it is not where the blackest Dirty South stories are enlivened most.

Dramatic narratives that pepper screens from lush landscapes of the Bayou to Miami's hood all point to a more poignant way of imagining the Dirty South and its Black residents. Tax credits offer incentives and continually cultivated and trained Black bodies provide below-the-line labor and narrative fodder in the case of reality TV. In this moment, as sociologist Zandria Robinson suggests, "The South has risen again as the geographic epicenter of authentic Black identity"[12]—a Black identity that flourishes as a mix of "I'll find a way or make one" and deprivation simultaneously. This notion comes both through narrative visioning and sonic tremors. Artists like Jermaine Dupri, OutKast, and Janelle Monáe in Atlanta; Lil Wayne, Master P, and Big Freedia in New Orleans; and Tobe Nwigwe in Houston suggest that the larger Black South no longer cowers and waits to be beckoned or identified, at least as far as Black popular culture is concerned. Examples of a Blacker, poorer, and more defiant South come through two significant narratives series flourishing in this moment: *Queen Sugar* and *P-Valley*.

"I'm Feeling Something I Haven't Felt in a Very Long Time . . . Free": Ava DuVernay's *Queen Sugar*

The series *Queen Sugar* performs a form of affective labor for grown Black women. Speaking to the confluence of complex Black women characters, familial support, and even problematically leading but tender-hearted Black men, the writers weekly demonstrate a Southern Black life rarely shown. It makes space for flawed and complicated relationships and love across generations, occupations, and consequences. For example, baby brother Ralph Angel's (Kofi Siriboe) actions often place his family's land and legacy in peril. Yet as cultural critic bell hooks muses with thoughts that characterize this series, "Forgiveness and compassion are always linked: how do we hold people accountable for wrongdoing and yet at the same time remain in touch with their humanity enough to believe in their capacity to be transformed?"[13] The seven seasons of *Queen Sugar* take audiences through this growth and transformation and allow for new possibilities for the Dirty South—in this case, Louisiana.

Queen Sugar chronicles the lives of the three Bordelon siblings Nova (Rutina Wesley), Charley (Dawn-Lyen Gardner), and Ralph Angel and their negotiations with relationships, land, community, history, and the Dirty South. An observation by Charley epitomizes the series' tension with and vision for whiteness and history. She remarks, "It's ironic, you know. The land that your ancestors killed our ancestors for will become the foundation for a new movement of Black empowerment."[14] The series appears on the Oprah Winfrey Network, and beyond *Queen Sugar*, OWN offers a preponderance of programs located in the Dirty South, including nonscripted *Welcome to Sweetie Pie's* (2011–2018) and *Iyanla, Fix My Life* (2012–2021) and the scripted *Greenleaf* (2016–2020). OWN also partners with Tyler Perry to include his mostly Southern-based works on the network. All this programming responds to the network recognizing the Black women twenty-five-plus market who comprise its largest audience. In their expanse of fictional Black narrative and nonscripted reality life, these OWN series and others around the televisual landscape laid successful ground for the 2020 release of Starz's *P-Valley*.

"Sometimes You Need Fiction to Tell the Truth": Katori Hall's *P-Valley*

Black Twitter fan favorite *P-Valley* became a mainstream press darling in part because of its creator, Pulitzer Prize–winning playwright Katori Hall. Describing herself to Elle.com, Hall says,

> First, I am a Black Southerner and wasn't born with a silver spoon in my mouth.
> Even though I went to those [universities] and understood all of these politics,
> my Blackness and where I was from was never far from my mind. I never felt
> any shame about where and how I grew up. I am proud of where I came from.
> My grandmother was a sharecropper, and we used to live in a very impoverished
> neighborhood in Memphis, and we moved out to be in a "better" neighborhood.
> But every weekend, I went back to visit Big Momma. And I learned that no matter
> where I lived or where I went or if I spoke a certain way, I'm still Black. They are

still gonna treat me like a nigga. So, I never felt that I had to put forward images that made people feel comfortable. And because I grew up on the fault line, I feel like it's my responsibility to shake the table. Actually, shake the ground.[15]

Hall describes the South she wanted to show as one with a "delta noir" aesthetic. She needed to expose the "shit behind the shine," letting audiences in on the work.[16] Like *Queen Sugar*, the first season of *P-Valley* featured all female directors, including Black women like Millicent Shelton, Tasha Smith, and Christine Swanson. For *Deadline*, Denise Petski reports, "*P-Valley* set a new record on the Starz App for most viewed series premiere at 17% above the previous high. . . . To date, *P-Valley* ranks #1 among 2020's new premium series with African American viewers . . . and is in the Top 5 of all premium series among African American households, according to Starz and Nielsen stats."[17] And following its second-season premiere in 2022, the series garnered 4.5 million viewers across platforms, eleven times its first season opener and more than its network-mate *Power Book IV: Force* (2022–). Starz executive Alison Hoffman boasts, "The series exemplifies our commitment to amplifying narratives by, about and for women and underrepresented audiences, and we are so proud of its continued success."[18] According to more pedestrian sources such as IMDB voters, women and men watch the series with a preponderance of the audience deemed millennials ages thirty to forty-four and more men than women in the forty-five-plus category. Thus, it seems also a series for Generation Xers. Coming from the Southern settings of dirt-poor Mississippi and languishing, rural Louisiana, *P-Valley* and *Queen Sugar* center unique Black stories and recognize people and subjects too long dismissed and ignored.

"I Did Not Come to Play with You Hoes": Queering of the Dirty South

Quiet as it's kept, the South has never been binary for Black folks. The queer finds itself expressed in many ways. The queer comes within work. The queer comes through bodies loving across and through gender and race. The queer comes through white respectability and Black raucousness embodied in one space, one body, one mind, settling together disquieted. The queer comes in sanctification and sinning snuggled right up together. Queering in these programs looks like oppression, ostracization, and invisibility alongside intersectional identities and loving with passion across communities. The twenty-first century returning to the Dirty South foregrounds those interstices where Black lives get lived, discussed, mimicked, hushed, and repeated. Thus, one significant and compelling aspect of these new Black series is their recognition of a queer Dirty South as part of the regular order of things.

P-Valley makes the queer commonplace as it tracks the budding, complicated love story of Lil Murda (J. Alphonse Nicholson) and Uncle Clifford (Nicco Annan)—nicely tying together their on-screen romantic journey with Al Green's iconic 1972 "Love and Happiness" as sonic validation in one episode.[19] Uncle Clifford is the nonbinary, gender-nonconforming manager of the Pynk, the strip club at the center of every character's world in the impoverished fictional town of Chucalissa, Mississippi. On playing Uncle Clifford, Annan maintains, "Within the [B]lack Southern community, to have that going on is really a big thing, and really a sense of movement." So when Uncle Clifford invites his customers to the club with his "The doors of the Pynk are open so come on in" refrain, he not only ushers in the clientele but also the audience to witness a side of the Dirty South that is often hidden from television narratives.

Queerality also gets elevated and demonstrated in the ways in which love and bodies, lust and work move not only in what often gets displayed as same-sex communities but also within hetero, bi, and trans ones, and across generations as well. When Coach (Sherman Augustus) "sponsors" a Mercedes Experience for himself (a private pole dance and sex), his wife, Farrah (Shamika Cotton), not only watches but also joins in and then schedules her own personal, private experiences with Mercedes (Brandee Evans), his "poon policing" notwithstanding. Demonstrating this desire for and of Black women across gender and class and allowing their voices and dreams to manifest help excavate a hidden queer Dirty South. It also helps temper the pervasive narrative of rabid Black homophobia.

In another example, the problematically biracial Corbin Kyle (Dan J. Johnson) operates as a conflicted outsider inside a prominent white cotton family whose Black mother was the family's maid. His identity and his behavior constantly poke at the past and challenge anyone who stands in his way to recognize and claim his birthright. This same fly in the familial and community ointment also (covertly) needs Uncle Clifford to periodically whip him inside the Pynk's Paradise room. Beyond its queer inferences, Corbin's particular history surfaces multiple wretched pasts in present-day form. It invokes and then overturns (or at least troubles) a master-slave dialectic that continues in the new Dirty South. In all its stories, queerness functions in *P-Valley* as part of relationships, work, and a spectacularized and present-day Blackness.

In *Queen Sugar*, DuVernay offers a queered rethinking of gendered norms, sexuality, and race through its youngest cast members, Blue (Ethan Hutchison) and Micah (Nicholas Ashe). In multiple episodes and seasons, the series explores societal assumptions, structures, and expectations of Black masculinity through Blue and his doll, Kenya. For *TheGrio*, George M. Johnson writes, "The dynamic of Ralph Angel (the ex-con) having the greatest understanding and capacity for who and what Blue might be is the most telling part of this narrative. The 'be a man' and 'big boys don't cry' narrative is something that is engrained in society to be synonymous with manhood. That Ralph Angel

FIG. 12.1 Blue playing with Kenya

serves as the protector of Blue's identity, whatever that may be, is a 101 on unconditional parenting, and how one should react when faced with the reality of a child exhibiting behaviors that don't align with a heteronormative society."[20] The tenderness Ralph Angel demonstrates toward and for Blue belies his bad choices / criminal behavior in ways that illuminate both the precarious conditions offered for Black men in the Dirty South and elsewhere and their embodied humanity simultaneously. In other words, this big Black man (mostly visualized as menacing and violent in mainstream culture), in *Queen Sugar*, turns out to be vulnerable, empathetic, intelligent, and human through his actions and his words, even while dealing with a community and larger society that imagine him as always-already dangerous.

In the example of Blue's big cousin Micah, his relationship with his fraternity brother Isaiah (Marquis Rodriguez) gives audiences an opportunity to witness how Black men can address and explore feelings outside of their assigned genitalia and perceived desire. After a public incident where Micah recoils from the presumption of their gay relationship, the two talk:

MICAH: To the extent that anybody can be sure about anything, I don't
    think I'm gay. But I do have feelings for you, and that's confusing.
    I feel like my sense of self, and my emotional attraction are at odds.
    Like, the way I feel for you in my heart doesn't match my feelings for
    you in other ways. . . .
ISAIAH: . . . You should know that I don't want anything from you, Micah,
    and I never did. Nothing except to be your friend, your brother. But
    society tells us that men can't love each other that way. You know, we
    don't do that. Women can be best friends, they can hold hands, they

can declare their love for each other, but we can't. And if we do, then we must be gay.[21]

Instead of a melodramatic scene of recrimination, uncovering, or even coming out, audiences find Black young men expressing their hearts to one another, tenderly. The closeness and quiet of the scene allow for undetermined and unboxed identities to linger, sit, and be left unresolved—"silences that allow for moral ambiguity."[22] Black stories in general don't get that freedom of indeterminate endings, and a Black queer story that doesn't end in tragedy, death, or pathos is nearly nonexistent. Making queer commonplace comes through not only the casting but also the characterization of actor Brian Michael Smith as transmale police officer Antoine "Toine" Wilkins in the series. His presence passes almost unmarked but recognized with joy by other Black men for walking in his truth. Both *Queen Sugar* and *P-Valley* provide a rarely seen sexual freedom and gender fluidity for Black folks in the Dirty South. This openness is not confined only to the narratives of these new Southern television series but draws on their aesthetics as well.

Musical forays sonify an understanding of and connection between Blackness and queerality with roots in the Dirty South and larger Black popular culture. In the past, artist Meshell Ndegeocello described how "beautiful brown bodies, pimp, switch, and sway" on her 1993 song "I'm Digging You (Like an Old Soul Record)." And in the twenty-first century, she serves as musical director for *Queen Sugar*. Selecting Ndegeocello, a queer bassist known for her musical artistry and collaborative and alternative visioning, was a dream for DuVernay. She wanted audiences to palpably experience different feelings with this series. In deciding what the musical score would sound like, the two had several conversations around color. Ndegeocello creates the series soundtrack with a team of musicians, and they dip into her own musical catalog often, using her 1999 song "Faithful" in the very first episode. In fact, her music and voice are the first sounds audiences encounter in the series opener while simultaneously seeing the black locs and the beautiful, deep-brown skin of Nova. As Bilal Qureshi writes, "The camera lingers on lips, skin, and hair in a manner that feels revolutionary in its heightened sensuality."[23] Knowing how to light and shoot Black skins and sonically meld rural and paced Black life mesmerizes audiences.

More, like Ndegeocello coming to public consciousness in the 1990s, New Orleans's Big Freedia brings bounce music and twerk to these series. As rapper and entertainer, Big Freedia champions a music and movement of identity underground that later gets recognized with concert tours and speaking engagements, her own reality television series, an ice cream flavor with Ben & Jerry's, a web series via Patreon, and color commentary for different areas of Black popular awards culture.[24] Big Freedia gets to rep herself in *P-Valley* on stage with her song "Explode" when she introduces Lil Murda and Miss Mississippi on their Dirty Dozen tour.[25] In fact, one writer characterizes *P-Valley*'s whole second season's musical score as an ode to Southern grit. So in 2016, when Big Freedia announces, "I did not come to play with you hoes," before Beyoncé calls Black women into "Formation," audiences "already know" how she has helped usher a new queer Dirty South into the mainstream. Overtly (and covertly) queer narratives centered in the Dirty South make space for a continued and perversely absent Black complexity and humanity on television. This perceived inhumanity often stems, at least in part, from (lack of) resources.

"Run Me My Stack": Informal Economies in the Dirty South

Queen Sugar and *P-Valley* foreground and elevate Black bodies that work in the fields and on the pole, showcasing the hardworking, quotidian life of the rural and poor Black Dirty South. In real-lived culture, Black folks shop for their groceries, run to the mall, pay bills, and pay respect at wakes all in their work uniforms. The 2022 Detroit-esque calamity of limited clean water in Jackson, Mississippi, confirms the paucity of basic services in real life beyond the sets of TV series and the residents they fictionalize. Within television narratives centering the Dirty South, viewers witness what essential workers look like at work. They feel the Black-body mandate to clean spaces, serve customers food, provide gas and convenience store goods, deliver packages, care for children, attempt to heal the sick, and bury those who cannot be saved. Real-world essential jobs are overrepresented by Black and Latinx workers and women. In fact, according to a 2020 report by the Center for Economic and Policy Research, two-thirds of frontline workers are women and 41 percent are people of color.[26] Nonetheless, for people in these communities, actual and fictionalized, there is no shame in work, no matter what it is.

Two types of informal economies manifest and are exemplified in these real-lived and fictional communities: one deals with the type of work available; the other deals with support systems needed for that work to happen. In both series, informal economies help folks survive living while Black and poor and rural in the Dirty South. Historian Robin D. G. Kelley introduced the idea of *Race Rebels* in the 1990s when he outlined how Black people, young Black people in particular, push back on problematic and inequitable work environments through their dress and behavior to carve out some pieces of dignity.[27] *Queen Sugar* and *P-Valley* imagine a little bit of that notion but tap into something larger. Building on the framework of several scholars before her, sociologist LaShawn Harris characterizes informal work economies as a "network of economic endeavors and community relations that support . . . both the generation of income and the exchange of goods and services outside officially sanctioned or regulated networks of exchange."[28] This definition suggests the types of work marginalized and impoverished communities must pursue and the necessary exchanges that must be constructed to maintain that work. *Queen Sugar* and *P-Valley* showcase a bit of this Black Dirty South informal economy.

Recognizing the work and livelihood precarity of the Dirty South, many Black audience members respond to these series manifesting such scenarios via Twitter, Instagram, and Facebook. They comment, "But fr, Mississippi is the poorest state in the U.S. Pandemic hits harder when you're already struggling" (love_mia_rue, June 17, 2022). Trustitsavirgo adds, "Chucalissa in a recession before the recession" (June 17, 2022). And kay_d_datopic writes in response to a detractor, "Screaming . . . clearly she has never been to Mississippi . . . where the ppl can live without but will have a mouth full of golds n big dreams" (June 18, 2022).

Working-class and working-poor Blacks deliver packages, farm, fish, park cars, operate machines, maintain senior care facilities, change bedpans, and teach in rural Southern communities. In places that exist on tourism of Black culture, the double consciousness of W. E. B. Du Bois becomes perniciously in play as tourists, often white in places like New Orleans, come to eat the food, hear the music, drink the liquor, and be entertained by the Other. For this setup to work effectively (and profitably), the Other needs to smile broadly while accepting long-term and planned low-pay and underresourced schools—both of which relegate them to said work. Dancers in the Dirty South largely fall into this labor category and because of their circumstances, must often consign childcare to whomever is not literally up on the pole. In *P-Valley*, audiences see not only the athleticism of the dancers and the Pynk's blinking lights but also the mundane—"strip malls, payday loan centers, [and] parking lot car washes" that "crackle with a realism that feels familiar and lived in."[29]

The collectivity of care to facilitate commerce can be seen all throughout the actual Dirty South and these series. In *Queen Sugar*, communities negotiate "da Rona" through free communal food package care enabled by Aunt Vi (Tina Lifford), sharing of resources to keep Ms. Parthena's (Rhonda Johnson Dents) farm and land from repossession, and burial of community members. In *P-Valley*, before his death from COVID-19, Mayor Ruffin (Isaiah Washington) operates as a "fuckin' Robin Hood nigga" by facilitating and paying a collective water bill that spouts from his home to his neighbors. Within its season 2 opener, the Pynk devises novel ways to keep operating. Turning the pandemic-closed club into a car wash with "titties" and free hot wings, the innovative "Pussyland" creates an experience for clients in their cars. With thoughtful and necessary cross-promotion to lure customers, they offer a choice between the right-now calamity of the pandemic, the cross, and carnal needs. This "nonessential" business turns into relief for both its blue-balls having former clients and the folks who work there. The equal division of monies made between all personnel ("pussy-having" or not), shared childcare, and making sure dancers have sufficient PPE and food (in order to not have to give head) demonstrate the ways this poor, Black, and Dirty South community enacts an informal economy, riding together to survive.

In the necessary scratchin' and survivin' of the Black Dirty South, the characters in these series are familiar and recognizable to Black viewers as almost

P-VALLEY | STARZ

FIG. 12.2 One of *P-Valley*'s crossroads (season 2, episode 1)

archetypal in function: one flourishes as part of their family; another's friend's cousin was locked up; someone else's niece is hiding her sexuality from an overly religious family, and her play paw-paw is barely making it. In *Queen Sugar*, Ralph Angel serves as lookout for someone who boosts goods from a warehouse. While in *P-Valley*, "booty money" saved for a more "legitimate and respectable" gym business gets laundered through the church and used as collateral for its loans. Absconded from her dancer daughter, Rev. Woodbine (Harriett D. Foy) subsequently uses this same money as a down payment for her new church. Later, Rev. Woodbine announces (and pole performs) in her mayoral run, "I hoed so you could fly, Chucalissa." Surviving in the Black Dirty South often looks unlike American bootstrap lies and, as media scholar Adrien Sebro theorizes, more reflects employment of hustle economics.[30]

The multiple modes of work and informal economies in these series also illustrate the simultaneous attitudes, convolution, and beauty of Blackness, Black women, and their relationship to the market. For example, in *P-Valley*, the tragedies and repercussions of colorism impact the dancers' earnings—making it a point of routine contention among them. It seems all the patrons want the light-skinned girl who stays getting her way despite her inability to dance well. In another example, when Keyshawn (Shannon Thornton) tells Lil Murda to "run me my stack," she recognizes that even on the back of their disenfranchisement, their collective work (in this case, using digital tools for fame and fortune as a dancer and budding rapper) sutures them into a freewheeling twenty-first-century informal (but increasingly formal and lucrative for some) economy. This new economy potentially moves them into more money and opportunity but with the need to maintain informal economic structures to make it happen.

I put these narratives and images in conversation with filmmaker Arthur Jafa's *Dreams Are Colder Than Death* (2013), where Jafa, a Mississippian, questions what Blackness means, especially in the South. The film arrests viewers with luxuriating scenes of Southern communities filled with Black bodies in life—swimming Black boys, walking-to-work Black girls, pontificating-in-the-yard Black men, and dancing-for-money-in-the-strip-club Black women. In this meditation on Southern Black life, one of the young dancers insightfully remarks, "The nakedness is the uniform. The costume is the accessory." Black people's need to lay bare, outfit, and provide for one another gets magnified in these Dirty South series unlike other places in visual culture prior.

Dreams Never Die

The confluence of Black migratory movement southward and Black massacre creates an opening for the stories of Black life to be redressed. Trayvon Martin's murder in Florida in 2012 and George Zimmerman's subsequent 2013 acquittal (along with many other Black deaths) launched the Black Lives Matter movement by three Black women. While televisual fictional narratives somewhat reflected the times with special episodes of the moment, nothing galvanized visual (and corporate) redress/reparations like the murder of George Floyd in 2020, while all were stuck at home because of COVID-19.

A cursory glance around the new water cooler for television talk, social media, finds some viewers identifying *P-Valley* as "ghetto," not sufficiently hard (or urban-like), or a series just for single men. Despite these critiques—or probably more accurately, *because* of them—its viewership continues to rise. Similarly, Reddit users castigate *Queen Sugar*'s Nova for putting her family's business in the book streets through her published memoirs. They accuse her of going down and up and around the ways of unrighteousness, disloyalty, and betrayal. Yet the undisputed understanding about Nova is that her connection to African traditional spiritual practices—shown to help, soothe, and heal Black women and men—as well as her activism forge a Dirty South alchemy that is steeped in not only the history, sweat, tears, bodies, and blood of Black people but also the loving, queer, and informal supports.

Reimaginings and commentary about a new Black Dirty South often come from millennials and Gen Zers using digital tools. Stories are being told and sold on the open market—with no dearth of content to enjoy, explore, and consume. The target demographic for all TV programming remains ages eighteen to forty-nine, which at this moment means Generation X, millennials, and Generation Z.[31] Yet according to the *Los Angeles Times*, only 10 percent of Generation Z would rather watch TV or movies as opposed to the other 90 percent, who'd rather play video games, listen to music, surf the net, or engage in social media.[32] In both *Queen Sugar* and *P-Valley*, their millennial and Gen Z characters take up the tools for consciousness raising (Micah's pictures of police brutality on Instagram) as well as making money (Keyshawn's in-home Instagram dance following and Micah's NFT pursuits). Both series incorporate and visualize what's happening right now alongside historic and systemic ways of keeping Black folks in their place in the new Black Dirty South.

In *P-Valley*'s series opening theme, "Down in the Valley," rapper Jucee Froot describes dancing at the Pynk as "climbing up the pole just to get out the bottom"—a sentiment that characterizes the necessity and viability of queer community and informal economies. Audiences might consider the emergence of multiple Black and dirty television stories and showrunners as a kind of return to the devil you know. They offer a glimpse of how a shifting culture imagines itself—insisting on recognition, value, and equity. The "for us by us" dreams explored in *Queen Sugar*, *P-Valley*, and other Southern narratives force the industry, audiences, and scholars to vision the Dirty South in new Black ways, freer of the concern for "them" and focused on concern for us. It might not be "progress" as measured in numbers and actualities, but it gives audiences and others an opportunity to imagine and see that dreams never die.

Notes

1   I thank scholars Kristen J. Warner and Salmon A. Shomade for helping me think through these ideas.

2   As noted in the *History of the Sitcom* documentary, episode 6, "Social Class," aired August 12, 2021.

3   Christine Tamir, "The Growing Diversity of Black America," Pew Research Center, March 25, 2021, https://www.pewresearch.org/social-trends/2021/03/25/the -growing-diversity-of-black-america/.

4   Charles M. Blow, *The Devil You Know: A Black Power Manifesto* (New York: Harper Perennial, 2021), quoted in Tanisha C. Ford, "Should Black Northerners Move Back to the South?," *New York Times*, March 2, 2021.

5   This affection predates Kanye's (Ye's) latest 2022 foolishness against Jews.

6   See Eric Pierson's "Audiences and the Televisual Slavery-Narrative" in this volume.

7   Named Best TV Show by the African American Film Critics Association, the series received four NAACP Image award nominations and was nominated as an Outstanding New Program by the Television Critics Association. It won three Cynopsis TV awards, was honored by *Broadcasting & Cable* and *Multichannel News* for

Diversity Discussion in Television and Video, and was nominated for an American Society of Cinematographers award for cinematography. Denise Petski, "'Underground': OWN Acquires WGN America's Historical Drama Series," December 3, 2020, accessed August 23, 2021, https://deadline.com/2020/12/underground-own-acquires-wgn-america-historical-drama-series-1234636068/. And still, it was canceled after two seasons.

8   See Brandy Monk-Payton, "Blackness and Televisual Reparation," *Film Quarterly* 71, no. 2 (Winter 2017): 12–18. I thank my Emory University "Black TV" freshperson seminar class, spring 2022, for thinking this through with me, especially Penelope Gallardo.

9   Regina N. Bradley, *Chronicling Stankonia: The Rise of the Hip-Hop South* (Chapel Hill: University of North Carolina Press, 2021), 104n13.

10 L. H. Stallings, *A Dirty South Manifesto* (Berkeley: University of California Press, 2020), 5.

11 In Parliament's 1975 song "Chocolate City," they talk about "gaining on" Atlanta in terms of emerging Black Power numerically, politically, and economically.

12 Zandria F. Robinson, *This Ain't Chicago: Race, Class, and Regional Identity in the Post-Soul South* (Chapel Hill: University of North Carolina Press, 2014), 1.

13 Melvin McLeod, "'There's No Place to Go but Up'—bell hooks and Maya Angelou in Conversation," *Lion's Roar*, January 1, 1998, https://www.lionsroar.com/theres-no-place-to-go-but-up/.

14 *Queen Sugar*, season 6, episode 10, "And You Would Be One of Them," written by Ava DuVernay, Anthony Sparks, and Natalie Baszile, aired November 16, 2021, on OWN.

15 Kellee Terrell, "*P-Valley* Creator Katori Hall Believes Cardi B 'Rolled Out the Pynk Carpet' for the Hit Starz Drama," *Elle.com*, September 9, 2020, https://www.elle.com/culture/movies-tv/a33966657/p-valley-katori-hall-interview/.

16 Libby Hill, "'P-Valley' Creator Katori Hall: 'You Do Have to Grit Your Teeth Sometimes to Get to the Top of the Pole,'" *IndieWire*, June 23, 2021, https://www.indiewire.com/video/katori-hall-p-valley-pole-grit-glitter-women-starz-emmy-1234641284/.

17 Denise Petski, "'P-Valley' Renewed for Season 2 By Starz," *Deadline*, July 27, 2020, https://deadline.com/2020/07/p-valley-renewed-season-2-starz-1202996294/.

18 As found in Rick Porter, "Starz's 'P-Valley' Posts Huge Viewer Gains for Season 2 Premiere," *Hollywood Reporter*, June 9, 2022, accessed December 29, 2022, https://www.hollywoodreporter.com/tv/tv-news/starz-p-valley-ratings-season-2-premiere-1235162035/.

19 Episode 3 of season 2 ends with Al Green's iconic, nondiegetically illustrating tune and Uncle Clifford's thinking about and looking at all the postcards Lil Murda has sent her on the road from the Dirty Dozen tour with Keyshawn.

20 George M. Johnson, "Through a Doll, 'Queen Sugar' Explores the Effeminization of the Black Man," *TheGrio*, July 19, 2017, https://thegrio.com/2017/07/19/queen-sugar-blue-kenya-doll/.

21 *Queen Sugar*, "And You Would Be One of Them."

22 This secondary thought expressed by Bilal Qureshi in his "The Cultural Consolation of Ava DuVernay's *Queen Sugar*," *Film Quarterly* 70, no. 3 (2017): 65.

23 Qureshi, 65.

24 Her TV series is *Big Freedia: Queen of Bounce* (changed to *Big Freedia Bounces Back* on Fuse, 2013–). She has been featured on recordings of Beyoncé, Drake, and Kesha. She authored her memoir, *Big Freedia: God Save the Queen Diva!* in 2015 with Gallery Books / Simon & Schuster. And she's done color commentary for *Vogue* magazine and the 2022 BET Awards. Artist Katey Red was doing this work prior to Big Freedia.

25 *P-Valley*, season 2, episode 3, "The Dirty Dozen," written by Katori Hall, Kemiyondo Coutinho, Jamey Hatley, and Tessa Evelyn Scott, aired June 19, 2022, on STARZ.

26 Hye Jin Rho, Hayley Brown, and Shawn Fremsted, "A Basic Demographic Profile of Workers in Frontline Industries," Center for Economic and Policy Research, April 2020, https://www.eeoc.gov/sites/default/files/2021-04/4-28-21%20Meeting%20-%2005%20Ramirez%20-%20Supporting%20Materials.pdf.

27 See Robin D. G. Kelley, *Race Rebels: Culture, Politics, and the Black Working Class* (New York: Free Press, 1994).

28 LaShawn Harris, introduction to *Sex Workers, Psychics, and Numbers Runners: Black Women in New York City's Underground Economy* (Champaign: University of Illinois Press, 2016), 19.

29 Hannah Giorgis, "The Southern-Gothic Stripper Drama That TV Deserves," *Atlantic*, September 5, 2000.

30 See Adrien Sebro, *Scratchin' and Survivin': Hustle Economics and the Black Sitcoms of Tandem Productions* (New Brunswick, N.J.: Rutgers University Press, 2023).

31 Erica Shelton Kodish in conversation with Dr. Nsenga Burton, Emory University, online, November 17, 2021.

32 Ryan Faughnder, "What Entertainment Does Gen Z Prefer? The Answer Isn't Good for Hollywood," *Los Angeles Times*, April 18, 2021, https://www.latimes.com/entertainment-arts/business/story/2021-04-18/what-entertainment-does-gen-z-prefer-the-answer-isnt-good-for-hollywood.

13

I Feel Conflicted as F*ck

● ●

Netflix's *Dear White People* and Re-presenting Black Viewing Communities

JACQUELINE JOHNSON

> Dear white people, please stop touching my hair. Does this look like a petting zoo to you?[1]
> —Samantha White, *Dear White People*

Netflix's *Dear White People* (2017–2021) gets its attention-grabbing title from the main character Samantha (Sam) White's incendiary and controversial campus radio show of the same name. A series about being a Black face in a white space, *Dear White People* has been lauded for its use of satire and wry, tongue-in-cheek humor to detail the unique experience of Black students at an elite white university. It chronicles everything from the regular microaggressions of having your hair probed by white classmates to the more macro institutional problems of campus police violence and the relationship between slavery and Ivy League universities.

In 2012, creator Justin Simien released the concept trailer for *Dear White People* to raise preproduction funds and build support for a future feature film project. Simien's *Dear White People* centers on the Black students at the fictional

Manchester (later Winchester) University and how they navigate elite white spaces and the intragroup tensions that exist among different factions of the Black student population. More specifically, the initial central drama revolves around a blackface party white students throw on campus. Since the viral concept trailer, *Dear White People* has successfully moved across mediums and platforms. After the trailer led to donors exceeding the $25,000 goal of Simien's Indiegogo campaign,[2] *Dear White People* (2014) the film, starring Tessa Thompson, Brandon P. Bell, Teyonah Parris, and Tyler James Williams, premiered at Sundance. The film was well received by critics, and Simien won Sundance's award for Breakthrough Talent. That same year, he released a companion book project, a satirical "guide to inter-racial harmony in 'post-racial' America."[3] Three years later, a television series of the same name premiered on Netflix to positive reviews. In each iteration, *Dear White People* nuances its portrayal of the characters. And while this chapter focuses on the Netflix series, I begin by charting the previous forms of the narrative to frame my analysis of how the series puts forth a more expansive vision of Black community and adds complexity to the narrative's engagement with questions of representation, visual culture, identity formation, and spectatorship.

Each adaptation of *Dear White People* positions the core set of characters as avid consumers of media. While both the concept trailer and 2014 feature film construct scenes of disappointment and disaffection at the box office of a local theater, the series makes communal television watching a foundational component of social life in the Black dormitory Armstrong-Parker. The series *Dear White People* uses parodies of recent or current shows with significant Black viewership like *Love & Hip Hop* (VH1, 2011–), *Iyanla, Fix My Life* (OWN, 2012–2021), and *Scandal* (ABC, 2012–2018) to demonstrate the inherent polysemy of Black viewing while simultaneously mocking televisual texts considered low-quality. Several scholars have productively addressed the gaps in scholarship on Black audiences in recent years, and I seek to add to this growing body of research by analyzing how Black audiences themselves are rendered on-screen.

Meta engagement with Black representation and reception embedded in *Dear White People* the series highlights key considerations that the scholarship on Black audiences probes. I further these insights by considering *Dear White People*'s use of parodies to deftly engage broader conversations about "positive" and "negative" media representations and their perceived effects while remaining cognizant of the affective pleasures of viewing media. Through an analysis of episodes from the series' second season, which begins with white students moving into Armstrong-Parker after another dorm on campus burns down, I assert that the series complicates the positive/negative representation binary. Further, I examine interviews with series creator Justin Simien to discuss the ways in which he wants the series to challenge notions of positive and negative images but, in the process, often reentrenches a hierarchical taste culture that positions reality television and melodrama as of lesser cultural value. Employing parody, Simien and the other writers of *Dear White People* use the medium of television as a form of television criticism and, in turn, contemplate their own show's place within the larger landscape of Black cultural production.

Polysemy and the Affect of Black Viewing Communities

In the Indiegogo campaign page that accompanied the concept trailer, Simien and his team introduce their project to potential donors by tapping into Black cultural memory through referencing cult texts:

> **Remember when** Black movies didn't necessarily star a dude in a fat suit and a wig? Or have major plot twists timed to Gospel numbers for no apparent reason? No? Damn . . .
>
> Well believe it or not there was a time when "Black Art-House" was a thing. When movies like *Do The Right Thing*, *Hollywood Shuffle*, and *Boyz n the Hood* were breaking box office records as well as making us laugh, cry, and think in ways movies hadn't before.
>
> The humble producers of DEAR WHITE PEOPLE, a satire about being a black face in a white place, long to bring those days back. But we can't do it without you!
>
> Here's the deal . . . we're looking to raise seed money that will go a tremendously long way in securing the capital we'll need to produce our million dollar indie feature. With our trailer, script and **your help**, we believe we can bring this exciting piece of cinema to life! Join us, won't you?[4]

This rhetorical framing positions *Dear White People* within a lineage of "quality" cinema and as the antithesis of the work of Martin Lawrence, Eddie Murphy, and Black media mogul Tyler Perry simultaneously. Here, *Dear White People* becomes a necessary and timely entry into a cinematic landscape that has flattened Blackness into caricature. As a corrective, the film promises to "bring back" the heyday of Black film—the late '80s and early '90s—in a way that will once again push audiences to "laugh, cry, and think." Moreover, the Indiegogo campaign page points to the economic success of these films as well as their social, emotional, and cultural resonances. Discussing the commercial viability of films like *Do the Right Thing* also addresses enduring industry "logic." "Black films don't sell" has long been used by Hollywood to rationalize the lack of industrial support for Black movies. The Indiegogo campaign page illustrates Rebecca Wanzo's argument that "African American fans make hypervisible the ways in which fandom is expected and demanded of some socially disadvantaged groups as a show of economic force and ideological combat."[5] The language used by Simien and his fellow producers attempts to hail Black audiences and donors by suggesting that supporting the film pushes back against the ways in which Hollywood has wronged Black viewers.

In a scene from the trailer—later recreated in the feature film—the Black students crowd the ticket window of a local movie theater and express their extreme displeasure to a white, unprepared ticket seller. The trailer opens with Samantha White stating, "Forget Hollywood and forget Tyler Perry."[6] And in case viewers needed clarification, one of her fellow students follows with "Can we get a movie with actual characters in it instead of stereotypes wrapped up in Christian dogma?"[7] Like the Indiegogo campaign page that accompanies it, the concept trailer for *Dear White People* immediately positions itself against Hollywood's current offerings and likens itself to films of the 1980s and 1990s, citing both *Election* (1999) and *School Daze* (1988) as influences.[8] The trailer's climax involves the white students of the campus humor magazine—clearly modeled after *The Harvard Lampoon*—hosting a party to mock Black culture complete with watermelons, gold chains, and white students in blackface.

The short, three-minute trailer suggests a clear connection between the (perceived) dearth of nuanced media representations of Blackness, how the white students conceive of Blackness, and finally how the Black students are marginalized on campus. While many scholars have dismissed the idea of a direct, causal relation between what audiences see in media and their thoughts and beliefs, Julia Himberg notes in *The New Gay for Pay*, "the notion has maintained a remarkably strong hold in popular thinking."[9] It is this belief that partially drives the fictional students of *Dear White People*. For decades, media effects dominated audience-centered research, especially in regard to television. However, scholarly formations and schools of thought popularized in the latter half of the twentieth century, especially cultural studies and postmodernism, brought forth new modes of thinking about the audience.

Stuart Hall's foundational essay "Encoding/Decoding" provides a useful frame for interpreting this particular scene from *Dear White People*'s concept trailer. The students operate in what Hall terms the "oppositional code."[10] For example, rather than readily adopt the dominant, encoded meaning in the films of Tyler Perry and *Red Tails* (Hemingway and Lucas, 2012; a film also maligned in the trailer), the students read their content as in line with the hegemonic, racist regime in American visual culture. In the introduction to her edited collection *Say It Loud! African American Audiences, Media, and Identity*, Robin R. Means Coleman summarizes a key component of Hall's theorization of audience. She writes that the "social, cultural, political, and power conditions that define the individual audience member will be brought to the engagement with media and collude, resulting in meanings informed by those conditions and positions."[11]

Aligned with this idea, several of the authors' works featured in *Say It Loud!* assess how Blackness—in conjunction with other axes of identity such as gender, age, and class—informs media reception. In Nancy C. Cornwell and Mark P. Orbe's research on Aaron McGruder's comic strip *The Boondocks* (1996–2006), for example, the scholars note, "African American responses. . . . are as diverse as African Americans themselves."[12] While some Black readers, especially those with more personal experiences in white suburbs, found the comic strip to

FIG. 13.1 Students in Armstrong-Parker gathered to watch television

be an accurate (and funny) form of cultural anthropology, others interpreted McGruder's satire as reinforcing problematic stereotypes.

The Boondocks and other media featured in Means Coleman's text such as *The Color Purple* (1985) have been understood as controversial since their debut. Similarly, the work of Tyler Perry has been dismissed by numerous Black critics who have critiqued it on the grounds of things like colorism, reliance on reductive stereotypes, and pervasive depictions of violence against women. In fact, Spike Lee famously likened Perry's works to minstrelsy. However, many of Perry's critics forget, as scholars like Miriam Petty have argued, a lot of Black people enjoy Tyler Perry.[13] Here, Tyler Perry becomes the bad representation boogeyman and a convenient focal point at which Black students can project their displeasure. The first two versions of *Dear White People* make clear that the story's Black students are not a monolith; however, in depicting media reception, the film flattens the real diversity of Black audiences and their viewing practices.

To contrast this positioning, the series depicts a larger range of affective engagements with media texts; specifically, the series foregrounds pleasure. As Richard Dyer has argued, "Pleasure remains a forbidden term of reference, particularly on the left."[14] Both critical and cultural scholarship employing race, class, and gender as central analytics and culture writing in the popular press has frequently been so consumed by what particular texts *do* that often the pleasure audiences derive from them has been obscured. From the first season, critics eagerly latched onto the *Scandal* parody, titled *Defamation*, which lampoons the melodramatic shifts and twists in Shonda Rhimes's prime-time juggernaut.

In an early episode of that season, the camera makes the viewing community and their experience and reactions the focal point. The cinematographer and editors use several medium close-ups juxtaposed with wider shots to track our core set of characters' faces and the larger group dynamic as they watch and talk at the television. Joelle (Ashley Blaine Featherson) moves quickly from affirming the protagonist's impassioned monologue with a vigorous head nod and a "That's my girl" to shock and disappointment when she gives in to the president with a ridiculous line of dialogue. Kelsey (Nia Jervier) snaps and says, "Yes coat. Oooh boots." Reggie (Marque Richardson), conversely, slouches deeply in his armchair with a slight grimace on his face, trying his hardest to convey that he is above the show. At the end of the episode, he wryly remarks, "Is this why the revolution dies? Because we were in here watching TV?" The editing and the framing of the shots in this scene position Black reception as active, varied, and communal.

Analyzing what drives Black women who are fans of *Scandal*, and its central romantic pairing of Olivia Pope (Kerry Washington) and Fitzgerald Grant (Tony Golding), Kristen Warner asserts that "black women are rarely allowed to be main characters in stories about choice, desire, and fantasy. . . . What this dearth of representation can produce in black women is a deeper craving to desire and be desired."[15] From the *Defamation* watch party scene, we understand how *Dear White People* demonstrates a range of viewing positions but is especially attentive to the ways that Black women respond to *Scandal*. *Dear White People* the series makes a significant shift from its earlier iterations through this emphasis on affect. In a different work on Black women, affect, and reality television, Warner draws on Lauren Berlant's formulation of affective communities. Warner states, "No representation can embody the totality of a multidimensional self, not to mention that the percentage of black female bodies on television is consistently low. Thus, black female audiences negotiate the characterizations that are available to them in a kind of liminal space where they can patch together facets of identity from which they derive pleasure or that resonate with their own experience."[16] As demonstrated in this *Scandal*-ized scene of *Dear White People*, many of the Black women, and several male students, must negotiate the texts available to them. These texts provide moments of pleasure and release, and they aid in forming connections with their peers. Most critically, the media texts are a part of their identity formation processes as they navigate the tension between their public and private performances of the self at a key life stage.

In the first episode of the second season, however, white students from another campus dormitory move into Armstrong-Parker and rupture the magic circle of Black reception. The new white residents immediately begin to take part in the Black dormitory's communal television-watching rituals. While watching a *Love & Hip Hop* parody, the white students raucously laugh at the antics of rapper P. Ninny (Lena Waithe in a cameo). Previously, our Black characters were able to laugh and joke at the over-the-top characterizations of the reality television characters; however, when white students enter their space, they become concerned with what exactly the white students find so funny. Al (Jemar Michael), one of the Black students, remarks, "This show is my shit, but this feels wrong." And later, he says, "I'm feelin' conflicted as fuck."

In an interview about the parodies, Simien discussed the shift when the white students enter the fold: "I think in a lot of ways, the show is about the dichotomy between the roles that we play and who we really are. And the thing that conditions us is our culture and the things that we watch on TV. And one of the weird quirks about being black is that we have our little problematic faves that we love to watch, and suddenly, when we hear white people laughing at different things than we're laughing at, and watching it, it suddenly makes us go, 'Wait a minute, I feel a little uncomfortable.'"[17] In the first season of the series, viewers are introduced to the social life at Armstrong-Parker. Though the characters are constantly negotiating their public performance of the self, it becomes clear to viewers that within the walls of Armstrong-Parker, many of the Black students feel they can lower their guard among other members of their community. When white students become a part of their "safe space," the Black students must negotiate themselves and their media representation and reception differently. They must now account for the possibility that seeing over-the-top, ratchet performances of Blackness on-screen might affect the real interactions they now have with their housemates. In her analysis of *Scandal* and viewing communities on Twitter, Dayna Chatman argues that the basis of critiques from a subsection of people that would live tweet the series when it aired every week was concern about how *Scandal* affected out-group perception of African Americans.[18] In embedding this type of anxiety within *Dear White People* the series through show-within-a-show parodies, Simien and the rest of the writers push the concept beyond a gag. They attempt to work through the key debates and anxieties about media representation and Black subjects that have circulated within Black communities for decades.

Further, the series attempts to engage how the politics of media representation create frictions among Black people. Rashid Bakr (Jeremy Tardy), the seemingly sole African student on campus, remarks that when he was growing up, ratchet reality television characterizations were his only frame of reference for Black Americans. So "when [he] came here, [he] was terrified" both of Black Americans and of being confused for one.[19] At the start of the series, Rashid is integrated into community life at Armstrong-Parker, but the television scene demonstrates another layer of intragroup tensions existing among the Black students at this elite university.

In another example, the middle of the second season finds Joelle meeting a fellow Black, premed student, Trevor (Shamier Anderson), who she invites back to Armstrong-Parker at the end of their date to attempt to show him what he is missing by choosing to live in a mainstream (white) residence hall. After showing him the dining hall and remarking on the addition of grits to the menu, she takes him to the lounge, which she describes as "where we get our weekly dose of escapist Black fantasy." They sit down to watch the *Empire* (FOX, 2015–2020) parody, *Prince O' Palities*, and Trevor argues that the parodic series is part of a long lineage of Hollywood's attempt to denigrate Black people. In fact, Trevor dismisses the series in its entirety, specifically citing its attempt to break down the Black family. Joelle, however, argues its pleasures cannot be completely written off or denied. We find out that Trevor's oppositional reading of the series is rooted in the larger ideological framework of the hotep.[20] As a hotep, he also spouts homophobic remarks and rejects mixed-race Black people, even calling Sam, Joelle's best friend, a "halfrican." Critically, Joelle recognizes his noxious ideas through how he responds to *Prince O' Palities*, and Trevor's ideological position is broken apart and dismissed within the text of the show. Positioning his oppositional reading through the lens of hotep ideology and media reception illustrates the problematic underpinnings of hotep-ism while simultaneously privileging Joelle's reading of the televisual text. Joelle's framing of the television she and her peers consume as escapist fantasy is echoed in interviews with Justin Simien; however, I assert that the types of series the students watch are more than escapism.

More Than Catharsis?

In addition to nuancing the depiction of Black reception in the television format, the series also attends to how genre and mode of production fit into the framing of both Black representation and reception in American media. *Dear White People* offers several parodies, but it is immediately apparent that the students of Armstrong-Parker have a particular television diet. With the exception of *Empire* and *Scandal*, none of the series the students watch in the first two seasons even approach the realm of "quality" television. Moreover, though *Empire* and *Scandal* are prime-time serials, uses of soap opera conventions also further divorce them from the label of quality, especially in their later seasons. Despite *Dear White People*'s attempts to account for the pleasure these television series provide, both the tone and their paratextual framing ultimately reinforce problematic taste hierarchies that devalue reality television and melodrama.

In the concept trailer, a white student criticizes Samantha's controversial campus radio show by asking how she would feel if someone made a "Dear Black People." Sam responds to the provocation by stating, "There's no need for a Dear Black People. *Cops* [FOX, 1989–2013, Spike 2013–2017, Paramount Network, 2018–2020, FOX Nation 2021–], FOX News, and reality television let us know exactly what you think of us."[21] Placing reality television on the same rhetorical plane as law enforcement and FOX News is a bold proclamation. In this framing, reality television is not only ideologically anti-Black but also has the power to materially affect (and even threaten) everyday Black people's lives. Further, it compresses reality television, perhaps better understood through the lens of production rather than genre, into a single entity despite the vast range of types of programming and subjects. In the feature film, Coco (Teyonah Parris) spends much of the run time trying to attract the attention of a reality television producer. This storyline is underdeveloped in the film. Simultaneously, it muddles Coco's character arc and fails to nuance reality television representations. In her review of the film at *The Wrap*, Inkoo Kang writes, "Coco is arguably the least coherent character; it's improbable that a girl so determined to join the preppy blue bloods would also pursue stardom on a reality show. A producer (Malcolm Barrett) tells [her] that she's not enough of a stereotype . . . to be on TV. Instead of taking the producer's comments as flattery, Coco uses it as constructive criticism."[22] As Racquel Gates notes, reality television is often positioned as the ultimate bad text of media, located in the televisual "gutter."[23] Thus in addition to trying to curry favor with a rapacious reality television producer, Coco also notably attends the blackface party white students put on without the same intention of disruption that drives her Black peers. In these two versions of the narrative, not only are the ideological underpinnings of reality television corrupt, but those that enjoy or invest time in reality television are portrayed as misguided and with less nuance.

The television series, conversely, understands the pleasures audiences can derive from watching reality television programs. Despite this knowing, the series reinforces a taste hierarchy, reinscribing anxieties about the power of negative representation on denigrated media forms and reinforcing the logics of respectability politics. Simien's discussion of parodies in interviews only solidifies this tendency. The Black students at Armstrong-Parker watch primetime serials rooted in soap operas, daytime talk shows, and reality television series. Throughout the series, many students clearly express their enjoyment of these types of shows but also sheepishly apologize for or qualify their enjoyment of these programs. In an interview with *Vanity Fair*, Simien stated that the television series parodied in *Dear White People* are all things he actually watches and enjoys himself.[24] He demonstrates his love for the programs by "being a little shady" and mocking their narrative structures and plotlines.[25] While the satirical, mocking tone *Dear White People* uses to construct the parodies is presumably done in jest, the over-the-top dialogue of the characters in the parodies constructs these series as inherently ridiculous. Further, in an earlier interview with *Vulture* about *Defamation*, Simien referred to Shonda Rhimes's ABC series as kitchen sink entertainment: "Honestly, I think her shows are great. Shonda knows what they are. I call them kitchen sink entertainment because they give you every possible thing that can happen."[26] While Simien begins by stating that he watches and likes Shondaland series, the kitchen sink analogy suggests the *Scandal* writers lack discernment. Simien further elaborated on his relationship to the series being parodied and the new white students in the 2018 *Vanity Fair* interview:

> There's no judgment against *Empire*, but there is a difference between watching
> *Empire* as the only black person in the room and watching it with all other black
> people. There is a difference, and it strikes you differently. And I just wanted to
> portray that. . . . I think it's a way to sort of acknowledge that some of the things

that I like to watch on TV may not be advancing the culture all that much, but it's a balance, man. These kids need to relax. They need to enjoy themselves, and it's just made a little bit more complicated now that white people have sort of invaded their safe space.[27]

Characterizing these types of shows as not "advancing the culture all that much" suggests that advancing the culture is something television series are supposed to do. Again, both the Indiegogo page used to raise funds and the eventual theatrical film trailer contain language that illustrates *Dear White People*'s desire to make audiences "laugh, cry, and think" in ways similar to *Do the Right Thing* and *Hollywood Shuffle*. Simien's discussion of the parodic series in interviews separates shows like *Scandal*, *Empire*, and *Love & Hip Hop* from the cultural and intellectual rigor of more esteemed Black media. Simien argues that the types of series Black students in Armstrong-Parker watch provide necessary catharsis for the mental and emotional toil of moving through an elite space as marginalized. However, might there be something else to them?

In her analysis of "negative" texts, Gates asserts, "Negative images encompass a wide range of politics and values: some challenge hegemony while others reinforce it. Yet what I find intriguing are the possibilities for queer, feminist, and otherwise nonnormative subjectivities in these negative texts, and the degree to which they are present without requiring 'reading against the grain.'"[28] Building from Gates's analysis, I would argue that many of the topics covered on the shows parodied on *Dear White People* actually engage facets of Black identity with limited representation on television and frequently speak to important issues. For example, storylines about Black queer people and their experiences are threaded throughout the parodies in *Dear White People*'s second season.

The *Empire* parody involves the family matriarch walking in on her closeted gay son having sex with another man. Similarly, on the *Love & Hip Hop* parody, rapper P. Ninny repeatedly declares that she is in no way shape or form a lesbian. Despite this proclamation, as the scene moves from her speaking directly to the camera and producers to interactions with another cast member, we realize that she is, of course, actually queer. The repeated cameos of Lena Waithe as rapper P. Ninny and her character's storyline present a subject largely absent from much of American media: the Black queer woman. While the white students who have just moved into Armstrong-Parker mock P. Ninny's assertion that she is not a lesbian and laugh uproariously as she argues with another Black woman whom she clearly has romantic and/or sexual feelings for, it cannot be denied that the *Love & Hip Hop* franchise has consistently made space for nonnormative, Black subjectivities and has especially allowed for a more expansive representation of Black femininities. The emphasis on affect and catharsis in both the series and in Simien's interviews does important work in adding nuance to the limiting (and frankly boring) framework of positive and negative representation. However, positioning escapism or catharsis as the primary contribution

FIG. 13.2 Lena Waithe as rapper P. Ninny in *Dear White People* season 2

of the series being parodied and Justin Simien's remark that these types of shows are not "advancing the culture all that much" hinge on the same idea that so-called negative texts do not progress Black Americans' social, political, or economic position and that they lack aesthetic or artistic merit.

Conclusion

Since its first episode, *Dear White People* has extended and nuanced the conversations that were introduced in the early trailer and feature film. When Simien first started to develop the concept and the characters, he was especially interested in articulating the challenges of being Black in a period where many Americans felt we had moved beyond race. Further, our current media landscape, with rising numbers of streaming services and platforms, was just beginning to take shape, and the recent increase in Black media had not yet come to pass. The concept trailer and feature film engaged other media texts from the position of dissatisfaction and frustration; the television series, in contrast, depicts its characters occupying a more negotiated viewing position.

The show's parodic series function as more than gags. In addition to shedding light on the communal viewing experience and reception practices of Black communities, the parodies reflect some of the challenges our core set of characters face. When Reggie, for example, is working through the aftermath of the campus police pointing a gun at him when a house party gets out of hand, the guest on *Dereca: Set Me Straight* is dealing with similar trauma. From the concept trailer to the film and finally to the television series, *Dear White People* has concerned itself with the state of Black representation in Hollywood and, importantly, found ways to question its own place in the media landscape.

The third season of *Dear White People* introduces viewers to new characters and expands its horizons to further engage Black and queer communities and Afro-Latinx identities. It also introduces us to new parodies like *US of Gay* (*Queer Eye*, Netflix, 2018–) and a hilarious spoof of *The Handmaid's Tale* (Hulu, 2017–) that Sam immerses herself in as she deals with grief and depression. While *Dear White People* is not the only Black show to utilize television parodies—*Insecure*'s (HBO, 2016–2021) *Due North* stands out as an example—the sheer number of television references is significant. The hyperreality *Dear White People* exists in affords the series space to experiment, and with that to critique, to be playful, to be contemplative. A culmination for the Black students at Winchester University was released in the fall of 2021, and the final season constructed a fitting conclusion for their television parodies.

Rather than mix and match different popular series with large Black followings, the season embeds a character into the parody and follows Coco as she competes on the reality television series *Big House*, a *Big Brother* (CBS, 2000–) parody. The show's ironic wink at *Big Brother* turned out to be incredibly prescient. While Coco navigated the racial politics of *Big House* and attempted to be the series' first Black winner, the Black contestants of season 23 of *Big Brother*, which finished airing a week after *Dear White People*'s final season dropped on Netflix, constructed an alliance (named The Cookout) that resulted in the first Black contestant to ever win. *Dear White People*, in all its iterations, has always been concerned with how the relationship between constructed personas and the true self has heightened stakes for Black people. Parodying a reality television show whose premise is rooted in surveillance and the performance of self is an apt conclusion for the series' utilization of the show-within-a-show. The parody television series the residents of Armstrong-Parker gather in the common room to watch are the writers' way of using the medium of television as a form of television criticism and a form of self-reflexivity. At a time where Black creative production has reached new heights and Black reception practices are more visible to broader publics, *Dear White People* illustrates the vitality of "Watching While Black."

Notes

1 "Dear White People," Indiegogo, accessed July 2, 2021, http://www.indiegogo.com/dearwhitepeople.

2 Indiegogo is a crowdfunding site founded in 2008. While people can use the site to raise funds for creative projects in addition to causes, the site markets itself as a hub for entrepreneurs with "groundbreaking" ideas. This contrasts Indiegogo with other crowdsourcing platforms like GoFundMe known for helping individuals raise money for things like health-care bills.

3   Justin Simien, *Dear White People: A Guide to Inter-Racial Harmony in "Post-Racial" America* (New York: Simon & Schuster, 2014).

4   "Dear White People," Indiegogo. Emphasis original.

5   Rebecca Wanzo, "African American Acafandom and Other Strangers: New Genealogies of Fan Studies," *Transformative Works and Cultures* 20 (September 15, 2015): n.p., https://doi.org/10.3983/twc.2015.0699.

6   Culture Machine, "Dear White People | Concept Trailer," YouTube video, accessed July 5, 2021, 3:02, https://www.youtube.com/watch?v=watjO62NrVg.

7   Culture Machine.

8   The framing of *Dear White People* necessarily elides Black independent films that were released in the 2000s like Barry Jenkins's *Medicine for Melancholy* (2008) and Dee Rees's *Pariah* (2011).

9   Julia Himberg, *The New Gay for Pay: The Sexual Politics of American Television Production* (Austin: University of Texas Press, 2018), 4.

10   Stuart Hall, "Encoding/Decoding," in *Media and Cultural Studies: Key Works*, 2nd ed., ed. Meenakshi Gigi Durham and Douglass Kellner, 137–144 (Hoboken, N.J.: Wiley Blackwell, 2012).

11   Robin R. Means Coleman, *Say It Loud! African American Audiences, Media, and Identity* (New York: Routledge, 2002), 15.

12   Nancy C. Cornwell and Mark P. Orbe, "'Keepin' It Real' and/or 'Sellin' Out to the Man' African American Responses to Aaron McGruder's *The Boondocks*," in Means Coleman, *Say It Loud!*, 39.

13   Miriam J. Petty, "'Old Folks at Home': Tyler Perry and the Dialectics of Nostalgia," *Quarterly Review of Film and Video* 34, no. 7 (October 3, 2017): 587–605, https://doi .org/10.1080/10509208.2017.1313060.

14   Richard Dyer, *Only Entertainment* (New York: Routledge, 1992), 168.

15   Kristen J. Warner, "If Loving Olitz Is Wrong, I Don't Wanna Be Right," *The Black Scholar* 45, no. 1 (2015): 17.

16   Kristen J. Warner, "They Gon' Think You Loud Regardless: Ratchetness, Reality Television, and Black Womanhood," *Camera Obscura: Feminism, Culture, and Media Studies* 30, no. 1 (May 1, 2015): 139, https://doi.org/10.1215/02705346-2885475.

17   Laura Bradley, "How *Dear White People* Crafts Its Hilarious Shows-within-a-Show," *Vanity Fair*, May 4, 2018, https://www.vanityfair.com/hollywood/2018/05/dear -white-people-season-2-review-show-within-a-show-lena-waithe-prince-o-palities.

18   Dayna Chatman, "Black Twitter and the Politics of Viewing Scandal," in *Fandom: Identities and Communities in a Mediated World*, 2nd ed., ed. Jonathan Gray, Cornel Sandvoss, and C. Lee Harrington, 299–314 (New York: New York University Press, 2017).

19   *Dear White People*, season 2, episode 1, "Volume 2: Chapter 1," directed by Justin Simien, released May 4, 2018, on Netflix.

20   While there is no one agreed upon definition for what a hotep is, *Dear White People*'s use of the word fits in with Ann-Derrick Gaillot's explanation in *The Outline*. As Galliot writes, "It's a figure born from the emergence of Afrocentrism in the wake of the Civil Rights Movement and its subsequent reemergence in the late '80s and '90s. It's easy to understand why—black nationalism emerged as an empowering system of belief in the face of centuries of subjugation and systemic oppression. But online, where the word has proliferated in recent years, hotep signifies a faux-wokeness associated with misogynoir, homophobia, toxic masculinity, and misguided understandings of history and science." Ann Derrick-Galliot, "The Rise of 'Hotep,'" *The Outline*, April 19, 2017, https://theoutline.com/post/1412/what-hotep-means.

21   Culture Machine, "Dear White People | Concept Trailer."

22 Inkoo Kang, "'Dear White People' Review: Critique of Race and Media Has More Than Satire on Its Mind," *The Wrap*, October 15, 2014, https://www.thewrap.com/dear-white-people-review-tessa-thompson-tyler-james-williams/.

23 Racquel J. Gates, *Double Negative: The Black Image and Popular Culture* (Durham, N.C.: Duke University Press, 2018), 145.

24 Bradley, "How *Dear White People*."

25 Bradley.

26 Jesse David Fox, "The Story Behind Dear White People's Perfect Scandal Parody," *Vulture*, April 27, 2017, https://www.vulture.com/2017/04/dear-white-people-trump-scandal-parody.html.

27 Bradley, "How *Dear White People*."

28 Gates, *Double Negative*, 20.

Notes on Contributors

CHRISTINE ACHAM is currently the chair and a professor of the School of Cinematic Arts at University of Hawai'i at Mānoa. She received her PhD in critical studies from the School of Cinematic Arts at the University of Southern California. Prior to joining University of Hawai'i, Christine was the assistant dean of diversity and inclusion and a professor of the practice of cinematic arts at the School of Cinematic Arts at USC. She previously held the position of associate professor in the African American and African studies program at the University of California-Davis. She teaches classes on film form, style, and culture, American television history and culture, and African American film, television, and popular culture. She has also taught documentary history and production in both the United States and Trinidad and Tobago. She is the author of *Revolution Televised: Prime Time and the Struggle for Black Power* (2005) and several articles on African American film, television, documentary, and web series. She codirected, edited, and produced the award-winning documentary *Infiltrating Hollywood: The Rise and Fall of the Spook Who Sat by the Door* (2011), which has been screened at over twenty national and international film festivals and universities. She is a member of the editorial board of the journal *Film Quarterly*.

BRIANA BARNER is an assistant professor in the Department of Communication at the University of Maryland and a former UM President's Postdoctoral Fellow. She received her doctorate in radio-television-film and a doctoral portfolio in women's and gender studies from the University of Texas. Briana also earned a master's in women's and gender studies from UT. She is an interdisciplinary critical and cultural communications scholar with research interests in Black podcasts, digital and Black feminism, Black cultural production, digital media, social media as a tool for social justice and activism, and the representation of marginalized people, specifically Black girls and women, in popular culture and media. Her work can be found in *Film Quarterly*, *Saving New Sounds: Podcast Preservation and Historiography*, and *Black Sisterhoods: Paradigm and Praxis*. Briana is a proud native of the southside of Chicago and an alumna of Bennett College, a small women's HBCU in Greensboro, North Carolina.

MICHAEL BOYCE GILLESPIE is an associate professor of cinema studies in the Department of Cinema Studies at New York University. He is the author of *Film Blackness: American Cinema and the Idea of Black Film* (2016) and coeditor of *Black One Shot*, an art criticism series on *ASAP/J*. His work focuses on Black visual and expressive culture, film theory, visual historiography, popular music, and contemporary art. His recent writing has appeared in *Regeneration: Black Cinema 1898–1971*, *Film Comment*, *Film Quarterly*, and *liquid blackness*. He was the consulting producer on the Criterion Collection releases of *Deep Cover* and *Shaft*.

HERMAN GRAY is an emeritus professor of sociology at University of California at Santa Cruz and has published widely in the areas of Black cultural politics and media. Gray's books include *Watching Race* (2004), *Cultural Moves* (2005), *Toward a Sociology of the Trace* (2010) coedited with Macarena Gómez-Barris, and *The Sage Handbook of Television Studies* coedited with M. Alvarado, M. Buonanno, and T. Miller (2014). Gray's most recent book is *Racism, Post Race* (2019) coedited with Roopali Mukherjee and Sarah Banet Weiser. Gray is a member of the Board of Jurors for the Peabody Awards.

SHELLEEN GREENE is an associate professor of cinema and media studies in the UCLA Department of Film, Television, and Digital Media. Her research interests include Italian film, Black European studies, and digital feminist studies. Her book *Equivocal Subjects: Between Italy and Africa—Constructions of Racial and National Identity in the Italian Cinema* (2012) examines the representation of mixed-race subjects of Italian and African descent, arguing that the changing cultural representations of mixed-race identity reveal shifts in the country's conceptual paradigms of race and nation. She has published in the *Journal of Italian Cinema and Media Studies*, *Italian Culture*, *California Italian Studies*, *estetica, studi e ricerche*, *Black One Shot / ASAP Journal*, *Feminist Media Studies*, and *ADA: A Journal of Gender, New Media and Technology*.

FELICIA D. HENDERSON is the creator of Showtime's Emmy Award–nominated and three-time NAACP Image Award Best Drama winning show, *Soul Food*, television's first successful drama to feature an African American cast. She is developing the WWII women pilot dramas *Avenger Field* and *45 Days: Rebel Girls of Americus*, a limited series set in 1960s Georgia. She was the showrunner–head writer–executive producer of the Netflix vampire drama *First Kill* and cocreated and executive produced *The Quad*, a one-hour drama for BET Networks.

She also co–executive produced the Netflix adaptation of Marvel's *The Punisher* and FOX's *Empire*. Henderson has written for and produced many high-profile shows such as *Gossip Girl, Fringe, Everybody Hates Chris,* and *Moesha*. Henderson is an associate professor in the Department of Radio/Television/Film at Northwestern University. Having earned BA and MFA degrees from UCLA and an MBA from the University of Georgia, she is a PhD candidate in cinema and media studies at UCLA as well. Her research interests include TV history; culture, class, race, and gender issues in television writers' rooms; the political economy of the 2007 WGA strike; and the "othering" of single women in the media. Her work has been published in textbooks and media studies journals. She has taught American film history, film editing, advanced screenwriting, writing for directors, TV history, TV drama, and TV comedy pilot writing at UCLA, the University of Texas at Austin, and Columbia University.

JACQUELINE JOHNSON is a doctoral candidate in the Division of Cinema and Media Studies at the University of Southern California. She received her BA in sociology from Boston University and her MA in media studies from the University of Texas at Austin, where her thesis project focused on Black reception and Twitter through an analysis of WGN America's *Underground*. Johnson is writing her dissertation on Black women as both the producers and subjects of romance narratives in television, podcasts, and novels. Her work is published in *Sartorial Fandom: Fashion, Beauty Culture and Identity* (2023) and *Rolling: Blackness and Mediated Comedy* (forthcoming).

NGHANA LEWIS is an associate professor of English and Africana studies at Tulane University, a faculty affiliate of the School of Law, and an adjunct professor with the Department of Psychology. She has published and lectured widely on her research, which cross-sectionally studies HIV/AIDS, hip-hop culture, and Black women's health. Lewis is the recipient of a 2020 NAACP Award for her outstanding work in "Education and Representation." In addition to her work in the academy, Dr. Lewis serves as district judge for the 40th Judicial District Court in and for the Parish of St. John the Baptist, Louisiana.

ALFRED L. MARTIN JR. is an associate professor of media studies at the University of Miami. Martin is the author of *The Generic Closet: Black Gayness and the Black-Cast Sitcom* (2021) and has published work in scholarly journals, including *Journal of Cinema and Media Studies, International Journal of Cultural Studies, Feminist Media Studies,* and *Television & New Media*.

BRANDY MONK-PAYTON is an assistant professor in the Department of Communication and Media Studies and affiliated faculty in the Department of African and African American Studies at Fordham University. Her research focuses on the theory and history of African American media representation and cultural production across television, film, and digital media. Her work has been published in edited collections such as *Unwatchable* and *From Madea to Media Mogul: Theorizing Tyler Perry* as well as the journals *Film Quarterly*, *Feminist Media Histories*, and *Communication, Culture and Critique*. She has also been featured on NPR's *All Things Considered* and *PBS NewsHour*.

ERIC PIERSON is a professor of communication and the director of the film studies minor at the University of San Diego. His work on Black images and audiences has appeared in *Beyond Blaxploitation: Documenting the Black Experience*, *Screening Noir*, the *Journal of Mass Media Ethics*, and *Watching While Black: Centering the Television of Black Audiences*. Expanding media literacy is the philosophical glue that holds together Professor Pierson's multiple strands of scholarly and creative work. He strives to create work that reflects academic rigor while also being accessible to those outside of the university setting. Professor Pierson's work can be found in a wide variety of venues as he strives to reach diverse audiences, including academic journals, edited book collections, film festival panels, and museum exhibitions. Professor Pierson holds two degrees from the University of Illinois at Urbana-Champaign: a BFA in fine arts and a PhD from the Institute of Communications Research.

TREAANDREA M. RUSSWORM (PhD, University of Chicago) is a professor in the Interactive Media and Games Division at the University of Southern California. She is also a series editor of Power Play: Games, Politics, Culture and was an inaugural associate editor of outreach and equity for the *Journal of Cinema and Media Studies*. She is the author or coeditor of three other books: *Blackness Is Burning: Civil Rights, Popular Culture, and the Problem of Recognition* (2016), *Gaming Representation: Race, Gender, and Sexuality in Video Games* (2017), and *From Madea to Media Mogul: Theorizing Tyler Perry* (2016). With research expertise in digital culture and popular African American media, Russworm is the founder of Radical Play, a games-based public humanities initiative and afterschool program. She is currently writing a new monograph on *The Sims* and new work on race and the politics of play.

ADRIEN SEBRO is an assistant professor of media studies at the University of Texas at Austin. His scholarship specializes in critical media studies at the intersections of television, film, comedy, and Black popular culture. Dr. Sebro is the author of *Scratchin' and Survivin': Hustle Economics and the Black Sitcoms of Tandem Productions* (Rutgers 2023).

BERETTA E. SMITH-SHOMADE is an associate professor in the Department of Film and Media at Emory University. Her research explores representational, industrial, and aesthetic aspects of Black television. She has two published monographs within this frame: *Shaded Lives: African-American Women and Television* (Rutgers, 2002) and *Pimpin' Ain't Easy: Selling Black Entertainment Television* (2007). She edited the first edition of this anthology, *Watching While Black: Centering the Television of Black Audiences* (Rutgers, 2013)—a *Choice* Outstanding Academic Title—and is the editor of the *Reboot*. She has published in leading media journals and anthologies on Black film, cable television, and Black spirituality. Her third monograph, *Finding God in All the Black Places: Sacred Imaginings in Black Popular Culture*, is forthcoming with Rutgers in 2024.

Index